UNIVERSITY OF
WITHD
ROM THE

D1646498

The Collapse of Globalism

John Ralston Saul's books have been published in more than twenty-five countries and a dozen languages. His philosophical trilogy – *Voltaire's Bastards*, *The Doubter's Companion* and *The Unconscious Civilization* – has had a growing impact on political thought around the world. The postscript to the trilogy is *On Equilibrium*, an exploration of the human struggle for personal and social balance. John Ralston Saul received a PhD from King's College, was President of the Canadian Centre of International PEN from 1990 to 1992 and was named by the *Utne Reader* as one of the '100 Visionaries of the World' in 1995. Appointed a Chevalier de l'Ordre des Arts et des Lettres in 1996, John Ralston Saul recently received the Pablo Neruda Medal.

'Skilfully punctures some of globalization's most cherished myths ... Informative ... provocative.' Andrew Lynch, *Sunday Business Post* (Dublin)

'Novelist, historian and philosopher ... John Ralston Saul is a Renaissance man in more ways than one: he's convinced that the West needs a new Renaissance to liberate powers of reflection, judgement and active citizenship that have gone to sleep under the weight of technocratic decision making.' *Utne Reader* 100 Visionaries of the World

ROM THE LIBRAR

Also by John Ralston Saul

NOVELS

The Birds of Prey

The Field Trilogy:

I. Baraka or The Lives, Fortunes,
and Sacred Honor of Anthony Smith

II. The Next Best Thing

III. The Paradise Eater

De si bons Américains

ESSAYS

Voltaire's Bastards

The Doubter's Companion

The Unconscious Civilization

Reflections of a Siamese Twin

On Equilibrium

The LaFontaine-Baldwin Lectures
(with Alain Debuc and Georges Erasmus)

The Collapse of Globalism

and the Reinvention of the World

University of Nottingham
Hallward Library

JOHN RALSTON SAUL

Atlantic Books
London

10 0661870 4

First published in Canada by Viking Canada, an imprint of the Penguin Group
(Canada), a division of Pearson Penguin Canada Inc. in 2005.

First published in Great Britain in hardback by Atlantic Books,
an imprint of Grove Atlantic Limited in 2005.

This paperback edition, with a new afterword, published by Atlantic Books in 2009.

Copyright © John Ralston Saul 2005
Afterword copyright © John Ralston Saul 2009

The moral right of John Ralston Saul to be identified as the author of this work has been
asserted by him in accordance with the Copyright, Designs and Patents Act of 1988.

All rights reserved. No part of this publication may be reproduced, stored in a retrieval
system, or transmitted in any form or by any means, electronic, mechanical, photo-
copying, recording, or otherwise, without the prior permission of both the copyright
owner and the above publisher of this book.

Every effort has been made to trace or contact all copyright holders. The publishers
will be pleased to make good any omissions or rectify any mistakes brought to their
attention at the earliest opportunity.

1 3 5 7 9 8 6 4 2

A CIP catalogue record for this book is available from the British Library.

ISBN: 978 184887 041 3

Printed in Great Britain by Clays Ltd, St Ives plc

Atlantic Books
An imprint of Grove Atlantic Ltd
Ormond House
26–27 Boswell Street
London
WC1N 3JZ

www.atlantic-books.co.uk

To

Hugh Probyn
Clarissa Ralston Saul
François Legué
William Ralston Saul
Alex Trench
Anna Trench
Talia Lewis
Myles Glaisek
Theo Lewis

the next generation in this strange world

CONTENTS

PART IV: THE FALL

PART V: AND WHERE ARE WE GOING NOW?

The Collapse
of Globalism

I still do not fully understand why it happened.
— Alan Greenspan, 23 October 2008

PART I

CONTEXT

[A law which prevents free trade is a] law which interferes with the wisdom of the Divine Providence, and substitutes the law of wicked men for the law of nature.

— Richard Cobden, speeches, 1843

— What do you need her for?
— What I needed God for, before I became an atheist. Something to worship.

— August Strindberg, *The Creditors*, 1888

To attempt to apply economic determinism to all human societies is little short of fantastic.

— Karl Polanyi, *Commentary* 3, no. 2, 1947

Ideology provides a lens through which one sees the world, a set of beliefs that are held so firmly that one hardly needs empirical confirmation.

— Joseph Stiglitz, *Globalization and Its Discontents*, 2003

1

A Serpent in Paradise

Globalization emerged in the 1970s as if from nowhere, fully grown, enrobed in an aura of inclusivity. Advocates and believers argued with audacity that, through the prism of a particular school of economics, societies around the world would be taken in new, interwoven and positive directions. This mission was converted into policy and law over twenty years — the 1980s and '90s — with the force of declared inevitability.

Now, after three decades, we can see the results. These include some remarkable successes, some disturbing failures and a collection of what might best be called running sores. In other words, the outcome has had nothing to do with truth or inevitability and a great deal to do with an experimental economic theory presented as Darwinian fact. It was an experiment that attempted simultaneously to reshape economic, political and social landscapes.

That very clear idea of Globalization is now slipping away. Much of it is already gone. Parts of it will probably remain. The field is crowded with other competing ideas, ideologies and influences ranging from the positive to the catastrophic. In this atmosphere of confusion, we can't be sure what is coming next, although we could almost certainly influence the outcome.

Leading figures who once said nation-states should be subject to economic forces now say they should be reinforced to face global military disorder. Prophets of Globalization who said "Privatize, privatize, privatize" now say they were wrong, because the national rule of law is more important. Economists are angrily divided over whether to loosen or tighten controls over capital markets. Increasingly strong nation-states, like India and Brazil, are challenging the received wisdom of global economics. Pharmaceutical transnationals find themselves ducking and weaving to avoid citizen movements.

Dozens of examples like these tell us that we are transiting one of those moments that separate more driven or coherent eras. It is like being in a vacuum, except that this is a chaotic vacuum, one filled with dense disorder and contradictory tendencies. Think of it as a storm between two weather fronts. Or think of those moments in fast-moving sports, like soccer or hockey, when a team loses its momentum and there is furious, disordered activity until one side finds the pattern and the energy to give it control.

These moments tend to begin with denial on all sides. The confusion frightens those who thought they were setting the direction. And it disappoints those who criticized that direction. There is nothing decisive or noble about the situation. The options are not clear.

Yet, a period of uncertainty is also one of choice, and therefore of opportunity. We cannot know how long it will last. Probably not long. And those choices that set the future will come insidiously, in fits and starts. Some have already presented themselves and somehow been processed, without our fully registering that a determining step was taken.

The shape of what comes next will therefore be decided — a conscious act — or it will be left to various interest groups to decide for us, or simply to fate and circumstance. It will probably emerge from a mix of all three. The soundness of the outcome will depend on the balance between these necessary mechanisms. The most dangerous disequilibrium will have favoured fate and circumstance over the other two. The most mediocre, interest groups. The soundest equilibrium would be led by conscious public decisions.

This book is about our ability to choose. It is also about where those choices might lead us.

To believe in the possibility of change is something very precise. It means that we believe in the reality of choice. That there are choices. That we have the power to choose in the hope of altering society for the greater good. Do we believe that our governments must inevitably tax the poor through stealth taxes such as state-controlled gambling? Or do we believe there is a choice? Do we believe that unserviceable Third World debt could be written off, if we chose to do so? The conviction that citizens have such power lies at the heart of the idea of civilization as a shared project. And the more people are confident that there are real choices, the more they want to vote — a minimal act — and of greater importance, the more they want to become involved in their society.

What does Globalization mean? Defining received wisdom is often a scholastic trap. Worse still, as the British Liberal John Morley put it a century ago, "If we want a platitude, there is nothing like a definition."[1] It is better to come at the subject in a context.

How much of Globalization will disappear? When a grand idea or ideology is fresh and the sailing is easy, even the most serious proponents make all-inclusive claims on its behalf. This grand view makes it easier for them to impose the specific changes they want. When things become more complicated, as they do, most of the same advocates retreat to more modest claims, while still insisting on the central nature of their truth and its inevitability. Many will angrily deny they ever claimed more.

Yet the papers, books, theses, speeches and articles on the subject, from country after country, are perfectly clear. For a quarter-century — at least until the mid-'90s — public and economic debate and the result-ing policies were driven by an all-inclusive vision of what Globalization was and why it was inevitable. Those texts are also a reminder of how computers have made economics even more dismal, and how much less this approach to economics is about thought than about statistics of uncertain value. That which never was a science struggles with difficulty to remain a domain of speculative investigation.

As to which parts of the Globalist belief system will disappear and which will stay, we have no idea. If everything went it would be danger-ous. The last thing we need is rampant nineteenth-century nationalism combined with old-fashioned protectionism as an international principle.

But once large forces begin to move about in a period of uncertainty, we cannot know the outcome. Look back. Put yourself in the context of times that led to great reversals. The people of those eras were usually amazed at how easily the once inevitable became the soon forgotten; and this whether the change in question was for the better or the worse.

If you look around today there are clear examples of Globalization as a success story. The most obvious is the growth in trade. And there are the examples of its failures. Think of New Zealand or, in a more comic vein, of the deregulated airline business. And then there are the running sores. The Third World debt crisis is now in its third decade.

Perhaps most important, there are other, broader forces at work — a growing para-political engagement of young people; the normalization of accelerated international violence; the re-emergence of nineteenth-century-style nationalism in a range running from the merely predictable to the most destructive; the emergence of new national models, for example, some which are not racially based; and the straight-forward reaffirmation of the nation-state, even inside the least expected of places, the European Union.

What these random examples tell us is that social and political realities since the early 1990s have not unfolded as predicted. These altered realities are now setting the course, in place of the economic forces that for the last three decades have been declared to be in charge. Or rather, to be inevitably in charge.

A shrinking number of people believe that economics could actually set a broader course for any civilization. I've noticed that not many people even bother listening when the old assertions of global economic inevitability are made. Inside the small, closed world of economists and officials and interest group associations and specialist writers, that sort of talk does go on. Why not? But most of us are elsewhere. And so, therefore, is the world.

What about our life in such an in-between time? I described this as a vacuum — an interregnum between two unreasonable certainties. If we use it as a short, positive moment of uncertainty when choice is privileged, well then, it becomes possible to emerge into a less ideological and more humanitarian era. This is not an unreasonable ambition or expectation. History is filled with interregnums — some military, some religious, some political, and many of them economic.

Ours is to a great extent a vacuum of economic thought, which adds an element of even greater uncertainty because economics is a romantic, tempestuous business, rather theatrical, often dependent on the willing suspension of disbelief by the rest of us. As with other fashions, its truths change more often than in more concrete sectors.

Civilizations, religions, languages, cultures, nations, even nation-states tend to last centuries. For economic theories a quarter-century is a good run. A half-century is unusual. More than that is something to boast about.

Most of these vacuums become filled with a swirl of concerns, not just military or economic or religious. They reflect the complexity of real life. Some of them have been used intelligently, some disastrously. And in some cases people are so convinced that the reigning ideology is inevitable that they never realize they are in a vacuum. So they are amazed to find themselves abruptly heading in another direction.

Admitting to the need for change is not the most common human trait. And the more power we have, the less change interests us; indeed, the more it frightens us. Nevertheless, eras do stumble, grind, pitch to an end and then, there we are, once again groping our way through an obscure vacuum.

There were those remarkable years in the early sixteenth century when religious reform movements in northern Europe might have led to a strengthened and inclusive *one church*. The complex tension between Erasmus and Luther illustrated that choice was still possible. Perhaps because so much depended on Erasmus's ethical leadership and he was simply too old, the positive turned negative and tension turned to violent division with hundreds of thousands of dead. Or there were those few years after the fall of Napoleon when a fairer European society seemed possible, at least until Metternich's influence over the power structures of the continent became dominant and he tied everyone up in a situation resembling peace without hope. Or those few years after the First World War when all seemed possible. Most of the smaller nation-states that saw in the Treaty of Versailles their chance for independence actually had to wait until 1989. Now some twenty-five of them, new nations or newly independent nations, are getting their first real chance to act as independent entities. They have finally become what many would call a Westphalian or others a nineteenth-century nation-state. They wish to express in the fullest possible manner their national existence. We don't know if this will be positive or negative. What we do know is that in one corner Globalists are declaring the nation-state to be a weakening phenomenon of the past, while in another corner two dozen nation-states stand fresh born, full of energy and ambition with at least a century's worth of frustration to work out.

John Maynard Keynes was on the British delegation at Versailles in 1919 and he resigned in protest when he saw the opportunities of that vacuum being thrown away in the negotiations. In 1919 he published his first explanatory protest. It began:

> The power to become habituated to his surroundings is a marked characteristic of mankind. Very few of us realize with conviction the intensely unusual, unstable, complicated, unreliable, temporary nature of the economic organization by which Western Europe has lived for the last half century. We assume some of the most peculiar and temporary of our late advantages as natural, permanent and to be depended on, and we lay our plans accordingly.[2]

The economic organization he was referring to was the first great modern experiment with free trade, perhaps even with Globalization, one that had risen out of the messianic struggle against the Corn Laws in Britain and then spread around Europe.

At this point you may well hear a chorus of true believers protesting that that was then. Now is now. And now we are far more integrated and in a far more complex manner, because technology, just for starters, binds us inevitably one to the other. And so on. To summarize the argument: that *particular* free trade situation was not like this *universal* free trade situation. But people in the late nineteenth and early twentieth centuries did not think their situation was particular. They thought it was universal. They believed this with as much conviction and sophistication as people do today. If anything, they were much more sophisticated about the world and how it works.

The true believers in today's chorus forget that nineteenth-century European free trade was double buckled by enormous empires, which held the world as one in a manner we can no longer imagine. Keynes went on to demonstrate the extent of economic interdependence inside Europe in 1914. Germany had been the leading customer of Russia, Norway, Holland, Belgium, Switzerland, Italy and Austria-Hungary; the second best of Britain, Sweden and Denmark; the third best of France; and the primary supplier to Russia, Norway, Sweden, Denmark, Holland, Switzerland, Italy, Austria-Hungary, Romania and Bulgaria, as well as the second largest to Britain, Belgium and France. Neither these investments nor this trade stopped these countries from slaughtering each other in an unprecedented way for five years.

The most haunting paragraph in Keynes's introduction, with a few alterations, might have been written today:

The inhabitant of London could order by telephone, sipping his morning tea in bed, the various products of the whole earth, in such quantity as he might see fit, and reasonably expect their early delivery upon his doorstep; he could at the same moment and by the same means adventure his wealth in the natural resources and new enterprises of any quarter of the world, and share, without exertion or even trouble, in their prospective fruits and advantages; or he could decide to couple the security of his fortunes with the good faith of the townspeople of any substantial municipality in any continent that fancy or information might recommend. He could secure forthwith, if he wished it, cheap and comfortable means of transit to any country or climate WITHOUT PASSPORT OR OTHER FORMALITY, could dispatch his servant to the neighboring office of a bank for such supply of the precious metals as might seem convenient, and could then proceed abroad to foreign quarters, without knowledge of their religion, language, or customs, bearing coined wealth upon his person, and would consider himself greatly aggrieved and much surprised at the least interference. But, most important of all, he regarded this state of affairs as normal, certain, and permanent, except in the direction of further improvement, and any deviation from it as aberrant, scandalous and avoidable. The projects and politics of militarism and imperialism, of racial and cultural rivalries, of monopolies, restrictions, and exclusion, which were to play the serpent to this paradise, were little more than the amusements of his daily newspaper, and appeared to exercise almost no influence at all on the ordinary course of social and economic life, the internationalization of which was really complete in practice.[3]

Instead the closest, most integrated of economic and trading partners went to war with each other in a particularly vicious manner. And immediately after that they variously embraced communism and fascism and the worst of racism and, almost incidentally, high tariff barriers. And then they went to war again. It was only on their way out of this second world war that they took greater care to seize the offered opportunities, Keynes being one of the most influential and the most conscious of the questioning, guiding hands. And they sought structures, not led by economics, but with sensible economics built in as supporting mechanisms.

That pre-1914 naively contented middle class was obviously a much smaller percentage of society than those who today are convinced that they are not naively contented, but are the clever beneficiaries of global economic destiny. For a reminder of reality, those clever beneficiaries might think of Keynes's five words describing open borders — *without passport or other formality*. Today only Europe has managed to remove the border barriers that didn't exist at all last time around. Elsewhere, it is not uncommon for travellers to be half stripped in airports. Looking at the steady evolution of security over the last thirty years — not just since September 11 — it is possible that this tendency will intensify. A few transborder incidents and it could easily spread back into Europe.

The stories of *civilization* in any place at any time have this in common — individuals feel they understand the mechanisms of their society. This sense of understanding implies that each of us has the self-confidence to wish to change our society for the better. Or at least we have the self-confidence to accept the possibility that we could change it for the better. Think of those who worked for clean water systems, public education, against slavery.

Do all of us have that self-confidence? Perhaps not. But many more of us do than our strangely meritocratic society often suggests. This understanding may come in many forms and at many levels. It may be conscious or unconscious or a bit of both.

To believe in the reality of choice is one of the most basic characteristics of leadership. Curiously enough, many individuals who think of themselves as leaders find this reality very difficult. They believe that their job is to understand power and management and perhaps make minor corrections to what they accept to be the torque of events. But they take for granted the reigning truths of the day and so are fundamentally passive.

As a result, change is eventually thrust upon them by reality. Or they are replaced. In either case, the strength of that particular civilization — its ability to choose — is weakened.

Let me turn the question around. What of barbarism?

There is more to it than physical violence. More profoundly, it is an assault on the individual's self-confidence. After all, it is our self-confidence that permits us to embrace the complexity and uncertainty of reality as a positive, so as not to be frightened by the possibility of choice. Barbarism can be thought of as violence done to the individual's understanding of herself as a citizen. That violence arises from the belief that truth has revealed itself. A religious truth, a racial truth, an economic truth. Even a scientific truth. The adjective hardly matters.

In the false light of truth, history withers and seems to come to an end. Destiny, it seems, is inextricably at work. And leadership shrinks to less than choice or citizenship. Instead it is centred on the sophisticated exercise of power, which can be gained and held by skillfully riding the wave of inevitability.

The more sophisticated, the more relentless the riding of this wave by those who seek or hold power, the more alienated individuals feel, the less interested in a society where real choices seem to have been marginalized and the mechanisms made to appear mysterious.

And so, as in today's societies, we vote less and are less involved in the mainstream structures of citizenship.

What could more certainly drive individuals away from citizenship than an endless chorus of leaders and specialists — a meritocracy of technicians and technocrats — proclaiming the inevitability of global economic forces and of technological forces, proclaiming the inevitability that these two forces will shape the way the planet works and therefore the way each of our societies works? The unstoppable progress of these forces can perhaps be managed. But even then, it will only be thanks to precise interventions by specialists whose methods can but remain obscure to most us.

If economics and technology are taken to be the great inevitable forces of our day, management is more like a support system that makes the other two seem inevitable. The abrupt rise to hyper-respectability of managerial schools and their matching with large corporations led by technocrats has had the astonishing effect of confusing management with leadership. And if leadership is reduced to management, well then, problems are not to be solved. They are to be managed. In fact, they are no longer problems.

What does this mean in practical terms? Take the self-evident example of the Third World debt crisis stretching on toward the end of its third decade. The debt is unpayable, unserviceable, of no use to a stable free market or to the debtors. Whole regions are literally incapacitated by it. This problem has been easily solvable for a quarter-century. We have centuries of experience dealing with equivalent situations in both the public and private sectors.

What stands in the way of a solution? Belief in the inevitability of a particular economic theory and an overly complex managerial method. Our society is filled with similar situations of all sizes. Such clever passivity cannot help but invite the rise of a yet more barbaric form of leadership. One in which the belief in revealed truth calls forth an ever-narrower devotion to highly peculiar types of economics or warfare or racial identification. With these, the most common expressions of citizenship are likely to be loyalty, belonging and acceptance, compensated by the rewards of self-interest and marked by the promotion of efficiency in the service of the inevitable.

This sort of world feels insecure and fears choice. It is a world of populism or, more accurately, false populism, of fast emotional flash-points. This is the unpleasant face of nationalism. What I would call negative nationalism.

But there are many other options. The belief that we do not have choices is a fantasy, an unfortunate indulgence in abdication. And so the curious thing about inevitability is that it tends not to last very long. The more the true believers in a reigning theory of truth insist that its growth is inevitable and therefore eternal, the faster the rest of us, who have a bit of distance, tend to decide that we do have the power of choice. And all things considered, we would rather choose some other approach.

The true believers and sophisticated managers go on riding their great wave ever more relentlessly and with remarkable but increasingly meaningless skill, while a growing percentage of the citizenry draw ever further back on the shore in a precautionary manner. To those up on the crest, so intent upon manoeuvring their surfboards, we must appear an unsympathetic lot, uninterested in their efforts, disengaged, strangely irritable, annoyed, alienated, dispirited, cynical.

Some of us even have our backs turned, too busy cashing in to watch, having convinced ourselves that humans unleashed at a global level with only their self-interest in play will produce a dynamic that spreads wealth and strengthens democracy. More and more I meet people who have followed the new rules, have done well for themselves and now seem adrift, as if asking, *Is that all there is?*

But most of us just seem to be disconnected, waiting for the wave to crash. We are waiting with the cruel, experienced eye of a citizenry that has lost respect for its leadership in general, yet hasn't quite worked out what to do about it and so waits for them to self-destruct.

Looking back, we see it has been a neat trick, presenting an economic truism as the prism through which civilization must be approached. But it doesn't change how reality works. The believers believe, but the world moves on.

After all, things do come to an end. Each of our lives is a testimony to this. Something else comes along — anything from a renewal to a simple death. In the meantime there has been a space of both time and emotion. A confusing vacuum. And however predictable each ending has been, it tends to be messy because it seems to us unexpected.

Think of that moment between adolescence and adult life — a time when the difficulty of imagining how to believe in a world and choose a future may produce everything from tension to high levels of suicide. Or think of love, so bright and certain, which often seems to evaporate. After a time, love may never reappear or new love may come.

There is no promise in any of this except that things do end. And the probability of renewal is dependent on our ability to use the interregnum to make choices that will help shape the next era of our lives.

To shape society we need to think about the origins of what is now passing — the origins of Globalization, its promise, its rise, and gradual collapse from the mid-1990s on. If we don't focus on that magisterial appearance, rise, hesitation and fall, we cannot understand what has happened to us, good and bad, and where we now are. And we need to look carefully at the other forces that increasingly set the pace today, from irregular warfare to NGOs to reinvigorated nation-states, from the reappearance of genocides and oligopolies and hidden forms of inflation to a new practical interest in ethics and positive forms of nationalism and a new interest in citizenship. Much of this is exciting. Some of it is dangerous. All of it is real.

There is one fundamental difference between personal and societal change. Families, for all their strengths, do have their own inevitable, demanding truths. The passage through time that is so difficult in individual lives can be easier for societies. If we do not lose ourselves in anger or despair or the ideology of certainty, society allows us to call upon the strength of community. That is the strength of the *other* whose reality confirms our own.

A Summary of the Promised Future

If you were to boil down the multitude of firm promises, suggested hopes, enthusiastic musings and deep beliefs expressed from the 1970s on by political leaders, academics, serious columnists, business leaders and their spokesmen, including myriad independent think-tanks, you would find that the promise of Globalization went as follows:

The power of the nation-state is waning.

Such states as we know them may even be dying.

In the future, power will lie with global markets.

Thus, economics, not politics and armies, will shape human events.

These global markets, freed of narrow national interests and inhibiting regulations, will gradually establish international economic balances.

And so we will at last have outgrown the eternal problem of boom-and-bust cycles.

Such markets will unleash waves of trade. And these waves will in turn unleash a broad economic tide of growth.

That tidal wave will in turn raise all ships, including those of the poor, whether in the West or in the developing world.

The resulting prosperity will allow put-upon individuals to convert dictatorships into democracies.

Of course, these democracies will not have the absolute powers of the old nation-states. And so we will see a shrivelling-away of irresponsible nationalism, racism and political violence.

On the economic front, the very size of the new markets will require ever larger corporations. And their size will raise them above the risks of bankruptcy. This will be another source of international stability.

Indeed, these transnationals will be on the cutting edge of the market's leadership of civilization. They will become like virtual states. And their aggressive dominance will make them impervious to local political prejudices.

All of the above will create the conditions for healthy governance, and so we will see the emergence of debt-free governments. The market will stand for no less.

Such stable public accounting will in turn stabilize our societies.

In short, freed from the fetters of wilful men, we will be able to follow our individual self-interests toward a life of prosperity and general happiness.

The cycles of history will have been broken.

History will indeed be dead.

What They Said It Would Do

What made the Globalist movement so original was not its internationalism or its international economics. History is full of both. From the Sumerian empire to the United Nations, we've had every form of political, military and religious arrangement. And international trading arrangements, even international production integration systems, have always existed. Rome had all these for centuries across a territory so large that it included most of Europe as well as today's Islamic world, with the exception of the Asian part.

The last time we tried free trade — from the mid-nineteenth century to the First World War — we were able to combine the dropping of commercial barriers in Europe with the astonishing reach of those same European countries around the world. The British, French, Dutch, Italian, Belgian, German, Russian and Austro-Hungarian empires, with the new American empire joining in at the end of the nineteenth century, were able to apply their political, legal, social and economic methods to the entire world. Along with those methods came a complex maze of regulations. As Keynes pointed out, raw materials, manufacturing and goods flowed in every direction.

So the remarkable originality of Globalization lay elsewhere: in its assertion that all civilizations from now on were going to be led by commerce. This premise came with a purity or simplicity that went far beyond the more nuanced economic ideas of thinkers like Montesquieu, Adam Smith or even Karl Marx. The other constituent parts of human activity — from politics to social policy to culture — were going to be perceived principally through the prism of economics, which, once released from most government interference, would find its own natural balances. The inherent discipline of unfettered markets would directly — according to the most optimistic — and indirectly — according to the more moderate — shape the key economic events, which in turn would shape the rest.

The advantage of this very new idea of market leadership was obvious: it would allow us to take full advantage of the last hundred years' technical and theoretical breakthroughs. The result would be a growth of wealth and general well-being through a multiplication of players, situations and factors.

There were no real precedents for such a system, except perhaps the small republican dictatorship of Venice. Even there, while the prism was commerce, the government maintained strict economic regulations directly related to the functioning of society. The expression of that civilization was also particularly revealing. Music, painting, sculpture, architecture were all encouraged, valued, admired. Writing, ideas and debate were discouraged and limited. The commercial republic saw freedom of speech as an expression of disloyalty and therefore dangerous.

There has never been a serious thinker in history on any continent who has suggested that commerce alone could lead civilization and that once given such prominence, commerce would therefore be capable of leading itself. Modern conservatives like Michael Oakeshott talked of unregulated competition as a chimera, while Karl Polanyi, among the most original of modern economists, said, "The idea of a self-adjusting market implied a stark utopia."[1]

What then of the problem of a definition? You can describe Globalization from a close-up technical point of view or draw back a bit for context or draw right back for context and consequence. It is disingenuous to insist on one without the others.

If you were to sum up the ideas of Globalization I laid out in the last chapter, the result would be this: an inevitable form of internationalism in which civilization is reformed from the perspective of economic leadership. The leadership here is provided not by people, but by the innate force of economics at work; that is, the marketplace.

There have been hundreds — thousands — of other definitions and promises and threats. The most technical is simply that the reduction of transport and communication costs would lead to an international integration of production and consumption. But the intent has always been grander than that. Alfred Eckes, the former chair of the U.S. International Trade Commission and an expert with great calm and *gravitas,* describes that intent as a "process in which technology, economics, business, communication and even politics dissolve the barriers of time and space that once separated a people."[2]

Anthony Giddens, the academic who has had so much influence on Tony Blair, sees Globalization transforming every part of society, politics and economics.[3] The economist Jagdish Bhagwati fixes his range at international economic integration without addressing the broader effects he nevertheless believes are there. Anne Krueger, number two at the International Monetary Fund, ends her definition of Globalization with: "all leading to the closer integration of the world including — but not limited to — the economy." Others talk of the "diminished competence of states." Thomas Friedman, the *New York Times* columnist, sees "the inexorable integration of markets, nation-states and technologies to a degree never witnessed before." The pro-market commentator Daniel Yergin says governments have lost control of the commanding heights of their national economies and with that their ability "to promote economic development, protect sovereignty and project national identity." He doesn't bother mentioning their ability to shape and finance the public good. Perhaps he simply doesn't believe that in a global world governments will be able to finance the public good. Or he sees the public good as a mere subsidiary outcropping of economic development. Businessmen who have become critics of Globalization, like George Soros, say it is all about the creation of uncontrolled global financial markets, the growth of transnationals and of "their increasing domination over national economies." A leading Japanese expert, Kenichi Ohmae, says, "Nation states are dinosaurs waiting to die." Others, spooked perhaps by the growing criticism of these non-economic projections, now protest that to claim "deeper economic integration would enfeeble national governments is a formula sold mainly by opponents of the liberal international order." You can't help noticing the political naivety that often surfaces when economists address the broader world. After all, any amateur with a few taps at the keyboard can pull up who has said what about Globalization. Even stranger, most economists are fast to dismiss any comment on Globalization coming from outside their professional corporation as, well, unprofessional. Yet they don't hesitate a moment to project their own technical theories and statistics onto every detail of every aspect of civilization and our lives within it.

Martin Wolf, one of the most intelligent and sophisticated of these economists who make themselves heard in public, likes to limit his Globalization arguments to economics, but that is because "they are the driving force for almost everything else."[4] In other words, you can focus on any piece of Globalization you wish, but in broader terms the argument always comes back to that of viewing civilization as a whole through an economic prism.

The general tenure of these dozens of definitions is that "international finance has become so interdependent and so interwoven with trade and industry that … political and military power can in reality do nothing."[5] But of course that was written in 1911, just before political and military power destroyed the reigning economic order.

Varied though these opinions may be, they produce a clear enough picture of Globalization's promise, whether in its technical details or in its broad effects on each of us. These themes have been repeated, elaborated on, studied and above all used for policy purposes by thousands of specialists, managers and leaders in every possible language over the last quarter-century.

What is more, a great deal of this promise has been delivered on. The statistics, like the definitions, are perfectly clear.

Since 1950 world trade has multiplied — depending on whose numbers you use — between twelve- and twenty-two-fold. Worldwide foreign direct investment has grown fifteen-fold since 1970. For foreign direct investment to developing countries, the multiple is twenty. The daily turnover in foreign exchange markets was $15 billion in 1973. Now it is over $1.5 trillion. Technology production has multiplied six times, the international trade in technology nine times. In 1956 it was possible to have eighty-nine simultaneous transatlantic telephone conversations by cable. Today, by satellite and fibre optics, there are one million, plus faxes and e-mails.[6]

All of this and much more is remarkable.

Why, then, is so much of Globalization and its promise slipping away? It isn't simply a matter of failures and unforeseen contradictory forces. The most revealing measurement is the system's own successes. Why? Because it increasingly feels as if even the promises fulfilled are not having the expected effect. A few questions will suggest the pattern.

Take the revolutionary explosion in money markets. Most of the foreign exchange movements are about speculation, not investment or wealth creation. The amounts involved are forty to sixty times that of real trade. Serious supporters of Globalization like Jagdish Bhagwati and partial critics like the economist Joseph Stiglitz and a growing number of others are horrified by what they see as a hijacking of the free trade movement to support open capital markets. As for the investments these capital markets may make in developing economies, the primary question must always be, Whose purpose do they serve? The 1997 Asia meltdown included $100 billion abruptly invested from abroad and then abruptly withdrawn within a year. Those countries had long had enough local capital for their own investment needs. Their economies were artificially inflated and then deflated — a classic boom-and-bust cycle, but imposed from the outside.

The question people are asking is, Do these open markets create growth? If they don't, what do they do? The effect cannot be neutral.

More rarely discussed is the lack of a sensible relationship between the spectacular growth in trade and the modest growth in wealth. Perhaps today's trade is not the same economic phenomenon as the trade of classic theory. Perhaps it can't produce wealth as expected.

Perhaps the high percentage of new trade that is merely movements inside transnationals does not create the same sort of wealth as the traditional sort across borders between separately owned corporations. The former is just a matter of shipping and tax planning. The latter is all about buying and selling. If transnationals have taken on some of the characteristics of empires, perhaps the old effect of colonies costing more than they are worth is also at play.

Is it possible that an over-obsession with trade — with the movement of goods and parts of goods — distracts us from the creation of wealth? Is it possible that trade taken out of a sensible economic and social equilibrium actually depresses wealth creation?

Is it possible that a sizable portion of our growth in trade relates not to a revival of capitalism, but to a decline into consumerism? Note how many of the leading modern economic historians equate consumerism not with wealth creation and societal growth, but with inflation and the decline of citizenship. Why? Because there is a constant surplus of goods that relate neither to structural investment nor to a concept of economic value, let alone to societal value. This in turn makes nonsense of the ideas of competition, comparative advantage and supply and demand.

Measuring success by gross domestic product is a dubious approach to life. But if you do, you discover that GDP growth per head over the last three decades has been quite modest — less than half that of the pre-Globalization quarter-century.[7] It has been particularly subdued in the Western democracies, disastrous in both Latin America and Africa, and remarkable in large parts of Asia.

Trade — with or without the capital markets — is meant to serve the economy. It is not a purpose. It is a service. If it does not serve, it may become a counterproductive distraction. It may even become an unusual form of inflation, one that we are not used to identifying, let alone measuring. And so we act as if something that is happening is not happening.

Klaus Schwab, the founder of the annual CEO gathering at Davos in Switzerland and a predictable echo of what the mainstream is thinking, now warns of "fragility" and of Globalization leading to "the first really synchronized world recession and the risks of economic implosion."[8] These days Alfred Eckes is quoting Keynes in the 1930s: "The age of economic internationalism was not particularly successful in avoiding war." Eckes's interpretation of Keynes is that "free trade, combined with capital mobility, was more likely to provoke war than to keep peace."

Meanwhile, a growing number of highly respected figures speaking outside of the Western democracies are turning their backs on theoretically scientific interpretations of global success such as trade statistics and cumulative GDPs. What they see are real people whose actual standard of living apparently must drop in order for them to appear to rise in Western-style statistics. How can that be? For example, these people may have been living a life beyond such measurements — perhaps rural lives. They are therefore technically existing on zero income. Then they move to a desperate urban slum where dirty water, sewage and alienation are the norm. But in such a place, even a dollar's worth of income can be measured. And so Western measurement systems say they have taken a step forward and upward.

What emerges from examining this sort of reality is that generalizations about free trade or even about protectionism are not terribly useful. Each comes in many forms. Each has its uses, in particular circumstances for particular lengths of time.

The Jordanian intellectual Prince Hassan now calls for a redefinition of "poverty in terms of human well-being rather than in terms of monetary wealth."[9] Malaysia has developed a Growth with Equity model. The Bhutanese, with their hard-headed yet ironic style, work behind something called GNH — Gross National Happiness. And China is now focused on a quality-of-life approach in the place of GDP. Why?

The easy answer is that none of these nation-states sees itself as an outpost of Western economic theory. Each regards itself as a centre and one with urgent needs. These needs have nothing to do with Globalization and everything to do with strengthening their particular nation-state by focusing, as in the case of China, on their explosive levels of poverty, but in a more stable and locally appropriate manner. The outcome of their market modernization will most probably be a stronger conviction of shared national belonging and a more confident exporting of what they think their national model is. Or as the writer and now Indian foreign minister K. Natwar Singh describes his country's view of its own economic reforms: "We are too large to be pushed around, too proud to be camp-followers and too independent to be clients."[10]

Spiritual leader and development activist, the Aga Khan, has his ear to the ground in a broader spectrum of places than almost any other international figure. He is a sharp observer of what is actually happening in the world. And when asked to describe what he sees, his focus is not on the economic success story of Globalization with positive trickle-down and welcome side effects. Instead he talks of "a world of increasing dissension and conflict" and focuses on the "failure of democracy" as our single greatest problem: "nearly 40 percent of UN member states are failed democracies." That is the greatest risk we face and the preconditions for dealing with this are first, "a healthy civil society" and second, "pluralism."[11]

And if all of this sounds like an anti-Western point of view, you can listen to Vaclav Havel, the Czech writer and political leader, a hero of modern democracy, strongly pro free market, calling on Europe to act "as inspiration for other parts of the world in order to counter the dangers of globalization." How? "I don't understand why the most important deity is the increase of gross domestic product. It is not about GDP. It is about the quality of life, and that is something else."[12]

Once you leave the hothouse of Western economic theorists and advocates, the world looks quite different — not at all the neat object of market-driven measurement.

Has then the whole Globalist ideology been a failure? Not at all. It's just that when normal people look at our situation they do not see a balanced relationship between the promise and the outcome. And they do not see a successful broader outcome, in good part because a growing assertion of economic wealth is matched by a growing realization of shrinking funds for the common good and greater instability in individual lives. Much of that instability is of economic origin. The mismatch between a spectacular growth in paper wealth, a marginal growth in real wealth and shrinking public and social capacities suggests some new form of inflation — a vaporization of money through an over-obsession with consumption economics and a whole range of imaginary market activities as highlighted by the money markets and the world of mergers and acquisitions.

In the midst of this growing feeling of discomfort with the evolution of events, sensible people like Samy Cohen, the director of France's international research centre (CERI), remind us that "the retreat of the state is neither general nor irreversible," even inside Europe.[13] And one of the central reasons for this illusion of general irreversibility is that the Globalization movement has produced myriad market-oriented international binding agreements at the global level and not a single binding agreement in the other areas of human intercourse — work conditions, taxation, child labour, health and so on. The deep imbalance of the movement, however successful in its own terms, cannot help but provoke unexpected forms of disorder.

4

What Somebody Forgot to Mention

Humans tend to see themselves as living in a civilization. And they understand civilization to be centred on a shared destiny, often called the public good. You find that identification in *The Epic of Gilgamesh* written over a thousand years before both Homer and the Old Testament. Or in Confucius. Or in the Koran. In Western civilization this idea has evolved in an unbroken line from the twelfth century. When you look carefully you find that the debate is always about seeking an equilibrium between societal obligations and individual rights. Repeatedly we are brought back to the natural relationship between the two — what I call responsible individualism. At the heart of that idea of civilization lies the certainty that responsible individualism implies the existence of real choices in the shaping of our destiny.

If in Siena you walk into the old council chamber of the Palazzo Communale — the city hall — you find it wrapped by an early-fourteenth-century fresco over forty metres long. The subject is good government. This was the first non-religious cycle painted anywhere in the West. You could say that Ambrogio Lorenzetti had produced the first modern visual expression of responsible, citizen-based government. Down one long wall are city scenes showing the results of good government, including peace, friendship, learning, the arts, general well-being and prosperous businesses; facing it are the results of bad government, images of urban decline, of fear, violence and suffering. There the only successful business makes weaponry.

And on the central wall is a representation of how a civilization actually works. A large woman called Wisdom floats above another, even larger, called Justice. The two arms of Justice's scale spring from her head, balanced by the influence of Wisdom. Suspended from each of the arms of the scale is a brass tray holding a small figure who distributes justice. And from these trays in turn two cords hang down, only to be grasped by a third large woman — Concord. She winds them together before passing this complex rope into the hands of the twenty-four magistrates who run the city. They are slightly smaller. They in turn pass the rope to a large male figure, Ben Comun, the common good, the Good Commune. Finally, on either side of him are seated six more large women — Peace, Fortitude, Prudence, Magnanimity, Temperance and, once again, Justice. These are the working elements of the common good. The humanist support system.

If you then look back to the figure of Justice, you notice that the small figure in one of the trays is handing down an object called a *staia* — a bushel — to two extremely small figures. They are merchants. The *staia* was an instrument of *just measure;* that is, of regulation.

So wisdom permits justice to produce concord through equilibrium. And the resulting shared common good is maintained thanks to the play between six humanist qualities. The whole process of civilization is driven by justice, and among the many beneficiaries are those who turn the wheels of the economy.

All of this we have always known, but we sometimes like to forget. We forget, for example, as the books of the Renaissance merchant of Prato pointed out, that "even the type of cover for their vats was regulated."[1] And in spite of or thanks to this regulation, the Renaissance was a great period of economic growth and international trade.

George Steiner in his biting way says that we sometimes grow tired of history, a state of emotion for which he cites a strange German word, *geschtsmüde*.[2] But history is always there, troubling and cyclical. We have been in the same strengthening international political cycle since the twelfth century. And much of it has non-Western roots. If you were to swoop down upon our process in the eighteenth century you would discover that the three largest international empires were Persian,

Ottoman and Mogul — all three Islamic. The fourth was probably Chinese. And at least three of them were in the forefront of experimentation in modern public administration.

This international political cycle has always been busy structuring the international economy. In 1815 at the Congress of Vienna, which brought a formal end to the Napoleonic era, you would find Enlightenment aristocrats busy installing "the regulation of superior and permanent interest,"[3] which included turning all the navigable European rivers that touched more than one country into permanent integrated trade zones. In effect, a borderless continent of nation-states.

The question over the last few decades has been whether one particular market theory driven by a technological revolution could overturn that great cycle of history. The philosopher John Gray says that our romance with economic determinism will be even shorter than the free trade period that ended in 1914, that with or without Globalization, the internationalization of our civilizations will go on and technology will serve.[4]

If anything, today's patterns are beginning to resemble the multi-layered complexities of the high Middle Ages, and not simply as played out in Europe.[5] Some people speak of this with admiration for the flexibility of the non-monolithic medieval mindset. There were no centres. Everywhere was a centre. Transferred to today's context, such a situation creates the perfect circumstance for renewed citizen powers. Others use medievalism as a warning of the fear-driven disorder that will arise if we slip into an internationalism shaped by narrow interests versus what humans living in civilizations actually share.

If an incapacity to deal with history is one warning sign of a transient ideology, another is the degree to which that ideology is presented as an inevitability. Westerners in particular seem to have a weakness for sudden absolute beliefs in rather improbable propositions.

In the 1815 Treaty of the Congress of Vienna the Town of Cracow was "declared to be for ever a Free, Independent, and strictly Neutral

City, under the Protection of Austria, Russia and Prussia."[6] *Forever* is such a long time.

But then we also convinced ourselves of the inevitability of the destruction of some 90 percent of the Aboriginal population of the Americas over a three-hundred-year period. In a not atypical example, the indigenous population in what is now the United States fell from 5 million to 250,000 by the late nineteenth century. It was as if, in the Swedish writer Sven Lindqvist's words, genocide had become "the inevitable byproduct of progress."[7]

Over the exact same decades of the highly moral drive to repeal the Corn Laws in favour of free trade — that is, to open British markets to cheap foreign grain in order to feed the new working class — Britain convinced herself that China had to accept a free trade in opium in order to regularize the inevitability of their trading relationship. Without the opium sales there would be an import-export imbalance. London went to war twice to prove this point. The death camp survivor Primo Levi lamented after the Second World War and the Holocaust "that a thinking man should be asked to believe without thinking? Was he not filled with disgust at all the dogmas, all the unproved affirmations, all the imperatives?"[8]

This small selection may present a rather violent portrait of ideological inevitability, particularly when what is in question today is mere economic determinism and its rather obscure, milquetoast spokesmen sitting in departments of economics and in bureaucratic institutions of international commerce, just trying to do their best. But such violent examples are the canary in a coal mine, which makes us conscious that we have slipped into the shaft of inevitabilities. There, we cannot know the outcome.

Much of what is said to be inevitable is little more than the result of linguistic initiatives. George Bush senior introduced a simple phrase into his presidential speeches — "free markets and free men" — which was quickly taken up by others. Thinking men did not seem to notice that the world had been stood on its head. It was not free markets that had produced free men. The story of democratic societies goes the other way around.

In 2004 Gregory Mankiw, chairman of the White House Council of Economic Advisers, made some rather passive public comments on job losses and found himself the target of widespread criticism. He later complained to an audience of fellow economists that "economists and non-economists speak very different languages."[9] He meant that he would never speak again to non-experts in such an open, frank manner.

He might have been mimicking Plato's slave doctor. On one side is the doctor of free men who "investigates the origin and the nature of the disease; he enters into community with the patient and his friends." Mr. Mankiw will go on doing that with his colleagues. The slave doctor, on the other hand, "gives an order based on empirical belief with the air of exact knowledge." Why? Because the slave lacks reason: "He can have true belief, but cannot know the truth of his belief." He is subject to the forces of inevitability: "Order is imposed upon [him] by a benevolent superior." "They lack *logos;* they do not know the Good, and cannot know their own good or the good of the state."[10] They speak a very different language.

The aura of inevitability surrounding Globalization has been so strong that even those *professionals,* who are to some extent in revolt against this ideology as a package, repeatedly feel obliged to begin their dissent with assent. For example, there are the two Nobel economists, Joseph Stiglitz ("We cannot go back on globalization; it is here to stay. The issue is how can we make it work") and Amartya Sen ("The one solution that is not available is that of stopping globalization of trade and economies").[11]

The historic truth about any change is that we cannot understand it if we accept what produced the need for it as an inevitable force. Besides, how much of this inevitability theory is little more than short-term utilitarianism? Is the remarkable growth in trade an expression of global inevitability, or is it simply about short-term cost advantage? If the latter, it can easily grow, alter shape or shrink for the most banal of reasons. A quarter to a half of today's trade involves transnational corporations moving pieces around inside each of their own international structures. Why? Transport is cheap and so is labour. But if you move transport costs up through the price of oil and improve wages, even a small amount —

for example, in China and India — most of the cost advantages are gone. Does that production then disappear? Not necessarily. It can restructure on a national or regional basis. After all, increased wages mean a large local market. Production doesn't need to be global to be successful. There is no noble global destiny in moving inanimate objects vast distances.

Or consider how national budgets were inevitably forced into fiscal discipline over the last quarter-century by the requirements of international markets. Over the last four years the United States, the country at the origin of this theory of inevitable fiscal balance, has thrown itself into the deepest deficits ever seen in any country in all of history. It was done for domestic — that is, national — reasons. Generally speaking, when a country does something for national reasons that may have a negative impact on people in other countries, it can be considered a nationalistic act.

Our desire to believe in the inevitability of things could best be summed up as "the sun will never set" syndrome. The problem is, it always does.

The transient nature of Globalization comes in part from the intellectual innocence or naivety that surrounds it. What could be more naive than to believe in one rather abstract approach to human life based on an expectation of economic leadership based upon a single and highly specific theory of economics? And what could be more innocent than to expect the world to sit back and watch that theory make its way uninterrupted for as long as it requires in order to succeed in its own terms? And even more naive: that everyone would wait expectantly for the trickle-down or discipline or inevitability of this approach to successfully reformulate all the other aspects of our lives.

The various civilizations on the planet have had experience with myriad other types of internationalism. Natwar Singh: "History is something organic, a phase of man's territorial density as essential for him as memory is for personal identity."[12] We are therefore perfectly capable of noticing while we wait that although some things are working, others are not. We see remarkable economic activity, yet difficulties in wealth creation and distribution. We note the return of oligopolies, even monopolies, yet they are the product of what is said to be modernization. We see something unusual and troubling — the growth of oligopolies at the international level. We see serious political and military slippage toward international violence and disorder; worse still, the return of genocides. From our broad experience of internationalism, we know that persistent violence always trumps economic systems. And leadership systems that cannot understand the causes of violence as a precondition to dealing with them are destined to fail.

Perhaps the original flaw of Globalization lies in its overstatement of the success of nineteenth-century free trade, along with an overstatement of the determinism of technology and the superiority of rational management systems. The certainty of all this inevitable change has distracted us from just how slowly civilizations move. The recent genocide in the Congo reminds us that they — we — are still dealing with King Leopold's violent, genocidal interference a century ago. Britain is still digesting its loss of world leadership. China still thinks and feels like the Middle Kingdom — the centre of the world. Canada, now the third-oldest continuous democracy in the world and the second-oldest continuous federation, is still emotionally and existentially hampered by its colonial insecurity; just as Australia remains confused by the tension between its European cultural origins, its Aboriginal reality and its Asian geography; just as German youth born forty years after the end of Nazism still struggle with the idea of who they could possibly be. Algerians are still attempting to reconstitute themselves after the loss of their great and appropriate leader, Abd-el-Kader, in 1848; and Americans are still scarred and hampered by the implications of their slave-dependent social and economic origins. The list is endless.

Humans change slowly. Societies are even slower. Neither is a client of any particular economic theory. Particularly when that theory, presented as a value-free, inevitable force of modernization, was so infected from the beginning by a particular political tendency known as neo-conservatism or neo-liberalism or economic rationalism.

There was — and is — no necessary or even natural link between ideas of international economics and an ideology that distrusts government's role in the development of the public good. There is no reason, for example, for the World Trade Organization (WTO) to find itself a target of those worried about citizens' rights. Nothing could be more useful to world trade than an international arbitration court. But from the moment that it was associated with a particular series of ideas, the organization could not help becoming a target. What ideas? That civilization must be perceived through the prism of economics; that international trade would tie the hands of governments; that intellectual property holders could use the WTO to protect themselves from more open national competition; that this could all take place in the intentional absence of other international arbitration courts to deal with the individual's human and working rights.

There was a hint of how all of this would unfold in the economist Milton Friedman's Nobel lecture. The year was 1976. "A highly static rigid economy may have a fixed place for everyone, whereas a dynamic, highly progressive economy, which offers ever-changing opportunities and fosters flexibility, may have a high natural rate of unemployment."[13] This is childish logic, unnecessarily divisive, pure Manicheism. Why accept that high employment can only be achieved through *rigidity*? Who says that permanent economic insecurity and disorder are *progressive*? Why can't stability and flexibility go together?

Friedman's assumptions were transposed into the Globalization movement. Global economics came to be presented as a tool to weaken government, discourage taxes both on corporations and on the top bracket of earners, force deregulation and, curiously enough, to strengthen private sector technocracies in large corporations to the disadvantage of real capitalists and entrepreneurs. That predilection for the large over the small meant that the Globalization movement would actively and quite naturally favour the limitation of real competition.

A great deal of this deforming of international economics was done through a remarkable level of conformism in departments of economics around the world. And much of this was the result of the international economic debate being flooded with work funded around the world by largely American neo-conservative foundations holding $2 billion in assets and neo-conservative *think-tanks* with $140 million to spend

every year.[14] This was and remains a gold mine for professors of economics everywhere. There is no equivalent funding or even sizable funding
for any other approach to economic thought. This situation is suggestive
of a one-party state of mind — the sort of thing Marxists dreamt of.

Before you knew it, national governments were forgetting or felt they
should pretend to forget Thomas Aquinas's old saintly joke that taxation
might be robbery, but it wasn't a sin, because raising taxes was the job
of the "sovereign ruler in accordance with the demands for justice to
promote the general welfare."

Equally, it seemed to be forgotten that economics is no more than a
dependant of civilization. Interpretations as recent as the thinker John
Ruggie's *embedded liberalism,* which clarified the role of modern
economics inside social relations, had to be put aside.[15]

Soon enough this pretence of forgetting was forgotten. One gauge of
our ability to remember has been the reaction of the economist John
Williamson, the author of "The Washington Consensus," to the way in
which other people used his 1989 ten-point description of what Western
bankers wanted from indebted Latin American countries. It quickly
became the ten commandments of the neo-conservative Globalist movement. At first he was bemused, then annoyed, then he actually began
explaining and protesting, and finally he made it clear that he had no
neo-conservative sympathies and disagreed with many aspects of
Globalization as applied — for example, the opening-up of capital
markets.[16] In 2002 he was still trying to make his intentions clear: "I, of
course never intended my terms to imply policies like capital account
liberalization, monetarism, supply-side economics, or a minimal state
(getting the state out of welfare provision and income redistribution),
which I think of as the quintessentially neo-liberal ideas. If that is how
the term is interpreted, then we can all enjoy its wake." You cannot help
feeling sorry for the man, trapped inside an international ideology. But
his disavowal tells us where Globalization is sliding. In early 2004 the
editor of *Newsweek,* Fareed Zakaria, wrote, "For almost every country
today, its primary struggle centres on globalization issues — growth,
poverty eradication, disease prevention, education, urbanization, the
preservation of identity."[17] He is right. Except most of these are not in

any direct way Globalization issues. They are international, regional and nation-state issues.

But why couldn't an ideology simply change bits and pieces of its definition of itself?

Because each ideology has a core belief that shapes the bits and pieces. The central perception of Globalization is that civilization should be seen through economics, and economics alone. If you add disease prevention or urbanization or preservation of identity (the characteristic of belonging somewhere) to a commercially driven view of human existence, you merely compound the confusion about how the world works. The difficulty is not in internationalism or international commerce. It is in Globalization's construct of how the two come about.

It was de Tocqueville in 1835 who said, "Can it be believed that the democracy which has overthrown the feudal system and vanquished kings will retreat before tradesmen and capitalists."[18] The equivalent retreat today would be before private sector technocrats, money market specialists, the dominant school of economists and, of course, those public commentators who fit the role of adoring courtiers.

5

A Short History of Economics Becoming Religion

There was little hint until the mid-nineteenth century that economics might be transformed into the source of civilizational truth. Only when God was said to have died did various leaders, professions and sectors risk pushing themselves forward as successors.

Even then, the market seemed an unlikely candidate, immersed as it has always been in the short-term needs of utilitarianism. After all, the weakness of the marketplace, when it comes to great issues, is the possession of a memory somewhat longer than a dog's, slightly shorter than a cat's. But that is also its great strength — its ability to pick itself up after every fall, to recapture its enthusiasms, to move in circles without being bothered by the self-evident repetitions, even the repetitions of error. That dogged, not overly reflective, willingness to just keep on trying is admirable.

What is the memory of the stock market? About that of a dog.

The money market? What was the question?

The great economist Joseph Schumpeter therefore insisted on the need to grasp historical facts, the need to have a historical sense or a historical *experience*. Without these, you couldn't get any idea of how whole economies work, let alone societies. But that historical sense is not a natural market function. And it most certainly is not a function of microeconomics or even of today's macroeconomics. The practitioners of both are awash in the sort of facts that carry them away from memory.

So in place of context, economics has slipped toward truth of the insistent, religious sort. In their defence, most serious economists, whatever their beliefs, when faced by the public policy conclusions drawn from their work would protest that their position is more nuanced. But their incapacity to explain these limitations and nuances in a responsible, public manner is not a sign of how complex economics is. It is a sign of their unwillingness to make the effort to be nuanced in a clear, public manner. Worse still, it is a sign of their unwillingness to disagree with each other in an accessible, constructive public manner.

Margaret Thatcher used to say that "nothing is more insidious than a fashionable consensus." And "surely there is something logically suspect about a solution which is always correct whatever the problem."[1]

Nothing is more comfortable than a consensus that has the answer to every problem. It is as if Karl Marx's historical determinism had been transmogrified directly into the brains of Globalists, particularly the neo-liberal sort.

In Athens, from which the West so insistently claims paternity, the market was understood to be essential, although not of primary importance for the citizen or the civilization. Those in trade were not even citizens, although they had to pay full taxes. Later, in the pre-Hellenistic period, the capitalists might be citizens, but their role was minor in the concept and running of society. In Rome — another popular source of Western historical paternity, and a pretty successful system — the market was probably weighted more to public enterprise than private. But again it was not central to the civilization's understanding of itself. Business was a utilitarian matter, not ideological. Neither business nor trade was about truth. The same sort of attitudes and structures could be found in the Buddhist world and the Confucian. Islamic civilization — an integral part of the Aristotelian, Greco-Roman, Mediterranean West — brought Europe out of its slumber in the last centuries of the first millennium. Muslims carefully regulated manufacturing, trade and taxes. But they were more interested in urban planning, social obligation, science, mathematics, philosophy and literature. In the European Middle Ages, as the economic historian R.H. Tawney pointed out, "at every turn, there [were] limits, restrictions, warnings against allowing economic interests to interfere with serious affairs."[2] The warnings were very specific. "Labour — the common lot of mankind — is necessary and honourable; trade is necessary but perilous to the soul; finance, if not immoral, is at best sordid and at worst disreputable." The high Middle Ages and the Renaissance were filled with complex professional guild and trading systems. The trading systems were Europe-wide, but they also ran from Europe through Africa, from China to Europe, and before long involved crossing the Atlantic from Europe to the Americas. There was no suggestion that these represented the core of civilization or an ideology or a truth.

A great deal has been said, in general negative, about controlled trading systems — the mercantilism of the next couple of centuries. But most of that commentary has involved free traders rewriting history to represent their idea of truth. Looked at dispassionately, the great battle of the mercantilists versus the free traders wasn't much of a struggle. Most countries used both systems and still do. The terms actually distract us from that which interested countries: their ability to build their own industries and their own economies. And so societies mixed and matched the two systems. The result was an intentional confusion of state monopolies with international trading companies, which also often had monopolies. State industries were confused with private industries. Protectionism was welcome wherever it could buy time to strengthen local industries; open borders were welcome when that helped. Various taxes and other incentives were developed to help create and strengthen specific industries. The constant argument was really about how to balance the mix. Nothing could have been further from an ideological methodology and a conviction of economic truth.

If there was one lesson learned during this period, it involved Spain. Awash in Latin American gold and silver from the sixteenth century on, the Spaniards mistook bullion — money — for wealth, that is, for a form of reality, and so undermined their own economy. Because they had the money, which is normally the outcome of making and trading something, they didn't think they had to bother with the production side of their economy. So once the bullion was spent, there was nothing left. They had mistakenly seen some divine providence in the ease with which so much had fallen into their hands. Here was an early warning of the dangers attached to confusing economics with belief systems. Spain didn't understand that the only purpose of money was as a grease or glue for reality. Today that Spanish imperial childishness seems very modern. It is an almost exact parallel to our belief that in a technological, global era, money markets have in and of themselves become a form of trade and so a source of wealth creation — that money has at last become real.

In the seventeenth and eighteenth centuries most other countries and empires used money with greater care than Spain. Their desire was to produce goods that in turn produced wealth. The Dutch for a very long time mixed mercantilism, complex supports for local industries, and free trade, as did the British. The British carefully used protectionism during the early Industrial Revolution to get their new-style economy up and running without interference during its fragile stage. They didn't even seriously consider free trade until well into the nineteenth century. By then they were so far ahead of everyone else that they couldn't help but win by opening their border to the non-manufactured produce of others, while convincing them to open their borders to British manufactured goods. During this whole period the French were much more mercantilist and intent on protecting local industries. They fell behind in some areas, went ahead in others, consolidated their agriculture, public services, public education, communication systems — roads and railways in particular — experimented with free trade for a decade and came into the First World War as the leading Allied power. The particular route they chose can hardly be seen to have been a disaster for them. After all, to this day they remain one of the two leading powers in Europe.

There was a wonderfully hypocritical debate in the eighteenth century involving the trade in English cloth versus Indian. It was often said to be about open markets and free trade, but it was always about specific rival interests. It stretched on through the nineteenth century, when even at the height of the free trade moralizing furor, the

Manchester merchants — the true believers of true believers — saw no contradiction in yet again not giving India its fair trading chance.

In 1981, with an almost endearing lack of historical memory, Margaret Thatcher stood up in Bombay to lecture Indians about free trade: "May I just say a word about international trade because in a way one of the great contributions that we in Britain try to make to international prosperity is to keep our markets open, and to persuade other countries to keep their markets open." It would be nice to think of the audience, sitting there with 250-year-old fixed ironic smiles.[3]

Mrs. Thatcher's tone was a typical product of the sort of economic religious belief that arose from the middle of the nineteenth century on. But it was also a reminder that there are a limited number of economic ideas. So they keep coming back.

Each return, if sensibly handled, lasts only so long as it is useful, and blends into the next fashion, thus consolidating any progress made. Unfortunately, most are not handled sensibly. So they create an economic and social imbalance. And they drag on, outliving their welcome and in the process damaging their real accomplishments, if not provoking an indiscriminate erasing of everything that has been accomplished, good and bad.

In the case of modern free trade, it began with a confusion of religious beliefs — both Protestant and economic — among the leaders of the movement, Richard Cobden and John Bright. Upon their first great victory — the repeal of the Corn Laws in 1846 — nine thousand people crowded into Manchester's Free Trade Hall to hear Cobden. "[H]aving the feeling I have of the sacredness of the principle, I say that I can never agree to tamper with it."[4] What did he mean by the sacred nature of free trade?

Cobden, 1843, in the House of Commons: "Our object is to make you conform to truth."

Bright, 1845, in the House: "[I speak on behalf of those people] into whose hearts free trade principles have sunk, and become, verily, a religious question."

Cobden in 1846 explained that the buy-cheap, sell-expensive principle was not about selfishness, but was a matter of "carrying out to the fullest extent the Christian doctrine of 'Do ye to all men as ye would they should do unto you.'"

Cobden, 1845: "I believe we are at an era which in importance, socially, has not its equal for the last 1800 years." "[W]e have a principle established now which is eternal in its truth and universal in its application, and must be applied in all nations and throughout all times, and applied not simply to commerce, but to every item of the tariffs of the world."

Cobden, 1843: "[A law which prevents free trade is a] law which interferes with the wisdom of the Divine Providence, and substitutes the law of wicked men for the law of nature."[5]

These are the deep, now largely unconscious, foundations of today's free trade movement. If you wanted to be unkind you would simply cite Flaubert's cynical observation: "When people no longer believe in the Immaculate Conception, they will believe in turning tables."[6] There is a resemblance to the *ex cathedra* declaration of the 17th Ecumenical Council of 1447: people, not within the one faith — whether Jew, heretic, schismatic or pagan — "cannot become participants in eternal life, but will depart 'into everlasting fire which was prepared for the devil and his angels' (Matt 25:41)."[7]

Of course there was a great deal more to the free trade movement than absolute belief. Given the right circumstances, free trade worked. In 1846 Britain had the right circumstances and so profited. If Gladstone survived as prime minister for so long, it was because his severe religious belief and economic convictions were limited by political intuition. And he was convinced that free trade was cheapening goods, spreading wealth and helping the growth in public education. Nineteenth-century free traders were in favour of higher wages, an interesting contrast with today's. They wanted strong infrastructures such as public post offices, closely regulated railway companies, and so on. Without effective public infrastructures and toughly regulated private services, they felt they could not do business efficiently.

The movement spread to France in 1860, where it lasted a decade with decent results. Germany was divided in its response. The trading cities like Hamburg were in favour, but Bismarck was busy building a national industrial infrastructure, as the British themselves had done before opening up to free trade. That done, the new German Empire created reciprocal relationships with most of Europe. Like today's European Union, it was a system that worked for large and small.[8] The First World War was the step too far that brought it all crashing down.

There was another unexpected advantage to the British-led religious approach. The Protestant ethic surrounding free trade had the effect, even in Catholic countries, of encouraging saving — the exact opposite of today's consumerism. The result was to strengthen the base for wealth creation.

Many philosophers supported the movement — Montesquieu first among them, as well as Hume and Kant.[9] They were convinced free trade would bring prosperity and peace. Hume wrote of trade and international "benevolent sympathies," Kant of "the power of money" as a force of "mediation" for peace; Montesquieu believed that "where there is commerce, people are better behaved."

Unfortunately they were wrong. Parallel with the growth of unregulated and untaxed international commerce in the second half of the nineteenth century came a growth in war; wars on the continent, wars around the world, all culminating in a disastrous world war. This is strangely similar to the evolution of the last quarter-century.

Along with these wars came another parallel growth — that of nationalism. Some of the implications were positive — democracy, for example, and regulations designed to support the public good. Neither had been high on the free trader's agenda. After all, the pro-democracy Chartist movement arose in Britain at exactly the same time as the free trader Anti-Corn Law League. The Chartists wanted precisely the democratic rules that Western democracies all have today. The free traders were not supportive. The Chartists were gradually marginalized, which pushed them into violence. Many were arrested, tried and deported. As for industrial regulations, the free traders — and specifically Cobden and Bright — were against both unions and legislation regulating work conditions. They were for high wages and well-run factories, providing the owners made those decisions. Dissatisfied workers should emigrate.[10] There is an interesting contemporary parallel here with the question of work conditions in developing countries. Today those workers play exactly the role played by the Western working class in the nineteeth and early twentieth centuries. Then as now the standard argument was that any attempt to regulate the workplace would damage the market and hurt the workers. Employment was their opportunity to better themselves. If do-gooders were allowed to interfere, the market would go elsewhere.

Tied to these nineteenth-century attitudes was the gradual conversion of machine-age theory into management theory, best known as Taylorism or Fordism or time-movement management. What it meant was the intentional confusing of men with machines.

When you put all of this together you can see why the free traders, lost in a religious conviction that they were going down the only possible road to progress, missed how social policies and regulations might have helped their cause, missed the great advancing political force of the working class, scarcely noticed the rise of populism, socialism, communism, false populism, fascism, all rolling up behind them. They even missed the simultaneous rise and formalization of modern racism.[11] The accumulation of these forces couldn't help but catch free trade up in its dynamism and dash it on the rocks of nationalism.

There was a fourth parallel growth, along with war, nationalism and management theory. The rapid rise of empires. International, integrated free trading markets were supposed to make empires go away. Instead one became the handmaiden of the other. Which for which is not clear. But it was soon obvious that empires were organized conduits of natural resources for industrial centres. Led by the British, this approach was expanded into what have been called informal empires — empires of trade treaties, special access, protection.[12] This was the last thing free trade economists had expected. All of them, right up to Schumpeter, were certain that "the principles of free trade economics ... left no room for imperialism,"[13] just as their successors over the last quarter-century have been convinced that Globalization would weaken nation-states and favour impartial international relations.

There is one free trade issue that is rarely mentioned in the context of Cobden and the great movement. During the eighteenth century, the British, followed by the French and the Americans, wanted to buy high-quality Chinese goods — tea, silk, porcelain. The West could not produce these goods, or at any rate could not match the Chinese level of excellence. The problem was that the Chinese didn't want any Western goods. There being no two-way trade, the West had to pay cash. The British used silver they received in trade with Spain. In 1781 there was no silver, so Warren Hastings, the first governor-general of India, sent off Indian opium to be sold in China to pay for British imports. This eventually led to two Opium Wars in which the West — pretending to be at war over the treatment of their traders — fought China to force the country to go on importing opium, thus addicting its citizens. By 1830 this trade was probably the largest single commodity business in the world.[14] The same House of Commons, so enthusiastic about the moral virtues of free trade, defeated motions to ban the opium trade in 1870, 1875, 1886 and 1889. The trade ended in 1913 as part of the winding-down of the first free trade experiment.

Put bluntly, Britain in particular and the West in general asked themselves whether the moral principle of fair trade trumped the well-being of a people. They answered that it did.

That is a question valid for all time; even if we refuse to raise it at appropriate moments, history will, when the time comes to describe our actions for future generations. In what possible context could a question relevant to the opium trade be raised today? What about the pharmaceuticals essential to combat AIDS, malaria and tuberculosis in the developing world and the way in which their prices are artificially kept high by the Trade-Related Aspects of Intellectual Property Rights (TRIPS) regime in the WTO? Or what about Western industrial agriculture and its effect on fragile societies? Or the destructive effect of unregulated financial markets on weaker economies?

By 1900 the record of free trade was increasingly unclear. The United States, using a combination of tariffs and national policies, was growing faster than Britain under free trade. Germany, using a combination of tariffs, national policies and bilateral arrangements, was growing faster than Britain.[15] Ex-colonies like Canada were putting their own industrial infrastructure in place, thanks to national policies — which combined tariffs with other support systems. Without such policies they would have been caught in the commodity producer trap. And they resented Britain's last attempt, early in the twentieth century, to gather the empire up into an economic free trading unit designed to send raw materials one way and manufactured goods the other. The Canadians led the Dominions in saying no. Meanwhile, Washington saw the unregulated, international system as simply old-fashioned. Teddy Roosevelt felt that overall the free trade approach had produced growth without equity. He did not believe in its moral virtue of truth. He felt it was time to try to rebalance the sharing of profits.[16]

What you discover in all of these patterns are two different types of conviction. The first is economic internationalism, most clearly expressed as free trade. This is the formal belief, but its minimalist clarity has a Protestant, even Pentecostal, feel about it. Here is a cause that good, straightforward men can embrace and preach.

The second conviction is more diffuse, perhaps an outcome of the first. It is all about what goes without saying. This is the conviction that among sophisticated, worldly people certain things should be taken for granted. You shouldn't need to preach them. Thus, in the context of economic internationalism, governments will be more constricted; regulations of a local sort less likely; regulation in general less likely; formal particularities tied to local conditions less frequent. These outcomes are meant to indicate sophistication, related not primarily to belief but simply to administrative practices. Belief is all very well, but a church must be run.

Imagine how difficult it must have been, first in 1914 and then through the troubled '20s to the broad collapse of 1929, for such a fervent and well-organized group of believers as the free traders to accept their multiple defeats. How could they accept as *revelation* that they did not speak for a divine force?

The first stage in a balanced detoxification process would have been to stare into the mirror of the preceding decades and ask themselves questions about the contradictory outcomes of the experience. North Americans, obsessed with the collapse of 1929, forget how much of the bad had already hit elsewhere in the world. Throughout the 1920s there had been inflation, deflation, the collapse of employment, much of it dealt with at great human cost to create an appearance of order, only to have it collapse again in the 1930s. What did it all mean? These questions were not asked. And so neither was there the sensible argument that could have begun with a simple question: Do economic theories work best when there are multiple approaches, some of them contradicting others, thus reflecting the complexity in which we actually live?

Instead of doubts and soul searching, quite the opposite happened.

Free traders around the world gradually chose not to glance in any mirror. Instead, they began to demonize a single law of the American Congress as the source of all evil. And so by shifting the blame for the collapse of the 1930s, they also erased any memory of the collapses of 1914 and 1929 and maintained their beliefs intact.

What happened was this: in the aftermath of the 1929 crisis a tariff act went through Congress in the United States. It was named Smoot-Hawley for its two sponsors, Senator Reed Smoot and Representative Willis C. Hawley. The act raised tariffs. Opponents of President Coolidge began to claim that this act had turned a small market shock into a depression, that he should have vetoed it. This politically motivated chorus was picked up by the free trade believers and turned into the sort of accusation appropriate to heresies. Smoot-Hawley, they claimed — and claim to this day — had raised tariffs to historic highs, provoking first protests from around the world and then retaliation, and so had thrown all of us into the catastrophe of protectionism. The unspoken assumption was that this, not the deregulated marketplace, had caused the Great Depression.

Over the last few years, calmer people like Alfred Eckes have carefully examined those events.[17] They discovered that the tariff rates had not been raised to historic highs. In fact, two-thirds of American imports were left untouched. There were very few international protests and even less retaliation. He found no convincing evidence that Smoot-Hawley caused the stock market crash or made the Depression worse.

These revelations will have difficulty displacing the established discourse. Whenever anyone wants to say something that sounds knowledgeable about the Depression, they trot out the villainy of Smoot-Hawley. And in a world of public figures reading speeches they haven't prepared and may not have thought much about, Smoot-Hawley fairly leaps off the speechwriter's internet trade files as something that will make the boss sound informed. It has become the equivalent of citing a few words of Adam Smith in order to support the sort of interest-driven civilization in which Smith actually did not believe. How can you stop them from libelling the poor man? How can you take away such a handy bogeyman as Smoot-Hawley?

Some, like Susan Strange, accuse the free traders of purposely creating "the myth that protectionism caused the Great Depression."[18] Eckes says that "they successfully transformed a molehill into a mountain." At the very least, they distracted attention from the catastrophic ending of the unregulated period, first in 1914 and then in 1929. And in doing this they distracted themselves from the need to ask some simple questions about their time in power.

This is the context in which I read the economist August von Hayek's Nobel lecture. It was 1974.[19] The Keynesian era was in ever greater difficulty — difficulty that should have provoked a serious examination of what was going right and what wrong. Instead, the father of the new international economic Pentecostalism chatted on, as if dealing with a given matter of truth, about "the superiority of the market order." "[W]hen it is not suppressed by the powers of government, it regularly displaces other types of order." This was the new religious language. That of the specialist — dispassionate, surrounded by battalions of what seem to be factually based arguments. Jesuitical, yet susceptible to a populist interpretation. Think of it as a disembodied version of "Onward Christian Soldiers." The facts of God sweep the heathens aside. You will recognize the Cobdenesque absolute assurance that truth is possessed, that forces of inevitability are on the march.

Note the pernicious assumption in his argument. Only government could stop the market, but because the market is the superior force of the two (natural superiority? moral? intellectual? or simply the inevitable superiority of the divine?) the government's actions would in every case be irresponsible. Remember Cobden's summation of international economics as morality: a law which stands in the way is a "law which interferes with the wisdom of the Divine Providence, and substitutes the law of wicked men for the law of nature."

There was no hint anywhere in Hayek's lecture that the preceding quarter-century had produced historic rates of growth or unheard-of degrees of egalitarianism. Instead, there was an absolute conviction that would lead the political economist Francis Fukuyama twenty years later to restate this certainty of one truth: "There is a fundamental process at work that dictates *a common evolutionary pattern* for all societies."[20]

The philosopher George Steiner feels that today "fundamentalism, that blind lunge towards simplification, towards the infantile comforts of imposed discipline, is immensely on the march."[21] What is different now is the way specialists use their version of facts to support these blind lunges. If what we are dealing with is a type of religious fundamentalism, then these facts are the modern equivalent of scholasticism. I'll concentrate on one example.

In October 2000 the American National Bureau of Economic Research put out a press release to deliver dramatic news:

ECONOMIC GROWTH IS REDUCING GLOBAL POVERTY

A new study showed that the number of people living on $1 a day or less had plummeted to 350 million. The press release insisted that these numbers, arrived at through the latest techniques, ended the argument by anti-Globalization "academics, journalists and multi-lateral organizations of all stripes ... that poverty and inequality are on the rise."[22] The period covered by the study was precisely that of Globalization.

The research fellow who did the study, Xavier Sala-i-Martín, demonstrated through his work that the number of people living on less than $1 a day had dramatically dropped. So had the number living on less than $2 a day. The report and its numbers immediately entered into the daily catechism of those who speak out for Globalization. As the release had made clear, that was the intent.

How wonderful if it were really true. I immediately got hold of this long study and read it through carefully.[23] The happiest stories in it were China and India. The most depressing sections dealt with Africa, but even there "not all the news … is bad." In thirteen countries the $1 poverty rate was reduced. The same was true for the $2 poverty rate.

I couldn't help noticing that five of the thirteen could also be found on a quite different list — the short list of countries suffering most from AIDS, a disease destructive of social and economic systems precisely because it strikes people down in their early to prime careers. Even more peculiar was the star country of Sala-i-Martín's African prosperity — Botswana — which had cut its $1 poverty rate from 35 percent to 1 percent and its $2 poverty rate from 60 percent to 9 percent. Botswana is also number one on the AIDS emergency list, with some 40 percent of people aged fifteen to forty-nine HIV positive. How did it become an international statistical star at the same time? Sala-i-Martín doesn't explain, but the answer is simple. Botswana has a very large diamond mine, a very small and, thanks to AIDS, shrinking population to share the wealth, and a reasonably good government. None of which has anything to do with the post-1971 theory of global economics.

Rwanda was also on Sala-i-Martín's hopeful list. An AIDS emergency country, it went through a terrifying genocide — somewhere around 800,000 murdered — and societal collapse during precisely the period when Sala-i-Martín was finding statistics of economic success.

What could these success stories mean? Is it like the outcome of the Black Death? So many people had died that the survivors by the simple act of surviving and inheriting the property of victims became richer. Does this mean that his facts contain basic assumptions about the value of a particular economic theory? Or perhaps his African statistics are a statistical aberration, while the rest are accurate. Or are not accurate. Mr. Sala-i-Martín declared that the number of people living on under $1 a day had dropped to 350 million by 1998. Yet in 2004 the World Bank calculated that there were still 1.1 billion people living on less than $1 a day.

I asked two internationally known African experts with a great deal of experience in global economic negotiations what they thought of Sala-i-Martín's report. If anything, their tendencies would have led them to an optimistic view of Globalization. They said Sala-i-Martín's numbers were skewed by China and India — two examples not of countries becoming less driven by national policies as a result of Globalization, but of countries using international markets to strengthen their internal focus and status as nation-states. And his international numbers were doubly skewed because he had used national statistics that can be subject to political interference, numbers much less accurate than the more down-to-earth Household Survey method. Even the latter are incomplete and often inaccurate. Overall, they felt the whole report was pretty meaningless. Nevertheless, it has become another important building block in the assertion of global economic certainty. The economist Paul Krugman: "Anyone who has seen how economic statistics are constructed knows that they are really a subgenre of science fiction."[24] But then what use are they, except for ideological assertions? Margaret Thatcher used to say she found that "much economic writing, though academically respectable, seems to the politician to have little relevance to the problems he has to solve."

But then, what is academic respectability? A fashionable consensus? Conformity?

The World Bank says the number of people living on $1 a day has fallen over the last two decades from 1.5 billion to 1.1 billion, but those living on $2 a day has grown from 1 billion to 1.6 billion. So the total of those living in basic poverty has actually grown from 2.5 to 2.7 billion under Globalization. The evolution from the $1 category to the $2 category might mean a marginal improvement or nothing at all or a worsening in poverty. What a sensible person would say is that there are no clear signs of progress, and there may be serious slippage, except in India and China. And even there the rich-poor divide has become so serious that it destroyed the last Indian government and is the single most important obsession of the Chinese government.

The more fundamental question is whether such statistical propositions as the $1-a-day-life reflect any reality that real people live. Perhaps that is why people like the Aga Khan have so little time for GDP measurements and now propose looking at people's Quality of Life.

After all, people at $3 a day could be living a life of pure despair in a savage slum of Lagos, a life far worse than that at $1 a day in a stable slum like Klong Toey in Bangkok, where there is a societal structure.

Our obsession with a certain kind of austere, abstracted measurement is closely tied to the idea of a civilization that believes it is being led by economics. That sort of leadership involves a bizarre contradiction: an aggressive certainty that these economics can be measured with great precision versus a passive certainty that they can only very marginally be shaped. Aggressive on the details, passive on the larger picture.

Where would this idea come from if not from a technocracy of administrators and economists who resemble an old priesthood but think of themselves as very modern, thanks to the mass of details by which they surround themselves?

PART II
THE RISE

All of our countries have been in the throes of recession and inflation more severe than at any time since World War II.

The post-war era of international relations is ended.

— Henry Kissinger, address to the
Pittsburgh World Affairs Council, 1975

Clericalism is a disease of all organizations.

— Andrea Riccardi, founder, Sant'Egidio, 2004

6

1971

It would be simplistic to tie the arrival of Globalism to the failure of Keynesianism. And it would be wrong to see it as a mere reaction to the multiple crises of the 1970s. Other more profound changes had prepared the way.

Not that the crises were imaginary. As in a nightmare they tumbled out, one after the other, leaving no space to breathe, no time to rebuild stability. They rocked the self-confidence of everyone in leadership positions, which in turn unnerved the citizenry. John Kirton, director of the G8 Research Group, writes of six seminal shocks that forced the West to reorganize itself at the leadership level by creating the G7.[1]

They began with Richard Nixon's decision to handle American financial problems by destroying the Bretton Woods monetary system. Bretton Woods was a key part of the post–Second World War international jigsaw puzzle. It was designed to maintain stability by tying other currencies to the U.S. dollar at fixed exchange rates. Suddenly, on August 15, 1971, Washington let the dollar float and the system was gone. The other Western powers had no choice but to try to adjust to a unilateral act.

This new-style currency devaluation was accompanied by a second unilateral act — in effect, the raising of American tariffs. It's hard to know how many of the dozens of different sorts of crises that followed would have happened anyway and how many were the result of these two big pieces being moved and so setting off a complex series of chain reactions.

The next seminal crisis was the failure of the General Agreement on Tariffs and Trade (GATT) negotiations in 1973. Many people were convinced that the only way out of their economic troubles was a growth in trade, so the Tokyo Round failure was a great letdown. It was followed by the Yom Kippur War in the same year, which led directly to the oil embargo and a first steep oil price rise. In 1974 India exploded a nuclear weapon. Suddenly the most dangerous of arms was no longer under the control of a small club.

How much larger would the nuclear world become? The risks were far more distant, even vague, than those created by the new economic problems, but nuclear weapons are an automatic source of immeasurable fear, which can cast a pall over everything else — a fear of the unknown, a fear of the rogue player.

As if to encourage that fear, new- and old-style communist parties were becoming so popular across southern Europe that they were within reach of political power, needing only to be invited into coalition governments. Then, in 1975, the United States withdrew from Vietnam, defeated — its first defeat since 1814.

These six seminal crises, surrounded by myriad others, created the general belief in the West and around the world that the post-war system had broken down, that American power was both shrinking and faced by a growing rivalry with Europe and Japan. And that much of the developing world — only ten to twenty years earlier mere colonial possessions — was evolving in an unexpected way.

Out of these crises came a terrifying combination of inflation and depression. It was called stagflation. All of this together produced a sense of powerlessness among the elites, which they communicated instinctually and even openly to their citizenry.

7

The Vacuum

Were things as bad as all that? Not really. There were a multitude of positive developments going on at the same time. Two of Western democracy's fundamental ambitions — inclusive education and egalitarian health care, both seen as the foundations of society's freedom and well-being — made historic strides forward, mostly thanks to public systems. Old racial prejudices and barriers were falling on all fronts. Women were breaking into the male bastions and so infusing the public and private domains with new energy and new approaches. People who had been marginalized for a wide variety of reasons were gradually being included to varying degrees. Public debate in the Western democracies — and at that point in the majority of the recently freed colonies — had rarely if ever been so open and so broadly based.

And in spite of the abrupt way in which the colonial powers had both freed and abandoned their empires, many of these new nations were experimenting with fresh approaches to governance. Much of this experimentation would soon go wrong. But the West now carefully forgets how much of that failure was imposed from outside through Western development theories from the 1960s to the 1980s. Even the origins of today's success stories are now discounted. For example, today's utilitarian eyes look back with disapproval on the thirty years of centralized planning in India. Everyone knows it wasn't efficient. It can easily be argued that India was held back by this. Indians will be the first to say that some of the bureaucratic heavy-handedness remains. But what

Western critics forget is that this relentlessly stable approach permitted Indians to catch their breath after the disorder and violence of independence. And when combined with Delhi's complex international policy of non-alignment, this period gave Indians time to think about their broad ambitions instead of being subjected to the reformulated ambitions being projected from the West. And so they developed a certain internal logic upon which they are still building, while those parts of the ex-colonial world that immediately gave themselves over to Western planning techniques — in which I include Soviet techniques — are now largely in ruins.

Whatever positive developments there were, the general atmosphere in the 1970s as the crises struck one after another was one of discomfort and fear of disorder among the Western elites, whether political, administrative, intellectual or business. Sometimes this amounted to a sense of incapacitating fear.

Their societies had entered into a vacuum — a confusing period between two eras. No one seemed able to rise above events so as to make out what was happening or what new direction might be taken. Henry Kissinger, then in his last years as secretary of state, had perhaps the clearest view: "[T]he postwar era of international relations is ended. No single upheaval marked this transformation.... But the cumulative evolution of a generation has profoundly altered our world."[1]

Most senior politicians and officials were frightened of such clarity. The acceptable position was to insist on the urgent need for the situation to be managed. This was the new technocratic approach toward crises, one that had great short-term advantages and great long-term disadvantages. It meant that those in power were discouraged from providing leadership.

Had they referred back to the preceding vacuum — that of the late 1940s — they would have discovered an idea of leadership that involved both taking risks and searching for the meaning in a time of uncertainty. The most obvious example was the Marshall Plan, although it is now intellectually fashionable to minimize the general's intentions by demonstrating how confused the origins of his plan were. It had not been first carefully worked out in order then to be properly managed. The intent was therefore an accidental outcome.

But George Marshall's sort of leadership rarely does stand up to contemporary technocratic analysis. It wasn't designed to. The primary interest of Secretary of State Marshall and others was not to manage disorder. It was to find a new reality that would make the disorder go away. He and others were convinced that Europe needed to be jump-started. His program would pour $1.3 billion (in dollars of the day) into sixteen countries between 1948 and 1951. In June 1947, when he gave his famous Harvard speech launching the whole idea, there was no plan. The speech had been cobbled together at the last moment from an unsynthesized intuition of what reality required. He and his advisors had managed to grasp the sense of history, so the future he imagined verbally at Harvard became the real future. You could say that he had found the way — or a way — out of the vacuum.

This is not a eulogy to the leader as the lone hero. His speech did not come out of nowhere. Marshall was surrounded by hundreds, thousands of inchoate questions, possibilities, risks. Once he had formulated the way, these elements, which moments before had appeared disparate, seemed to form up behind his imagined idea. And so, suddenly, "the Marshall Plan mushroomed into a program with so many stated objectives, purposes and motives as to make these virtually meaningless as a list of reasons for its origins. The contradictions alone are enough to boggle the mind in search of rationality."[2] Therein lay its genius. It could not have emerged from a management team, much less from a think-tank or consultants.

Which brings me back to the underlying evolution toward the supremacy of management — an evolution that was not at the origin of the West's response to the crises of the '70s. But the steady expansion and rise of a new technocratic class in every corner of civilization, public and private, would shape that response. This was one of the practical conclusions to come out of the two world wars. A new kind of management was needed to run ever larger operations — whether these dealt with public health care or private factories.

Yet there was no debate about the central nature of management. After all, management must be based on the assumption that there are broad forces at work. At best, these forces are represented by leadership. And leadership needs to be rendered concrete through management. On the other hand, leadership was not supposed to weaken its capacity to shape or change these forces. If you confuse leadership with management, you remove the idea of choice — the choices that the citizenry express through their leaders. Gradually you find in the place of leadership a growing assumption that the broader forces at work are of mysterious origin. Indeed, they are inevitable. They can't be shaped.

The crises of the early 1970s coincided with this deep confusion between leadership and management. It is still with us, fed by an astonishing inflation in the number and size of management schools and a narrow silo approach toward higher education. That silo approach is central to the assumption that broader forces cannot be shaped. In practical terms, this is one of the reasons that leaders, who want to exercise their power to choose on broad policy questions, have so much trouble getting supportive advice from their technocracy.

The sequential crises of the 1970s coincided with the arrival at the top of the political ladder of the first generation of these technocrats — Harold Wilson of the United Kingdom, France's Valéry Giscard d'Estaing, West Germany's Helmut Schmidt, even Henry Kissinger in his own unusual way. What that meant in Europe was only too clear. Even before the last world war was over people like Albert Camus were saying, "France and Europe must today create a new civilization or perish."[3] Sixty years later, Spanish thinker Victor Pérez-Diaz was lamenting that the reality of a politically united Europe was slipping away in the absence of "a European political culture of active citizenry." "The European public space and the European demos," the two key "components of a European *civitas*" remain elusive. Why? Because the Union was built around administrative, professional, political and economic structures. Nothing was done about the idea of citizenship, let alone civilization. So when the crises began, the Union, under its fresh technocratic leaders, was pushed yet further in the direction of management and away from leadership, away from civilization.

As so often happens, confusion is revealed in language. For example, this first generation of technocratic leaders was unable to admit the world had slipped into a depression. They were so far from being able to think and act at the level of the problem that they couldn't even say the word. Instead of action they embraced reaction by concentrating on the management of what they insisted on calling a recession. But then there was another recession and another. Throughout the 1970s, one after another after another after another. An energy crisis, followed by inflation, unemployment, economic stall, debt, more inflation, unemployment and so on. Sequential recessions, but never a depression. After all, if there were a depression there would also have been a major leadership failure as well as an urgent need for dramatic leadership initiatives. A recession, on the other hand, was something managers could handle, because the broader forces were not assumed to be out of control. Even Kissinger couldn't quite say the word: "All of our countries have been in the throes of recession and inflation more severe than at any time since World War II."

He had prepared all his life for just such a crisis. Kissinger was guided by his detailed study of how, from the vacuum produced with Napoleon's defeat in 1815, a way out had been found by the Austrian statesman Prince Metternich and the British foreign secretary Viscount Castlereagh, who created a continent-wide balance of power known as the European Concert. Both men were brilliant, but Metternich was the ultimate systems man, who "confused policy with intrigue [and tried] to substitute cunning for strength of character." "So agile was Metternich's performance that it was forgotten its basis was diplomatic skill and it left the fundamental problems unsolved." Castlereagh, the perfect humanist, sought "a peace of equilibrium," saw peace as "a moral act," developed policies which, as with Marshall, "did not reside in the *facts,* but in their interpretation." He was a statesman who could "recognize the real relationship of forces" and so accepted "the precedence of integration over retribution." Kissinger seemed to wish he were Castlereagh, but fate had made him a reincarnation of Metternich.[4]

The fear our contemporary elites have of admitting an unmanage-able reality like *depression,* while operating under the conscious or unconscious inspiration of Metternich, suggests just how autocratic the new style of leadership might be when it came to technocratic correc-tions, and how timid, fearful even, when faced by the full force of social and human reality out of control. Their concept of *efficiency* was all about streamlining thought rather than dealing with the idiosyncratic nature of society. They wanted two things: some sort of abstract approach capable of limiting big situations that were difficult to manage, and the right to tinker with the minutiae of administrative systems. Joseph Stiglitz would much later describe what their methods were already leading to: "The institutions have come to reflect the mind-sets of those to whom they are accountable. The typical central bank governor begins his day worrying about inflation statistics, not poverty statistics; the trade minister worries about export numbers, not pollution indices."[5]

In other words, these new-style leaders were an almost passive pushover for the revived neo-liberal movement with its devotion to larger solutions through deregulated structures. The technocrats were ill prepared for an apparently straight, open public debate. They were caught up in their management, dealing with each other, ever less able to speak intelligently to the citizenry.

You might say they were constantly in close-up. They tinkered or they slashed. As tinkering didn't work, they increasingly accepted the logic of the fresh and limpid ideologues so insistently on the horizon: only slash-ing could save the day. In Viscount Castlereagh or General Marshall's terms, they failed to lead because they failed to imagine. In contempo-rary terms, they inadvertently strengthened the critique of publicly administered programs. Instead of focusing on their own failure, they increasingly accepted the rather simplistic argument that public programs were inefficient if not subjected to free market impulses. And global free market impulses couldn't help doing the job even better.

On the other side, even Hayek, ancient as he was in the 1970s, had a clear view of exactly what was needed: "The influence of the economist that mainly matters is an influence over laymen: politicians, journalists, civil servants and the public generally."[6] And so as the period of vacuum progressed, the only clear words firmly expressed were those of the Globalists, who were often redefined nineteenth-century free traders, certainly utilitarian and increasingly what became known as neo-conservatives or neo-liberals.

Those who held power were simply too busy tinkering in an obscure specialist way to talk to us. And in any case they saw themselves as too sophisticated to talk to us in an open, intelligent manner. The ideologues weren't. There were great differences among those who spoke up, between the intellectual and moral sophistication of a Hayek or the careful reflections of a Samuel Brittain as opposed to the rather brutal simplifications of a Milton Friedman or an ideologue like Robert Nozick, to take just four. There were also great differences between each of the neo-liberals and among all of them as a group versus the simple free traders. But what linked them all was some idea of a possible global balance that would be more or less natural, thanks to released market forces. That in turn implied weakened governments, therefore weakened nation-states. And what linked them in turn to the non-communicative technocrats in power was a shared utilitarianism.

What the public saw was an odd debate between ebullient, optimistic, amusing, theatrical Globalists and lugubrious, self-absorbed, techno-cratic and obscure liberal managers. This produced a vague public feeling that government was increasingly a failure. On that basis, parts of the West slipped out of the vacuum into a new era. Although much slower to come in much of Europe, even there this idea began to take hold. And whether in government or business, the key to leadership would be economics. Which, *sotto voce,* meant self-interest. This was a curious outcome, because the original free traders had thought the opposite. When Cobden said, "[No] class could be trusted to legislate in favour of its own interest, for it generally mistook its own interest,"[7] he was echoing Adam Smith's central belief in the individual's ability to empathize with the *other* and the need, therefore, to organize society around that identification with the *other*. And indeed the rise to respectability of self-interest was followed by a sharp rise in corruption in both the public and the private sector everywhere in the

democracies. There hadn't been anything quite like it since the financial free-for-all of the later nineteenth century.

The natural link between the Globalists — even the neo-liberal
Globalists — and the modern technocracy goes beyond simple utilitarianism. Think of the European technocracy's success in managing
the Union's integration on a fairly egalitarian and inclusive basis. Yet
there could be no more eloquent illustration of the problem than their
incapacity over a sixty-year period to even begin to address how
Europeans would actually live together. They couldn't face such a broad
and non-utilitarian issue as European culture, with its multitude of
levels and possible relationships.

And think of the curious case of the American liberal hero John
Rawls, whose theory of society as a maze of contracts actually strengthened the utilitarian argument of those he opposed. By providing an
unrealistic, but nevertheless ethical, argument for modern interest-
driven utilitarianism, he gave credibility to the libertarian arguments.[8]

The intellectual, ethical and political failure of the elites who said they
believed in an inclusive egalitarianism; their fear of rising above the
crises to set a new direction; their incapacity to reform the ever larger
management structures on the basis of their purpose rather than simply
defending their technical structures — all of this was part of what led us
out of the vacuum in the direction of a Globalism heavily influenced
by utilitarian assumptions and methods.

Curiously enough, those first steps were filled with themes that today
seem familiar. Why? Because they are now being repeated as Globalism
ebbs away. The U.S. dollar devaluation that had precipitated so much
change in 1971 was repeated in 2004, this time with greater sophistication. The technocracy has learned how to pretend it isn't doing something it is doing. With the situation in Iraq, there are once again the

dangers of a war economy, as there was in the 1970s. Once again there is an energy price rise, although the context is much more complex and broad this time around. In 1973 there was much talk of Western societies being undermined because of transnationals exporting jobs, what we now call *outsourcing*.[9] There was also talk of disorder in the international monetary system. And then as now there was a belief that the economic weakness of the United States meant it could maintain its dominance only by military and diplomatic means.

Robert Jackson suggested then that we were faced with a choice between three ways of organizing our societies and the world: a *Realist* approach, a *Functionalist* approach or a *Rationalist* approach. The Realist was all about the play between nation-states seeking international balances. The Functionalist spoke for itself. This was the road taken in the Globalist era. The Rationalist was a grander version of the Functionalist — it involved a legalistic, individualistic approach that somehow was supposed to lead everyone in the same direction. John Rawls's prose is a good illustration of the Rationalist school and why it simply degenerates into the Functionalist.

What is surprising is how clear the direction taken seems to have been when you look back now. It certainly didn't seem that clear at the time.

8

The King's Fool

Just as classic plays with kings, virgins, love and betrayal must have their fool, so Globalization had Davos. That this would be its role was not immediately clear. The first gathering, in January 1971 in that small town in the Swiss Alps, was a serious attempt to galvanize the European business technocracy into stronger competition with the United States. This was the twenty-fifth-anniversary celebration of the Centre d'études industrielles, and the gathering was very much built around a triple vision of life — nations were dying and deserved to die; business was to be led by managers, not capitalists; and business must lead society. Or, as the 160-page report of the conference put it:

> By contrast with the visibly decrepit condition of most European states, industry and commerce have had to adapt more quickly to the new realities, partly because they are closer to life and cannot go on for long dumping the consequences of their mistakes in the laps of others.... Normally speaking, it is the function of those in charge of policy to seize the initiative, but on this occasion industry and commerce are marching in the van.[1]

This sort of overstatement would become only more extreme as the organization fell increasingly into the hands of a young management professor, Klaus Schwab, who began reaching out to the international business technocracy.

That first meeting included a thirty-point plan for European executive managers. It was quite an interesting plan, very inclusive on how to deal with both social issues and Eastern Europe. But above all, that gathering involved a remarkable bit of foresight. The European Management Symposium, soon to become the World Economic Forum, or Davos, was the first organization in the early 1970s to detect which side of the vacuum Western civilization was going to exit from. It met seven months before Nixon dismantled Bretton Woods. And from the beginning it proposed viewing society through an economic prism and viewing economics through the prism of the managers of large corporations, rather than through the eyes of capitalists.

Eventually the core funding of Davos was taken over by its corporate membership, thus facilitating the use of the meetings as a public relations exercise for the themes that the controlling members wanted attention paid to that year. All of this has always been perfectly transparent to anyone who cared to look, which made the growing attendance of senior elected politicians all the more peculiar, and eventually fascinating.

Mr. Schwab had succeeded in creating a modern version of a court, with all the characteristics of palace life — an absence of power but a hope of possible influence; courtier-like behaviour, now called lobbying or networking; and powerful dukes and princes humiliated by the apparent need to pay court to the king or those close to the king, who in this case had taken on a more abstract form. The king of Davos was a concept. The concept of society seen through the prism of economics. And those to be courted were the managers of the big firms. The humiliated princes were the elected leaders.

If you step back to view this in a historical context, you might at first laugh at Mr. Schwab's egocentric claims of originality and influence. He is reminiscent of one of those pretentious salt tax collectors become duke in the days before the French Revolution.

Or you might become intrigued, even annoyed, by so much power gathered in a place of such narrow and uninteresting ambitions, a place that had no citizen imprint. But that is a bit disingenuous. The intentions were always clear.[2] The purpose of Davos was and is to advance the policies of those who own it. They themselves would explain that that is to advance a deregulated, business-led global system. It is an organized, concentrated lobby system. And since most Western democracies have normalized the lobbying process by bringing it inside their managerial system, thanks to registrations and declarations, it is hard to suggest that any of this is technically unethical. Davos is merely a global expression of the normalization of unethical behaviour.

The only troubling thing about the gathering was that so many elected leaders felt they should accept the organization's logic in order to become courtiers there. It is one of the curious things about the atmosphere that courts create. There is always an abundance of mirrors, but courtiers can't really see their own reflections. The dukes at Versailles also tried to convince themselves that the process of attending court was not designed to humiliate them. But it was.

9

Selected Romantic Enthusiasms

So great a revolution as the rethinking of the world through an economic prism required more than mere trade to build its structures. Dozens of supporting theories and experiments were initiated.

new zealand. the petri dish. the trojan horse.

New Zealand is a small, highly centralized democracy. Until the mid-1990s, it followed the first-past-the-post parliamentary system, and anybody who won a majority held almost unquestionable power. The upside of this was that governments had the ability to take clear political risks. And so early in the twentieth century, New Zealand had led other countries both in legislating women's rights and in experimenting with public programs.

In the early 1980s, the international economic problems that had struck people around the world combined with some overly enthusiastic spending by the governor in Wellington to produce a financial crisis. A labour government won an election in the midst of this, and quite unexpectedly its minister of finance responded aggressively to the crisis with intense economic rationalist — that is, neo-conservative — policies, none of which had been mentioned during the campaign. This included the full range of trade and financial liberalization; broad deregulation; the selling-off of state corporations, in majority to foreigners; heavy tax cuts; a shifting of the tax burden from the top to the bottom. And so on.

It is hard to know if the crisis was quite as bad as the minister, Roger Douglas, claimed. Some feel that the senior finance department bureaucrats — themselves converts to neo-conservatism — had decided in advance what measures to recommend. Unexpectedly, they found themselves with a true believer as minister. Together they rushed ahead, Douglas shouting that *there was no alternative,* panicking people, including the rest of the cabinet, few of whom knew much about such policies. The idea was to create a fait accompli before anyone could work out what was happening.

One of the treasury officials, Roger Kerr, resigned in order to take over a corporate lobby group, the Business Roundtable. It became the public voice, organizer and indirect source of funding for the reform movement's ideology.

There should be no doubt that the economic crisis was real. The constant questions were simply, *was there such a need to panic,* and *were there other alternatives for dealing with it?* Douglas, Kerr and their allies were so certain and so driven that the non-believers never had the time to work out what other alternatives there might be. The members of both major political parties were in constant reaction. As the historian Michael King puts it, "By the time they had concluded that the social cost of the policies was too high, it was too late: the policies were entrenched."[1]

These included the Public Finance Act, which integrated government accounts with private sector methods. The State Sector Act involved running government departments as if each were a separate private corporation, with a CEO hired on a performance-related contract. Government research was mainly put on a commercial basis. Forty state-owned corporations were sold off. Some said the overall fiscal approach resembled an IMF (International Monetary Fund) recovery program.

Overnight, New Zealand became the world's poster boy for Globalization and neo-conservatism. There were strong claims over the next fifteen years that this was a successful model. The most immediate financial crisis retreated. International market standards were applied on all fronts. In 1996 New Zealand was ranked third in international competitiveness by the World Economic Forum. Inflation was defeated.

On the other hand, poverty soared — a shock in such a middle-class country. The international debt also soared. Twenty percent of working-age adults were dependent on benefits. Real wages dropped. By the end of the century median wages for young people had dropped from $14,700 to $8100.[2]

Roger Douglas and his most impassioned successor, Ruth Richardson, took the long view. They felt that only part of their task was done.

Looking back on those fifteen years, the New Zealand economist Brian Easton summarized it as an artificial choice between the threatening whirlpool in 1984 and the way in which Douglas and Richardson "almost smashed us on Scylla's rocks" with their absolute solutions.[3] But the Business Roundtable continues to repeat that the reforms were all about taking the long view and "paying attention not [to] the particular nuts and bolts but the overall framework. Only a sound, consistent framework, and continuous improvements to it will allow New Zealand to become a high-productivity, high-income, high-employment economy."

Or as international cheerleaders like *The Economist* put it, "[T]he longer New Zealand's reforms are allowed to bear fruit, the harder it will be for others to ignore their message."

deregulation. a form of freedom.

Regulations have always been the nuts and bolts of societies that want to move beyond brute violence and clan loyalties. They were therefore central to the development of democracy and took on an increasingly complex role after the Industrial Revolution. A few decades of experience with unregulated factory owners and wild financiers demonstrated to citizens and political leaders that market leaders, if left to themselves, would, on average, act badly. Modern economic regulations were developed to help those market leaders act properly, while still making a profit. It was hoped that the resulting stability would save society from the worst of the boom-and-bust cycles proper to any unregulated economy.

But how much regulation was needed to do this? And in what form?

By 1971 a community of frustrated businesswomen and -men had built up, beyond those who had never accepted the principles of the public good in an organized form. There was also a broad scattering of citizens who had been annoyed or insulted by the effects of one regulation or another.

That was hardly surprising. The disorder and suffering during the Depression had convinced most people that advanced civilizations required more and stricter regulations. The very size and complexity of the world war had already been an education in how complex democracies must organize and manage themselves. The unprecedented post-war expansion of public services, egalitarian intentions and economic growth had confirmed that need. Progress and regulations went hand in hand, as they had in every successful long-term civilization in history.

People had come to believe that monopolies and combines were unacceptable. They came to expect higher levels of honesty and justice and fairness in the way society operated. Regulations were designed to facilitate this.

In the day-to-day, year-by-year reality within which all of us live, these new regulations were put in place the way democracies typically reform themselves: much of it ad hoc, invariably a bit at a time, here and there, conditioned by political trends, needs and crises. If you stepped back to get an overview, the result would resemble a disorderly pile — at worst an opaque mountain and at best a brilliant patchwork or maze of rules and regulations. However well it worked, however much it helped, this maze could not help but annoy people.

If only we'd had good old-fashioned dictatorships we could have redesigned the whole thing overnight into a neat and tidy, streamlined, efficient system. After all, that's what Napoleon theoretically did with the French legal system. He just stayed up late and dictated the new rules to a scribe and then imposed them as a set piece. Well before the Industrial Revolution, efficiency could be counted on to appear up front in the promises of a reforming dictator. Caesar was perfectly clear on the subject in his run-up to overthrowing the Roman Republic.

Since that doesn't seem to be the democratic way, citizens just have to struggle with reform. It is particularly tough when they are trying to reform their own or someone else's earlier reforms, each of which had been put into place to strengthen the public good. Even if this is successful, the risk is that the patchwork becomes steadily patchier.

The particular problem in Western democracies from the 1970s on was that those highly specialized technocrats who had been put in place to make the patchwork work couldn't help, even inadvertently, getting in the way of improvements. Once in place, they became the natural defenders of the systems in which they were expert.

The amazing thing was how well this opaque mountain did manage to function, even without reforms. Mrs. Thatcher herself boasted in 1981 that the average income per head in Western industrialized economies had multiplied two and a half times between 1950 and 1980. Much of this "was due to the performance of the miracle economies of Japan, Germany and France." These were the three most prominent examples of highly regulated democracies. A few minutes later, however, she was attacking overly "planned and controlled economies."[4]

If there was certainty among ideologues, there was confusion in the minds of most thinking people. The citizenry of twenty or so Western democracies had built a system that had produced miracles. And it still worked, even if that required quite an effort. Yet it was in desperate need of reform. Of streamlining. Yet the system from which everyone benefited and was reliant on could not help being run — managed — on a day-to-day basis by a technocratic leadership, which was the chief obstacle to its reform.

In such a contradictory context, Globalism presented itself as the solution. By taking economic relations to a broader level — an international level — it would destroy the nationally based obstacles to reform. And by focusing on private sector regulation and taking a slash-and-burn approach, Globalism promised that a broader, unstoppable force of initially market energy and then human energy would be released. Air travel, trucking, transportation of all sorts, energy rules, employment rules, financial rules were among many sectors that would be affected. It would be different on different continents. But it was all about releasing forces. Societies everywhere would have to follow, unleashing this energy in every domain.

The only problem was that this approach included no recognition of how successful the previous regulatory period had been. And there was no understanding that that period had, in turn, been preceded by an unregulated era of normalized human tragedy, rich-poor extremes, destructive boom-and-bust cycles and the rise of political radicalism.

The deregulation movement saw itself pushing society straight ahead on flat ground in order to deal with real problems. A prudent approach would have involved remembering that the world is round. If you remove one stage of human organization to correct its shortcomings, do you progress forward or do you swing right around to the problems of the preceding stage?

privatization. releasing our energies.

This is the Siamese twin of regulation/deregulation. By 1970 governments around the world each owned a good percentage of their nation's economy. They had started corporations to fill holes the private sector wouldn't touch. They had started others by going out on the cutting edge of new developments. They had taken over basket-case industries from the market rather than let them collapse. They had nationalized some in what they believed to be the national interest.

Had they gone too far? Was the balance wrong? Should governments own anything? Or should they move into new areas as the public good required and get out as soon as the situation stabilized?

Governments have always owned or indirectly owned an important percentage of the economy. Traditionally, most governments owned the whole armaments sector. During the Industrial Revolution they tended to take over communication systems — telegraph, post office, roads, ports, sewage, water — because the business community didn't trust their own sector to handle such natural monopolies fairly, effectively and efficiently. So the smart businessmen lobbied for publicly owned communication and service monopolies.

Uncertain how to handle the public/private balance, governments often tried to invent private but closely regulated situations to get the best of both worlds. The largest railway in the world — the Canadian Pacific Railway — was built in the 1870s and '80s by the government through a carefully chosen and shaped private market. The CPR was given privileges and obligations. But this sort of monopoly quickly became the focus of populist fury and required another layer of regulations to control such things as freight rates. This was an era that theoretically thought of free trade in opposition to specific policies of national development. Those national initiatives meant there were more and more public-private combinations that were intentionally monopolistic or oligopolistic. The situation resembled that of the mercantilist era with its great trading corporations.

The real crunch came in the early part of the twentieth century when private monopolies were flagrantly exploiting society. Franklin Roosevelt, then governor of New York, focused on the electric power producers. In 1929 sixteen natural monopolies controlled 92 percent of private electric power production. They were charging well above the rates of neighbouring public power authorities in Canada.[5] In various parts of Europe, the offenders were the owners of the coal mines or the railways or the steel mills or dozens of other industries.

Even conservatives agreed about the solution in such cases. Michael Oakeshott: "[U]ndertakings in which competition cannot be made to work as the agency of control must be transferred to public operation."

As with deregulation, the atmosphere surrounding privatization in the 1980s and '90s was quite different. Some public firms were basket cases. Others — such as water and energy — often ran so smoothly that they could be seen as an unnecessary distraction for governments with a great deal to do.

There was no real analysis of what to privatize and why. The dominant argument was simply to shift the balance of general economic ownership from the public to the private as a way of energizing a stagnant, crisis-ridden situation. A few of those sold off were confirmed money losers. Many were businesses that carried guaranteed long-term sources of revenue. A few were privatized into situations of natural competition or competition constructed through strict regulation. Many — such as water — were natural monopolies whoever the owner.

A junior cabinet minister in New Zealand's Globalist revolution became the finance minister in the very different atmosphere of the early twenty-first century. As Michael Cullen now puts it, "There's no reason why you should assume that because something owns something privately, it's going to be any better run."[6] If a natural monopoly is privatized, only draconian regulations can maintain fair prices. It is important to remember that in many cases where natural monopolies have been private for some time — water, for example — they have often become institutionalized centres for political corruption.

But there was something else driving the enthusiasm for privatization. The private sector was coming out of three decades of growth during which it had been heavily regulated and taxed without negative effect. Suddenly, in the 1970s, growth evaporated. There was need for a new kick-start. The dominant business leadership was increasingly technocratic, managerial more than either creative or risk oriented. People like Schumpeter had long noted the trend. It was no longer a trend. It was the dominant reality. The public sector contained a wide range of safe sectors, essentially requiring little more than solid management, whether public or private, and almost guaranteed to produce long-term royalties. Privatization in this scenario was not at all about releasing the market to compete. Or introducing market toughness into lazy public corporations. To the contrary. It was all about shifting the free market away from capitalism and toward coupon clipping — a more passive lifestyle well suited to managers.

Whatever the driving force — and no doubt there was a mixture of impulses — some forty corporations were sold off in Britain, forty in New Zealand, equivalent numbers in many other places. Energy, electronic communications, railways, roads, water, post offices. The total sale value was some US$600 billion. There was and remains great controversy as to whether many corporations were undervalued, and if so, whether this was honest incompetence or intentional handouts to friends.

The other simple question was one of long-term value. The state — the citizenry — had spent decades building up these industries, in some cases with great success. Their real value lay in long-term returns. Privatization meant a one-time payment, which the state could not invest with equal success. And so the citizenry lost the advantage of the long-term capital worth of their nation-state.

However, in those days, the dominant theme was one of freeing up the people's energies through a looser, more agile economy. The basket cases would be fixed by market demands. Lazy behemoths would become lean. Prices of energy, water, travel and communication would drop. And so on.

deregulated money markets. a new type of real trade.

Perhaps the most original or strange or profoundly ironic of the Globalization movement's romantic dreams involved the normalization of the capital markets. Here was a sector that had played an identical role for the last twenty-five hundred years of recorded economic history. That is, since Solon rescued Athens from the moneylenders, who had incapacitated their own society through a broad network of unserviceable debts. Solon, the leading poet of the city, was given twelve months of power to solve the problem. He "broke the chains" — cancelled the debts — and launched the city into a creative freedom that would produce the Athens from which all of the democratic West claims to be descended.

The millennia that followed were filled with similar crises and similar cancellations, either through the effects of war or economic collapse or massive devaluation. The second half of the nineteenth century was particularly exciting. The free trade, imperial empire generation of bankers often had a good understanding of how global speculation could work. They "made their fortune in the financing of wars"[7] rather than lost it, because they allied themselves with those destined to win. Karl Polanyi saw them as "a permanent agency of the most elastic kind." When John Maynard Keynes and the American Harry White put Bretton Woods together, they had this history clear in their minds. Even clearer was their experience of the 1930s. They wanted to protect democracy "from the disruptive impact of capital flows motivated by 'political reasons' or by a desire on the part of elite groups to evade the 'burdens of social legislation.'"

None of this dampened the enthusiasm of the Globalists. From the 1970s on, they saw new communications technology, new financial sophistication and a more managerial approach toward capitalism as an opportunity — the first ever — to convert money into a real trade good. It was as if, in John Ruggie's words, international capital markets had "been cut loose from their role as servants to international trade."[8]

Money, in whatever form, was now an asset in its own right. There were tangible assets, like classic trade, and "intangible assets," like money. But they were all assets. David Hume had written that money "is none of the wheels of trade. It is the oil which renders the motion of the wheels more smooth and easy." This was no longer true. Adam Smith and David Hume had been overthrown.

Could this change in character be true? To be exact, could money change its character? Or could the new global economy change the character of money? Could the historic failure of alchemy be reversed in a new domain, as money was converted from one substance to another? The market decided to act as if this were so.

In the 1970s there was six times more currency being traded than real trade goods. This was a not untypical multiple of oil to the wheel. Then it began to ooze out, faster and faster. After 1980 it was as if the currency market were working with water and it burst out like a flash flood. By 1995 it was fifty times real trade and still growing. This was no servant. This was somebody with an exciting life of his own.

All along there was a Greek chorus warning of disaster. Fingers were pointed at the unprecedented levels of speculation. Unproductive. Inflationary. But the global truth of Globalism insisted that money was the new, hot, real trade good.

Arguments as to whether this was so went on everywhere. But countries wanted it to be so, because they wanted to benefit from this new international market.[9] International corporations wanted it to be so. The neo-liberals declared that it was so. They wanted democratic governments to be appropriately disciplined by international financial markets. It was not surprising, given the multi-millennia record of those markets, that the effect was often the opposite. Already in the early 1980s you could watch the U.S. trade deficit move from $9 billion to $100 billion while the dollar appreciated 60 percent in real terms.[10] In other words, there was now a need not only for good national financial management but for strict international financial management, because the money markets were developing an intangible logic that had to do with themselves and not with any geographic reality. Currency value was no longer a reward or a punishment.

By the early 1990s this experiment in pretending the unreal was real had gathered even more momentum. The best-paid people on Wall Street were all involved in currency speculation through hedge funds or commodity funds. George Soros, halfway down his road to Damascus, headed the lists and spoke of the money speculator's life: "It is a sort of disease when you consider yourself some kind of god, the creator of everything, but I feel comfortable about it now since I began to live it out."[11]

Money market crises rattled the confidence of even the most convinced deregulators sooner and more often than any other sector. Yet the international organizations responsible for this were slow to react. In the 1992 annual report of the Bank for International Settlements, in the midst of a European financial firestorm, its directors still asserted that "deregulation should proceed speedily." There were a few weak caveats.

In the face of the self-evident, one technical argument seemed to keep the believers on track — *there was no alternative*. Why? Because communications technology linked markets around the world twenty-four hours a day. They now constituted a perpetual motion machine of unstoppable energy. No nation and no agency could therefore prevent the market from acting as it thought best.

deregulating flight. dissatisfaction with success.

We sometimes have to admit to ourselves that the most romantic of our dreams will appear comical to others. After forty years of constant growth and success, the airline industry decided that it wanted more. More of what? Well, just more.

Here is a case where Globalization and deregulation clearly began within the United States, with the Airline Deregulation Act of 1978. As a result, even the Civil Aeronautics Board was gradually eliminated. It is worth remembering today that the original regulations of 1938 had been put in place because the sixteen airline corporations then in existence were heading for bankruptcy. It seemed that in its simple early life this was a business ill-suited to the open market.

But in the more sophisticated era of the 1970s the conviction was that everything had changed. Besides, "forty years of tight regulation had resulted in an inefficient, stultified scheduled airline industry."[12] The idea that to be *scheduled* was a weakness tells us that the primary dream of the new school was not to serve the public but to gain larger profits. "The clear expectation of those advocating total economic deregulation was that the sector would be transformed into a highly efficient, competitive and consumer-oriented marketplace." The consumer in this theory was not the same thing as a customer or a passenger.

The curious detail is this. The business had never stopped growing. Passenger kilometres have increased almost a hundred times since 1950. The airline business grew before deregulation. It grew after. It grew all over the world.

The only change is that up until the 1970s this growth had delivered fairly predictable profitability.

corporate gigantism. size matters.

If the world were going to be one big market, corporations should be as big as possible, otherwise they wouldn't be able to float or make waves on the shoreless ocean. It was as simplistic as that.

This is immediately recognizable as a mercantilist anti–free market argument. It takes us back to the great trading companies of the seventeenth and eighteenth centuries. The East India Company. The Hudson's Bay Company. La Compagnie française de l'Orient et de la Chine. The Dutch East India Company (Verenigde Oostindische Compagnie). It relates directly to arguments in favour of oligopolies and monopolies. It is also not a conservative argument. Michael Oakeshott: "Even if the much advertised economies of gigantic financial combinations were real, sound policy would wisely sacrifice these economies to preservation of more economic freedom and equality."[13]

The modern obsession with size is managerial, not capitalistic. Technocrats, given a choice, will seek power through structure and the extension of structure rather than through the direct development or sale of goods. For a manager, success is measured by structural size and confirmed by bonuses.

Their biggest problem as the structures grow larger is slowness, lack of creativity, risk aversion, stagnation at the top. The easiest way to energize such a structure is to buy another structure. This is managerial shock treatment. Bang two organizations together.

The result has been a new world of mergers and acquisitions in which nothing is actually done, but large pieces are moved around, resulting in the effective printing of new sorts of money to finance it all. By 2000 the yearly world total value of mergers and acquisitions was $3.5 trillion. That is $3.5 trillion of debt, often attributed to the corporation taken over. The next year ended badly and the number was down to $2 trillion. One-third of this involved banging pieces together across borders; it could therefore be called Globalism.

One fascinating aspect of gigantism is the marriage between the most superficial sort of financiers — looking for *targets* and *megadeals* and *payoff bonanzas* and *shooting for a big score* — and the most serious of business managers, who don't even like selling, because it is beneath them as working professionals. In their world, size replaces risk and innovation. What links the speculators and the managers is the shared assumption that size replaces the need to think.

the transnationals. the virtual state.

This new idea of power was the most serious of dreams and intimately linked to that of gigantism. The force of Globalism, through trade agreements, deregulation and privatization, would seriously weaken the ability of nation-states to act with any political independence. The resulting power vacuum would be filled by the obvious modern alternative, the transnational corporation. Richer than a majority of the nation-states on the planet, free of the geographical and social obligations of these old states, beyond the embarrassing demands of nationalism, freed in fact from the emotional, immeasurable demands of the citizenry, the transnational would be able to organize world affairs in a more rational, efficient manner. As for individual citizens, they would find themselves freed from those emotional limits encouraged by national life, and so would benefit from this new transnational regime led by more practical self-interest.

It does all sound a bit silly when you lay it out like that. But the world of senior international management has been talking that way since the '70s. Davos has been abuzz with that message from the beginning.

Even today management professors tell this story to their students. The transnational "is the greatest learning engine in the history of the world." From "competing with the authority of the nation state" to becoming the "engine of productivity," this is the future. "Whether it likes it or not, the multinational corporation is a political actor."[14] Half of George Soros's two-part critique of global capitalism is devoted to global financial markets, the other half to the transnationals' "increasing domination over national economies" and their "penetration of market values into areas where they do not traditionally belong."

If you looked at the sheer financial numbers as early as the 1970s, they already supported such an argument. They are even more convincing today. Wal-Mart's gross annual revenues of US$250 billion dwarf those of most developing or small nation-states. Jagdish Bhagwati, passionate defender of Globalization, nevertheless worries about "the possibility that the multinationals have, through their interest-driven lobbying, helped set rules in the world trading, intellectual property, aid, and other regimes that are occasionally harmful to the interests of the poor countries."[15]

In quite another vein, Hedley Bull saw the return of "a modern and secular equivalent of the kind of universal political organization that existed in Western Christendom in the Middle Ages." At that time no structure was sovereign or independent as understood from the nineteenth century on. There were overlapping authorities of all sorts — religious, baronial, dukedoms, kingdoms, professional (the guilds), trade systems, international commercial fairs. There was little sense of exclusivity. This idea of non-exclusive, overlapping authorities is certainly back and often for the better. Europe is a perfect example — a continent of overlapping authorities.

But Bull also saw something darker in the return of the medieval model: a combination of the growing disintegration of established states, the return of non-state violence — which is now narrowly and often inaccurately described as terrorism — and the rise of transnational organizations. It could certainly be argued that today the most prominent transnational organizations are the gigantic corporations. And the only effective international rules and courts in place at the global level have been designed principally to referee their overlapping authorities.

Part of this argument involves the return of the medieval idea of trans-border allegiances and fiefdoms. The American writer Lewis Lapham: "Consanguine hierarchies of international capitalism imitate the old feudal arrangements." You could also say that today's system resembles the old Roman *clientship* arrangements. If it is true, as the dominant Globalist theory argues, that individuals are primarily driven by self-interest, and their civilizations are therefore also driven by self-interest as well as being guided by transnationals that have power without responsibility, well then, the Roman approach to *Clientela* would make perfect sense. But in late-medieval terms, all of this would be seen as an aberration of their concept of interwoven responsibilities. Today's transnationals are like guilds without responsibility and so designed to reduce the citizen to client.

But perhaps all of this is a bit premature. The vast majority of the transnationals are creatures of the West. The rest of the world sees them as instruments of the West. They are physically centred somewhere. The bulk of their particular leadership will come from one area — a nation-state or a region. Their corporate culture reflects their country of origin. And their employees around the world really do live elsewhere. How far could they shift their loyalty so as to fit wholly into a virtual structure that does not even offer them guaranteed employment?

Much more convincing is Mussolini's argument in 1935 that "super-capitalism finds its inspiration and its justification in a utopia, the utopia of unlimited consumption."[16] What is convincing is his understanding that situations in which civilization is reduced to a commercial perspective offer an opening to false populists such as himself who can claim to speak for the abandoned need of local attachment.

balanced budgets. projected moralism.

This is one of those improbable moral — not ethical — assertions that came with the tidal wave of Globalism and swept over many countries with such force as to make calm comment impossible. Well-run public accounts, it was said, must be balanced. Public debt is stealing from our children. If you can't run government programs without going into debt, cut the programs.

And so, here and there, nations, as well as state and provincial governments, passed laws denying themselves the right to be in debt. Others set what were said to be responsible debt limits. They were not necessarily wrong. In the long run there are irresponsible debt levels. And there had been irresponsible levels in the 1970s, which led to an apprehension of international crisis. There are also more or less responsible reasons to incur debt. The most obvious responsible reasons relate to a crisis in the public good, investment in improving the public good, and military urgency. The most irresponsible would probably involve the misrepresentation of military urgency — or the misrepresentation of how best to deal with a military urgency — to justify shifting money to arms manufacturers.

There was a double improbability to outlawing debt or setting permanent limits. First, the moralizing message came from the private sector and from economists who didn't believe in public programming. Yet the Globalization era would see the most extravagant and irresponsible indulgence in debt by the private sector since the days of the South Sea Bubble. But then moralizing, as opposed to ethics, is usually something that is good for other people. The shifting of market energy to the servicing of its own debts related in good part to the restructuring of corporate ownership rather than investment in new or developing areas. This may be one of the keys to understanding how little real growth there has been during the era of Globalization in spite of a market awash in money. The money has been wasted on megalomaniac managerial tinkering as opposed to capitalist risk taking.

Second, debt had always been a tool central to political power. The battle for democracy had in good part been about elected officials struggling for control of the right to raise taxes and to raise debt as they wished for what they wished. These days we rarely think about the right to be in debt as a *right*, but early democratic leaders did. To deny yourself this was to revert to the seventeenth and eighteenth centuries, when aristocratic elites or the king controlled the power of debt and could therefore interfere with the raising and spending of money.

Debt has always been a complex tool that works best in moderation. But in an emergency a government might have to abandon moderation. Historically there was only one moral aspect to debt. And that applied to the private, not the public, sector. To live off interest was always, and in almost every civilization, considered at best disreputable and most often immoral. In almost every major religion around the world rules forbade it. Perhaps the anti-debt moralizing of the Globalization movement was about more than simply shutting down government. Perhaps it involved those in the financial business taking revenge for centuries of being looked down upon.

nature as a machine.

Add up the preceding eight enthusiasms and a natural conclusion is our desire to treat agriculture as a pliant yet recalcitrant child of the market. The aim is clear. Industrialized production methods and open trade will encourage growth and the production of cheap agricultural products, which is what poorer people need: more for less.

The industrial theory of agriculture is a reminder that Globalization is not a simple invention of the private sector. More often than not the big solutions of Globalization are just privatized versions of the big government solutions of the post-war period.

It would be a mistake to condemn either of these grand approaches as failures. After all, big government drained swamps to defeat malaria in the West; organized sewage disposal and clean water delivery, which did more for life expectancy than any medical innovation; rebuilt Europe after 1945 in under a decade; created the Japanese miracle in even less time; and produced a worldwide surplus of food, even if it has never been distributed fairly. And Globalization has made us rethink production; taken economic opportunities into unexpected areas; demonstrated that technology can be used in unexpected ways and that we need not be the prisoners of any particular structure, even if that was an unintentional message.

The Keynesian and Globalization eras have both been about big solutions. There is a utilitarian difference between them: the public solutions tended to be quite practical — dams, roads, ports — while the solutions of Globalization have been more abstract. They have been more about a theory of how everything works, which can be applied anywhere to anything. Curiously enough, for a movement that was declared to be the enemy of bureaucracy, Globalization has turned out to be a system devoted to systems. Form over content, the case study, admiration for the abstract skills of structural experts, distrust of more practical people who adapt to particular realities. In spite of the paternity offered to Hayek, Friedman and a crowd of free trade–neo-liberal economists, the real core of the theory is — boringly — much more about two administrative elements: management and risk avoidance. The third element has been an obsession with the accumulation of wealth, as opposed to competition, innovation and production. The revolution of Globalism has been the assertion that private sector management is a more efficient way to handle structure than public sector management, and the conviction that wealth accumulation should replace new investment, risk and growth.

We all know about the failures of the public approach: the dams that solved one small problem while creating a broad range of new problems, for instance, or the big industrialization programs imposed on the developing world by the World Bank, which destabilized rural areas and created vast slums.

The private sector's industrialized vision of agriculture — which is all about mass production, large machines, and a great deal of artificial additives — is in the same optimistic tradition. Curiously enough, this vision has always included large public subsidies. What those who live in the West have seen is that this industrialized approach to agriculture can produce food surpluses, but drives the farming population off the land, bankrupts smaller communities and, at the end of the day, leaves even the largest producers struggling to break even. The real profits of the last quarter-century have gone to the managerial organizations — the middlemen — wholesalers and large retail distributors of machinery, additives and bulk food.

The implications for the developing world are enormous. In low-income countries, 70 percent of employment is agricultural, in middle-income 30 percent. In the West it is 4 percent, and, even at that, the sector has been in permanent financial and human crisis since the '70s. The application of industrial agricultural methods to the low- and middle-income countries is a recipe for social catastrophe. Yet that is the dream of open markets. The most efficient will win out. Food will be seen as a secondary outcome of an industrial method. Or to say the same thing another way, this is a determinist approach toward agriculture as an industry, not a food source. Yet with 70 percent of the population in low-income countries on smaller holdings, efficiency is a very minor consideration. Food security for people without cash incomes, rural viability, natural disaster prevention, biodiversity, employment of older farmers — this is a short list of much more important issues that the United Nations Development Programme (UNDP) puts forward.[17] The message may be understated, but it is clear: agriculture "performs various non-commodity roles."

Such a layered, subtle approach is now so far away from our urban understanding in the West that our typical political answer to those societies operating outside the industrial agriculture model is to block the import of their goods. Why? Well, mysteriously, their products are said to be unfairly cheap, even though we also say they are inefficiently produced. Even more curious, we simply don't want to have any serious conversation about the *big solution, highly modern industrial agriculture* that functions inside our own societies. Nobody wants to talk about its contradictions. For example, even with ten to fifteen thousand acres of good grain-producing land in Western Canada or the United States and all the best equipment and chemicals, a farmer will have difficulty making a solid and predictable profit.

This doesn't seem to meet the expectations of current economic theory or management structure. No one wants to treat this most transparent of economic areas as a test of global theory, because the conclusion would have to be that, enthusiasms aside, it doesn't work. We should therefore be talking about another approach, perhaps a little less enthusiastically and a little more realistically.

10

The Gathering Force

Globalization didn't burst out of the gate in the early 1970s. It would be a good fifteen years before people felt they knew what they meant when they said the word. Those fifteen years were filled with attempts to define the international economic prism through treaties, the handling of crises, international organizations and a great deal of pushing and pulling among experts. There was not a great deal of public debate about the economic and social assumptions the Globalist approach might involve. Not yet.

Instead, there was a rather straightforward increasing emphasis on trade. Trade as the key to growth, to international relations, to democracy, to almost anything. From the status of an important utilitarian activity, it was gradually promoted to a position of such cultural nobility that it might have surprised even Cobden. It was as if trade had become the engine of civilization. For some it seemed as if the moving of goods across borders was the purpose of civilization. To produce goods for local markets was somehow old-fashioned, inferior, uninteresting.

Wherever fashion settles, the space tends to expand. So the meaning of the term *trade* gradually expanded. Not simply goods, but services. Not simply products, but employees. Fashion usually expands beyond its own capabilities, so today the space is already beginning to contract — driven back by the reality people live. For example, a growing number of economists and non-economists now question why a passive royalty collection business like intellectual property should receive the protection of the international trade regime. And by 2004 the World Bank had concluded that developing economies are often damaged by complex and strict trade agreements.[1]

Beyond the apparently simple idea of the importance of trade and what it should include there was another, perhaps more important, argument. Was the neo-liberal or neo-conservative economic and social program necessary to the international trade and growth package? If so, how much of it? For example, was it necessary to link the idea of deregulation to that of borderless trade? What about the MAI (Multilateral Agreement on Investment) idea of equal treatment for corporations in whatever country they chose to operate? In other words, was giving the interests of corporations primacy over the public good of particular nations an automatic or useful part and parcel of the idea of borderless trade? By continually insisting on these sorts of linkages, Globalization's boosters turned their movement into one necessarily seen as neo-conservatism. And so the language underpinning trade has gradually become that of the neo-conservative movement.

How much of that language was actually put into effect depended on the country and the issue at stake. But by the second half of the 1980s, even public social programs run by social democratic governments were often viewed through the neo-liberal intellectual lens of competition, self-interest, efficiency, *real costs* and so on. And the reason given was that this was the inevitable outcome of living in a global economy.

The first step down this road came with the creation of the G6, which would quickly become the G7 and later the G8. With the first of the seminal crises — Nixon's dismantling of Bretton Woods in 1971 — the finance ministers of the United States, Germany, France and Britain began meeting in private to talk about what should be done to stabilize the situation. They met in the White House library and were known as the Library Group. The Japanese minister was soon added. By 1974 two of them had taken over their national governments — Helmut Schmidt and Valéry Giscard d'Estaing — and they wanted to reconstitute their working group at the head-of-government level to deal with the major economic problems of the world.[2]

This was a sensible idea. But it was also revolutionary. Government leaders of the most powerful democracies were trumping existing international gatherings by creating a more senior structure and one dedicated to looking at civilization through an economic prism. This had never happened before. It was as if democratic concerns, social concerns, diplomatic and military concerns had been demoted. If these leaders were to come together in the most exclusive way, the principal reason would be economic management. And whatever other issues arose — terrorist crises, for instance, during the 1970s — they would approach them through an economic forum.

The implications of this prism can be found in the details. For example, the meetings were — are — organized through *sherpas:* one senior advisor to each of the government leaders. They are usually economists or trade experts.

There was, however, another view of why and how to create the G7. Henry Kissinger probably knew more about European history than either Schmidt or Giscard. He had been fretting about the declining political and economic influence of the United States, as well as the signs of growing international disorder. His idea was to reinvent the Castlereagh-Metternich European Concert that had met for five straight years from 1818 on. The Vienna Treaty said these meetings were "for the purpose of consulting upon their common interests and for the consideration of the measures … salutary for the repose and prosperity of nations and for the maintenance of the peace of Europe."[3] According to Harold Nicolson, they had wanted "some permanent institutional device which would enable the United Nations to co-operate indefinitely in preventing the threat of war whenever it might arise." Nicolson used the term *United Nations* to suggest a parallel with 1945. Kissinger saw a further parallel and imagined the G7 in exactly the war-prevention terms of the Vienna Treaty. That was exactly what Kissinger wanted. And given his broader geopolitical view, he insisted that Italy be added, because he worried about Italian communism, and Canada, because it was the key to world commodity markets, particularly in minerals. Thus, he didn't exclude economics. He wanted a body capable of "determined joint actions that give the industrial democracies a greater voice in economic decisions affecting their future." But he saw the political issues as primary.

The two European technocratic leaders didn't agree with him. Their model was a reflection of the Common Market concentration on economics and administration. And they, through Giscard, organized the first leaders' meeting at the French president's country residence in Rambouillet. The date was November 1975. The subject was exchange rates. The Khmer Rouge had taken power six months before and were already busy killing Cambodian civilians. By the time they were overthrown in 1979, they had executed some 2 million people. The subject would never make it onto the G7 agenda.

This unfair observation nevertheless gives a little foreshadowing of why a few years later the Yugoslav civil war would be so badly handled by Europe and the G7. Not that the leaders necessarily set out to avoid politics during their gatherings. Within three years they were struggling with what to do about terrorism. But when you analyze the agendas year after year over three decades, trade is by far the subject most talked about. In the early years, it had to compete with two other economic problems — unemployment and inflation. As classic inflation was reduced, the leaders seemed to forget both. The emphasis shifted to trade as the simplest true evocation of Globalization, so trade became the answer to every problem, including unemployment.

The curious thing, according to John Kirton's measurements, is that they didn't do particularly well at managing the sudden economic crises that fell upon them. They might have done better had they been more responsive to leadership based on ideas than to a management-driven approach based on acceptance of an inevitable context. The seven leaders often did better on the political front. As for the economic crises, these just kept on coming. Sequential Mexican collapses, a Third World debt crisis in 1982, an American debt crisis in '83, a stock market crash in '87.

⊕

In the midst of their arguments over economic management versus political leadership, something very revealing happened. Giscard had been a long-time and apparently successful French minister of finance. He was elected in mid-1974 as a young president who could bring his economic talents to the top job. He represented a new-style politician. The specialist. The man who would take your worries away with his financial expertise. Compared with leaders like Charles de Gaulle or Konrad Adenauer — who somehow involved citizenry emotionally in their grand schemes — here was a calm, dispassionate, modern leader. Even post-modern. This was the face of the post-nationalist nation-state.

But Giscard came to power in the midst of those seminal crises of oil, inflation, unemployment and no growth. He counterattacked as best a technocrat could and made no impact. Interest rates were so high that they were bankrupting the private sector without controlling inflation. Giscard became bewildered. Discouraged.

Then one night he appeared on television to address the people. He told them that great global forces were at work. These were new forces. Forces of inevitability. Forces of economic interdependence. There was little a national government could do. He was powerless.

This historic appearance was probably the original declaration of Globalization as a freestanding force escaping the controls of all men. It was also the invention of the new leader: the manager as castrato. This approach created quite a fashion among leaders at all levels. The easy answer to the most difficult problems was increasingly to lament publicly that you were powerless. Impotent. That your large budgets, your public structures, the talents and determination of your population could make little difference. These were not problems to be solved. These were manifestations of the global reality. With your leader/manager friends in other countries you would do your best to round the sharp corners through management of the details.

You might say that Globalization became an excuse for not dealing with important problems. Worse than that, this betrayal of the idea of public responsibility — that is, a belief in the possibility of choice — gradually undermined the citizens' confidence in their democracy. People like Giscard made the shibboleth of inevitability credible. It was the return of the fearful priests so central to the darkest moments of the Middle Ages.

In such an atmosphere, the clarity and determination of Margaret Thatcher and a few others were refreshing. In the early 1970s she could be found clearing the ground for neo-conservatives, constructing the emotional underpinnings of Globalism. In a famous incident she ended a discussion among Conservative Party members by thumping Hayek's *The Constitution of Liberty* down on the table. "This is what we believe!" She often used a simple phrase — *There is no alternative!* or TINA — to force people to get on with her policies.

But there was a contradictory undercurrent to this forcefulness. If there was no alternative, well then, she also was a victim of inevitability. A weak person. A believer. Someone afraid of that central human strength — that confidence to be uncertain. Octavio Paz: "Critical thinking cannot be sacrificed on the altars of accelerated economic development."[4]

Out of public sight Mrs. Thatcher was in reality much more open to uncertainty, persuasion and debate than the citizenry would ever have imagined. But her view of herself, of the era, of the crisis was that no doubt must show. Her public certitude reinforced the assertion that progress was being made, that it was inevitable, that it could never be rolled back. "Inevitable and irreversible" was the central assertion. She seemed to be saying, along with others, that this was one of those moments of historic systemic shift, like the end of feudalism or the birth of the nation-state.[5]

The reality was perhaps less mysterious. We were witnessing the arrival of the false rationality of managerialism. This was, in M.G. Smith's words, "the basic fallacy of the view that an all-dominating bureaucracy is a more rational or superior organ of government than a controlled bureaucracy."[6] Or Camus: "Nothing being true or false, good or bad, the measurement will be the most efficient, that is the strongest. The world will no longer be divided between just and unjust, but masters and slaves."

The master here was not the manager of efficiency. It was the invisible hand of inevitability. The managerial idea of big solutions was relatively banal, often monolithic and obsessive. Something called *productivity* abruptly became a great god of economic theory. Down-to-earth people like the management theorist Henry Mintzberg pointed out that productivity was — is — generally used to describe what a microeconomist can easily measure. Circumscribed in this way, productivity can't evaluate ideas, corporate memory or corporate loyalty or leadership. So the severe measures — usually slashing and firing — taken to increase productivity have tended to strip organizations of their medium- to long-term strengths.

What has given the managerial class such confidence in its role as the servant of inevitability has been the establishment of a global — a shared — idea of what they do. The real purpose of Davos may simply have been that there they could be surrounded by an echo of themselves — a self-valorizing experience for a leadership without direction. There they could polish their global vocabulary and adjust to the fashion of the year. The fact that those who finance Davos have consciously used it to shape these fashions, if anything, comforts all those who have come in search of a direction secreted through a club of the like-minded.

Technology is the other crutch that has been found — the inevitable truth of technological progress. International economists and managers became convinced that every region or country must embrace the efficiencies of new technology to improve their productivity. But as the demographer and economist David Foot has pointed out, labour-saving technology is really only of primary importance in countries with low population growth. Simply applying a severe idea of technical efficiency to every society may provoke social and economic disaster in the short to medium term.

None of this is new. The inevitability of technological progress was used against the artisan class in the early nineteenth century as a reason to exclude them rather than negotiate their reintegration. This exclusion provoked a political explosion that began with the Luddites in Britain and lasted a century — provoking communism, fascism, false populist dictatorships, urban violence. Yet a classic part of contemporary managerial vocabulary is to attack as a Luddite anyone who wants to work out a non-exclusionary approach to technical progress. In 2004 the acting managing director of the IMF, Anne Krueger, accused the NGOs of being

Luddites. "The progress they opposed stood to benefit a much larger cross-section of the population."[7] This is classic, official misrepresentation of Western history. Is Ms. Krueger ignorant or simply a passive repeater of what she once heard from her professors? Or, coming from someone at her level, is such repetition a form of wilful ignorance — a refusal to try to understand?

The Luddites were not opposed to progress. They just wanted to be included, wanted not to starve, not to be humiliated.

Today's version of the old technological determinism takes place within a much broader assertion — that of global determinism. This is presented as relentless modernity — uncontrollable technology driving mere humans. In reality the argument has nothing to do with modernity. Its central message is that humans are rendered passive by the logic of dumb machines. That this could be an argument in favour of modernist sophistication and progress tells us a great deal about the panic that technocrats feel when they are asked to lead.

Even more problematic is the degree to which this version of modernity is little more than a prolongation of the original Industrial Revolution idea of technology as an argument for exclusion. It is often an artless and disingenuous reworking of the old imperial technological determinism that Sven Lindqvist described: "[T]echnical superiority provides a natural right to annihilate the enemy even when he is defenseless." *Annihilate* can mean anything from *rationalize* to *marginalize* to *exclude* to *let fall into poverty* to *starve* to *kill*.

The heart of the global argument as an inevitability driven by technology probably lies in the continuing struggle over the internet and intellectual property. Lawrence Lessig, perhaps the leading activist and theorist of communication systems, worries that large communications and entertainment companies are gradually getting control over the network. It is as "if General Motors could build the highway system such that GM trucks r[u]n better on it than Ford Trucks."[8] The possibility of controlling the actual means of communication, as opposed to what is delivered on it, is one of the oldest managerial dreams, stretching back through all empires and religious systems. Here you see the national and historic link between absolutist leadership and controlling management.

It is central to the idea of monopoly and oligopoly. There is one question that needs to be asked each time there is a technological determinist argument. Is the aim to produce a justifiable protection for some new initiatives? Or is *inevitability* just a term designed to protect large, lazy, non-cutting-edge coupon clippers who periodically talk about how their advantages cannot be rolled back? Lessig calls the confusion surrounding the straightforward asking of this question "the fallacy of 'is-ism' — to confuse how something is with how it must be…. There is no single way that the Net *has* to be; no simple architecture defines the nature of the Net."

There was a disturbing hint in the early 1970s of how this managerialist global economic theory would work. Europe's technocratic leaders suddenly realized that their national working classes had disappeared. A century of social progress encouraged by public policy and regulation — in particular a highly successful quarter-century after 1945 — had increased education levels, developed skills, raised wages and living standards in general. In fact, the situation had been increasingly obvious through the 1960s. Rather than attempt to rethink and reorganize that part of the economy dependent on a traditional working class, the technocracy decided simply to create a new working class by bringing in hundreds of thousands of *guest workers* from the Mediterranean basin. Most of them were Islamic. Most of them came from major imperial civilizations such as Turkey and Morocco. Others came from ex-colonies such as Algeria, Tunisia and Somalia, which were also textured and complex civilizations. That those brought in came from the poorest, least-educated part of the population allowed the managers to pretend that these rich origins did not need to be taken into account. The technocrats' model was old-fashioned utilitarianism mixed with abstract management theory. It was a radical reworking of late-nineteenth-century Taylorism, with its conscious confusing of men and machines.

The theory was that these *guest workers* would arrive, along with their wives to look after them, and therefore their children. They would work, receive access to the social services offered citizens, but not become citizens — a combination guaranteed to provoke alienation and humiliation — and of course be prepared to be sent home whenever the host wished. Thirty-five years later, 17 million Muslims, including *guest workers*, many now retired, their children, grandchildren and newer workers, are caught up with 450 million other Europeans in the ethical, human contradictions that this global managerial approach has created. Many of them can now become citizens. Many now are. But the whole process toward inclusion has been based on a utilitarian maze of exclusion. The result tends therefore not to be the joy and pride of belonging, but much more complex feelings on all sides. Of anger, often sublimated anger. Of misunderstanding. Many differences have become unscalable mountains instead of rich opportunities. The advantages of complex human relationships have been replaced by the disadvantages of the simple. If nationalism of a negative sort is reappearing in Europe among both old Europeans and new, it stems in good part from this managerial approach to the reality of human lives.

At the heart of the problem lies the Globalist idea of viewing society through an economic prism. In practical terms this has meant demoting the values — ethical and moral — of community in favour of the certainty that humans are primarily driven by self-interest. They will therefore not mind being confused with machines, provided their income is raised. It would be difficult to find a clearer example of the self-delusion of Globalization theories.

This story of 17 million people is only one aspect of contemporary *worker mobility*. The word *mobility* carries a positive implication. But if they are on the move because their poverty drives them, then a more accurate phrase would be contemporary *worker instability*.

There are today over 120 million migrant workers with their families, of which only 20 million are in Europe. This level of displacement resembles a wartime or immediate post-war situation. It does not suggest a period of economic progress — let alone social progress — toward greater prosperity. On the other hand, it does resemble other eras of extreme economic change, which in general have led to periods of great social instability and violence, as happened in the nineteenth century. In other words, we live in a period obsessed by management, yet managed by people who are in general so unfamiliar with history that they are unconscious of the effects of their utilitarian methods.

Europe's *guest worker* experiment involved a fascinating alteration in classic free trade economics. Adam Smith, David Ricardo even more so, and most of the nineteenth-century enthusiasts all believed fervently that you should produce what you had a comparative advantage in. Everyone would somehow end up buying cheap and selling expensive. The early Globalist managers altered this theory by importing not cheap goods but cheap workers. Why? To maintain their old model of the buy-sell balance. How? By compensating for rising social justice within their own borders. How? By creating a new working class, one that could not rise socially. Why? Because, like the working class of the nineteenth century, it was bereft of citizens' rights. Behind a modern technocratic discourse, the aim was to preserve a nineteenth-century idea of how markets must work, an idea dependent on the existence of a working class — better still, a disenfranchised working class. In the 1990s there would be yet another reinvention of the old buy-sell idea. In the meantime, this highly original abstraction of human lives would become the foundation for a revival of Western racism, something we thought we had defeated in 1945.

The real triumph of the new age of Globalism clearly lay elsewhere. It lay in the explosion of international, multinational and bilateral trade agreements. This includes some 300 regional trade agreements since 1945, of which about 250 since 1995. Many of these are in the Americas or within Europe or between Europe and the outside. Some 50 of them involve developing economies, and that is a fast-growing component. Europe is the biggest regional grouping. North America is just behind. Third comes Mercosur, which began with Argentina, Brazil, Paraguay and Uruguay in 1991.

The enthusiasm behind trade agreements is so strong that there never seems to be an opportunity to sit back and coolly evaluate their impact. As long as trade grows, we are said to be on track. It was a pity, for example, that shortly after the Free Trade Agreement between Canada and the United States in 1989 — the biggest bilateral trade relationship in the world — the Canadian government lost its conviction that the deal would work or work fast enough for their political purposes. So mysteriously, the Canadian dollar was devalued from 89 cents US to 63 cents US. Of course it wasn't done abruptly, as Washington had done in 1971 and again in 2004. No one even acknowledged this was happening. If asked, officials would have protested that the changes related to inflation targets, not trade. Others would say 89 cents was an overvalued level, and they would probably have been right. Smart businessmen joked that at 89 cents the deal would fail, and at 70 cents it was irrelevant. Statisticians would point out that as the dollar sank, imports had grown along with exports, thus disproving the devaluation argument. But exports grew faster. And the mechanisms of production and trade changed because the cheap dollar meant Americans, flush in their own booming economy, could snap up Canadian corporations at a 30 percent discount and then convert binational trade into tax-strategy movements.

Whatever the conscious or unconscious combination of reasons, the dollar was devalued and trade grew. For more than a decade it was impossible to know if this was due to the accuracy of trade theory or to goods made cheap by a low dollar.

And then there is the case of Mercosur. It has gone from a free trade area to a customs union and hopes to become a common market. It now controls 70 percent of Latin American trade, has a GDP of US$1 trillion and a population of 230 million. Chile — a paragon of openness and middle-class stability since ridding itself of General Pinochet and the economic boom-and-bust cycles his Globalist neo-conservatism provoked — has signed eleven trade agreements and believes firmly that it benefits from this trade. In fact, the continent has had the sharpest world increase in intra-regional trade.[9]

The troubling thing about this continental success story is that none of it has had any effect on income disparities inside Mercosur. Thirty-seven percent of member-state citizens live below poverty levels.

Many would say it is too soon to judge the outcome. Others would point out that this successful trade regime has had no moderating effect on the economic and social crises in the region. Argentina's destructive collapses were unmoderated by growing trade. Record numbers of educated young people emigrated, discouraged by the incapacity of the new global regimes to bring any stability. In just one of the several separate Mexican crises, the average income of people was halved.

All of this has happened before. After all, the region has always been a major exporter of commodities. And commodity-dependent economies are automatically subjected to terrifying boom-and-bust cycles. This can be moderated only by regulations aimed at creating the stability and slowness to change typical of a middle-class society. These regulations need to be strict and tough enough to deform the market's natural tendencies. The less middle-class regulation there is, the more the booms will lead to busts, which will slip into full collapse. It is virtually impossible in such situations to consolidate the gains made during the boom periods.

Perhaps this time there will be consolidation. After all, trade continues to grow, as does, in some cases, the variety of exports. And general education has made some progress, which can help the economy diversify. On the other hand, until very recently, most commodities have suffered greatly under Globalization, precisely because the increasingly open markets have allowed the middlemen and the consumers to push the producers into overproduction and then to play those producers off one against another. A recent recovery in some areas has come not because of open markets but because of the nineteenth-century-style expansion in production in Asia.

Elsewhere the positive effects of trade seem clearer: Europe, Canada and the United States, East Asia, parts of South Asia. Certainly the growth in trade from the 1980s on is impressive. What is hard to measure is the effect. In some places the parallel economic growth is remarkable, in others painful. In some there is a growing international economic integration. In others the outcome is a strengthening nation-state. Perhaps it was too soon in the 1980s or '90s to judge the broader implications of such a dramatic growth in trade.

One example stands out above the others. Spain moved slowly into Europe and, in the process, moved from an underdeveloped economy lacking in social programs as well as in democracy to a state impressive on all three fronts. The key seems to have been the care and slowness with which Spain was drawn into the European Union, from a simple trade agreement in 1970, to its first proper democratic elections in 1977, followed immediately by a serious candidacy for membership in Europe. A decade later came membership.

What made this process so successful? In good part it was Europe's insistence on Spain's gradually adopting middle-class social institutions and regulations as part of strengthening its democracy and bringing up both the standard of living and the costs of living. Why both? Because raising taxes was central to funding the programs. That is the real level playing field of middle-class democracies. The reward to Spain for creating this successful social regulation was entry into the open European market.

The general outcome was the closest thing to what a non-ideological economist might call undisputable success. Yet none of this very real progress was accomplished by following the Globalization model.

It is worth comparing Spain's carefully constructed and monitored progress with that of the most confused part of Globalization's rise. This involved projecting a whole new set of Western economic models onto the developing world. I say *new* because this was already the second set of economic administrative models to be offered — in reality, imposed — since the independence of the former colonies. Thus, they were expected to absorb for the second time in a mere twenty years a brand-new ideology.

The first — in the 1950s and '60s — had revolved around big centralized government-driven management structures delivering gigantic projects. Then abruptly, they were being pushed by Western lenders and investors, along with international organizations such as the World Bank, to embrace big private sector management theories based on a new kind of centralization. This time it was corporate and international. With remarkable optimism and trust they set out to give it a try.

11

Crucifixion Economics

We whip the child until it cries, and then we whip it for crying.

— EDMUND BURKE

The first sign that Globalization might not be a global truth or even a globally applicable theory came in the developing world in the early 1980s. And it came in that most delicate part of human relationships — the repayment of debts.

In the 1970s the West was more in crisis than the Third World. Today's fifteen most indebted nations then owed only $18 billion and paid just $2.8 billion a year in interest or 9.8 percent of their GNP. By the 1980s their interest payments were $36 billion or nearly half their GNP.[1] The result was a first crisis early in the decade, with Mexico in desperate trouble. At the same time, a second wave of crises began to build, this time in Africa. By then international organizations such as the G7, the World Bank and the IMF had focused their attention on the forty-one most indebted nations. Their debt-to-export ratio in the 1970s had been between 100 and 260 percent. That is to say, it was not too bad. By the end of the century, it was between 1000 and 2500 percent.[2]

The effect was to bring their economies gradually to a halt. Most of them have now been stalled for almost twenty years.

Latin American GDP per person had risen a very respectable 2.4 percent per year from 1950 to 1980. During the heyday of Globalization, from 1980 to 2000, it managed a miserable total net increase of 4.3 percent. In Africa, from 1950 to 1980, GDP per person had risen 1.8 percent per year. Not dramatic gains, but still progress. Between 1980 and 2000 it fell 6.2 percent.

There are endless statistics of this sort. They all add up to the same message: the Globalist era has damaged large sections of the world. The most painful numbers tell us, first, that by the mid-1990s the poorest countries carried debts they could not service without damaging themselves. Second, these debts remain virtually unchanged today despite much talk in the West and a range of partial solutions. The political and social situation has degraded. Health and education programs have been cut, the international rule being, or so it seems, that there is little room for programs if debts are to be serviced.

In the West people talk more about whose fault all of this is than about the effects of the situation. There is an enthusiastic focus on the increasingly dysfunctional nature of these non-Western regimes. Franklin Roosevelt in the early 1930s simply said: "Social unrest and a deepening sense of unfairness are dangers to our natural life which we must minimize by rigorous methods."[3] Eventually unrest elsewhere will be dangerous to Western societies, as well as to those in which it originates.

And that is the central point of the developing world debt crisis. It has now gone on for a quarter-century. There have been ups and downs. The number of countries not properly servicing their debts is today about the same as it was during the Second World War, when so many nations were out of commission.[4] There have been endless meetings over the last twenty years. The G7 has gone over the situation again and again. Mrs. Thatcher opened the 1984 London Summit saying, "There are no easy or painless solutions, but we can set out ways both in which the commercial banks and the international financial institutions can help and in which the debtor countries can ease their own problems.... [T]he problem is manageable."[5]

It wasn't manageable. It was then, as it is now, a matter of leadership. Aleksandr Herzen, speaking a century ago to a group of anarchists about how to overthrow the czar, said, "We think we are the doctors. We are the disease."

The Third World debt crises, as seen from within the West, are all about pretending no mistakes have been made in managing the problem. The refusal to simply deal with it is always presented in a cool, detached yet concerned way, all from a utilitarian point of view. The *other* does not really exist. This problem is just an unfortunate matter of contractual obligations.

Actually, in the case of the forty-one most impoverished nations, the money is mainly owed to international institutions controlled and financed by the G7. So there is no complex conundrum involving commercial banks and the deposits of little old ladies in Düsseldorf or Columbus.

The stolid Western pretence of cool, detached utilitarianism is an almost exact reflection of the way the same civilization justified forcing the opium trade on China for 130 years. Respect for trade, debt, contracts and the market must unfortunately trump disease, suffering and social order. To make this logic less painfully obvious, small charitable programs are offered up in order to demonstrate the West's desire to help, without fundamentally changing the situation.

What is to be made of this incapacity to act, this alienation of sophisticated Western elites from simple realities? I remember flying in the late 1980s to Thailand. Beside me in business class was a sleek, urban young man with the air of an ambitious Wall Street junior vice-president of international banking. He was excited. He had never been to Asia before. He was going as the IMF representative to evaluate the economic and political situation in Indonesia. You could say he was going to decide the fate of the country. This didn't seem to weigh heavily on his shoulders. He hadn't bothered to read about Indonesian history or politics, let alone religion or culture. To make up for his ignorance, he had the file. Knew it. Knew the graphs. Knew the numbers. And he was confident of his ability to reduce any social complexities and the nature of Indonesian civilization to a *case study*.

Years later, Joseph Stiglitz spoke of the indebted countries and "[t]he success as an intellectual doctrine of the Washington consensus. [This] rests on its simplicity … its policy recommendations could be administered by economists using little more than simple accounting frameworks … a few economic indicators — inflation, money supply growth, interest rates, budget and trade deficits — could serve as the basis for a set of policy recommendations. Indeed, in some cases economists would fly into a country, look at and attempt to verify these data, and make macroeconomic recommendations for policy reforms all in the space of a couple of weeks."[6] All of this is in the tradition of the darkest of black comedy. But it is also classic technical aridity. The comedy and aridity together provide only a superficial indication of a much more profound problem.

After all, management theory is not enough to immobilize Western civilization for twenty-five years when faced by a financial problem that is small by our standards. Besides, there is a long tradition of how we ourselves have dealt with unpayable, unserviceable debts over thousands of years. We usually don't pay.

In 1971 Nixon tried to escape part of his financial problems by devaluing. That was a form of debt abrogation or default. He then tried to inflate his way out of the oil crisis. In 2004 the American government again devalued to deal with several problems, including debt in the form of foreign holdings in American dollars.

Every Western country has at some point escaped some of its obligations by somehow abrogating its contractual responsibilities. That's how you relaunch an economy. As for the private sector, bankruptcy is the most common way of escaping debt. That's what happened in the 1930s. Debt was destroyed in order to free national balance sheets.[7] In that case, it was a messy and massive destruction. Today governments have created a legal status of interim bankruptcy, which allows corporations to dispense with lender and employment rights without losing their corporation. All they have to do is reorganize themselves. The Third World debt situation could at any time have been erased in just such a calm and orderly manner. Commentators would point out that many of these indebted nations have incompetent, self-serving governments and don't deserve such an opportunity. But surely that is also the case of many troubled corporations. The characteristic of Globalization is that it will do for the private sector what it won't do for the public. In the mid-1990s, after yet another Mexican collapse, a growing number of economists were asking, Why save speculators? Instead, money was thrown at them, they were saved and no problem was solved.

Overall, hundreds of billions of dollars have been thrown at hopeless debt situations to animate what would happily have died. At the 1987 G7 meeting in Venice it was decided that the industrialized countries could help by allowing payments to be stretched out over a longer period. Later there were various strategies — the Brady Plan among them — to charitably chip away at the edges of impossibility. All of this to keep heavily indebted countries manacled to these impossible illusions of contractual moralism.

In 1996 the G7 met in Lyon and attempted to agree on a $5 billion debt-relief scheme to bring down the $200 billion owed by the poorest countries. Today the figure is still above $200 billion. In 2000 President Chirac called for an "ethic of solidarity." He said France was ready to propose at the G7 summit in Okinawa the cancellation of 100 percent of this debt.[8] Frustrated though Monsieur Chirac was, that is not what happened.

Yet he did have a hold on the edge of Western reality. He spoke of *ethical solidarity*. That ought to be easy in a sophisticated civilization that considers itself rational. But we have operated on this question in a fatal confusion. Those who preach Globalization can't seem to tell the difference between ethics and morality. Through ethics the health of the public good can be measured. Ethics would lead us to solve this problem by simply cancelling the debt. Morality is a weapon of religious and social righteousness. Moralism is usually the last step in the decline of a civilization. Globalism from its very beginnings shoved ethics to the side in favour of moralism. Why? Perhaps because it inherited such a strong conviction of moral righteousness from the original free trade movement.

So the West has imposed on its former colonies a rigorously moral approach to debt — one it has rarely applied to itself. And if Catholics might have carried this moralism toward interpretations of guilt, the strongly Protestant sources of free trade and utilitarianism have carried us toward an insistence on redemption. The inevitability, the no-going-back of Globalism, are part of this redemptive process. People who fail must learn their lesson, be disciplined, be punished.

We have insisted upon hair shirts and self-flagellation and self-imposed suffering. Gerard Baker mockingly writes of the sado-monetarism of the ruling school of economists.[9] But we have gradually taken it further still, as if seeking in a voyeurist manner to watch the economic and social auto-crucifixion of these societies. Then, when death has cleansed them of their sins, they will be reborn, healthy, strong and able to balance their national accounts because they will have learned the importance of responsible growth.

In the meantime? Well, in the meantime, who knows?

Mind you, this problematic situation has never been considered central to the Globalization success story. That story resembles a fast-moving train. People who don't pay attention may well fall off the caboose. What can be said? Perhaps there'll be another train coming along the way.

In the meantime, the real world moves on.

The situation of the crucified countries is brought up from time to time. There is a flurry of headlines. Tragedy is evoked. Nice little urgent programs are thrown together to encourage them to do better. Encouraging things are said in public. Not often. This is not a problem that often comes to mind when important people are discussing big questions. There are more important things to do to keep the train of global civilization barrelling down the main track.

PART III

THE PLATEAU

[C]oalitions begin to disintegrate from the moment that the common danger is removed.

— Harold Nicolson, 1948

Success

There was good reason for believers in the idea of Globalization to feel satisfied with their success. Through the 1970s and '80s and on into the '90s they anchored in place reform after reform. Tariffs were right down. Trade was growing at a remarkable pace. The idea of what trade included had been radically expanded. Trade treaties of every sort and other economic binding agreements were being signed. There was broad deregulation, privatization, a lowering of tax rates at the top half of society, and a shifting of the tax burden from the top directly and indirectly through stealth taxes to the bottom. Governments were feeling seriously squeezed as their tax base shrank and the moral pressure to balance their budgets grew. Big public programs were in trouble, underfunded, and those in charge of them were desperate to sort out the confusing messages about how they might be reformed. All in all, it was a remarkable success story. For the global idea. For the marketplace.

In every direction there were signs of a changed world, a world listening to the new message. As you would expect from an ideological movement, these changes were carefully installed in a new vocabulary of received wisdom. The public sector had taken on much of the language and structural logic of the private sector. Public servants were making fools of themselves paying a lot of money to private consultants — and paying repeatedly — to be taught how to use private sector logic.

Soon these servants of the public good had memorized the new vocabulary and were calling citizens *clients* or *stakeholders* or *taxpayers,* using the narrow utilitarian word *efficient* as if it were a core idea, while losing the more relevant concept of whether a law or program was *effective*, apologizing for taxes, undermining public finances by using versions of *real-cost accounting*, a system developed by the private sector to maximize its costs in order to reduce its taxes, and so on. Somehow these public servants couldn't focus on why the more *efficient* they became, the fewer services they could deliver.

Observing such confusion was all quite fun for the consultants who profited financially. And, of course, no one pointed out to the apparently gullible public servant victims of language that all of this market logic was predicated on actually being in the market, in competition. Why? In order to make a profit. So all three factors — being in the market, in a state of competition, in order to make a profit — were irrelevant and inappropriate to the public good. Why explain? Far better to egg them on with yet more expensive and fashionable advice, while pretending progress was being made.

And there they were, the elected leaders and officials, so pleased to be invited to Davos, trying to curry favour with the new powers — the corporate technocracy — listening intently to the PR as if it were ideas, learning like little children. Whether they were social democrats or liberals, they were all becoming Globalists, of a kinder, gentler sort.

Then in 1989 came the collapse of the Soviet system. Simplistic voices claimed this was the intentional outcome of President Ronald Reagan's arms race. The Soviets had been cleverly bankrupted. But this reasoning came largely from people tied to the arms industry — people who approved expanding weapon production.

It was more likely that, after a long decline, the Soviet system failed because it didn't work, surely a more self-confident explanation to be coming from the democracies.

Russia and a number of the old Warsaw Pact countries then rushed to embrace classic capitalism of the late-nineteenth-century sort. Perhaps they were merely going back to where they had left off before becoming communists. They were also embracing the discourse that had been pouring out of the West since the early 1970s. And there was no short-age of Western consultants and academic economists eager to push them into experiments with market purity. Imagine how exciting it was for these theoreticians to find countries prepared not merely to engage in reforms, but to risk the entire well-being of real people — of entire peoples — in order to act as existential case studies.

Variations on crucifixion economics were imposed, usually with results that damaged these real people, and often prompted the return of the communist party to power, this time by the ballot box. But from a theoretical point of view, it was fascinating to watch, just as it had been in parts of Africa and South America. After all, this was the sort of thing the West, even at its most ideological, had long abandoned as too prone to political and economic instability for its own societies.

The end of the Soviet system was nevertheless a great victory for Globalism. It was therefore all the more unfortunate that those key years of metamorphosis were allowed to pass without the G7's stepping forward to give serious help to the Russian president, Mikhail Gorbachev. Instead they left Russia to find its own way with little more than the advice of the theorists and a bit of help when it was too late.

The result was the sell-off — or rather the giving away — of most massive state enterprises to Communist Party technocrats and secret service strongmen. Russia was left with 70 percent of its economy in the hands of thirty-six corporations — that is, thirty-six men. It had been converted from a highly centralized public system into the most concentrated private sector system of the world's big economies. Every traditional Western notion of the dangers of oligopolies and monop-olies had been ignored. And the unregulated manner in which this mass privatization took place had the effect of erasing all lines between the marketplace, corruption and violent criminality. Yet when you look at the gradual return of oligopolies and monopolies in and among the democracies as a result of Globalist policies, it is hard not to see the Russian development as a logical outcome of the privatiza-tion advice given by Western experts. The overall effect was to build organized crime right into the new system.

Ever since then, Russian leaders have been seriously handicapped by the need to struggle against this corporate/criminal power structure. To take the cynical view, this handicapping of the Russian leadership was a clever way to force their acceptance of the loss of Russia's status as a primary power, as well as the loss of the buffer zone between it and the West. Whatever shape Russia was gradually falling into, it would no longer be the opposing bloc.

The Western victory was remarkable. Not surprisingly, if you looked closely around the democracies, you could already see Harold Nicolson's dictum gathering force: "[C]oalitions begin to disintegrate from the moment that the common danger is removed."[1]

It wouldn't happen for all to see until early in the twenty-first century. But the old political and military structures of the post–Second World War period began to pull and creak, and the effect was not to strengthen Globalization but to pry open its fault lines. Why? Because in spite of its global assertions, the movement had come out of the West. Its roots and assumptions came out of nineteenth-century Western assumptions, political experience and economic theory. Its long-term success was dependent on a continued Western unity of view and the capacity of the West to reach out in an inclusive manner to the rest of the globe.

Perhaps the most dramatic part of the collapse of the Soviet bloc was the rapid disintegration of social programs inside both Russia and the surrounding countries. A number of leading thinkers, with ties to that world, now see the removal of the old social protections — as opposed to their conversion into a middle-class Western-style safety net — as a projection of what will happen in the West over the next decade. They see the radical stripping-down of the communist system as an experiment in neo-liberal Globalism, demonstrating that you can dismantle such a costly machine without paying any real political price. "Eastern Europe served as a laboratory for a second important test — how far can one push labour without significant social protests and dislocations?" "[Y]ou can make labour flexible enough to diminish their collective demands to a bare minimum."[2] Again, this disintegration was tied to the advice being urgently given by Western consultants and economists.

The principal counterweight to this social decline was the gradual integration of the ex-Pact countries into the European Union with its still-complex safety net. Even if multiple attempts were under way to make the European system more flexible, lighter, less opaque, none of them were intended to strip it down to the Globalist market model.

This was the atmosphere during the late 1980s and early '90s. It was largely positive. Where there were disappointments, the reply was *Give it time. These are big changes. Take the broad, long, structural view. It will all come right soon enough.*

But if you looked closer with a dispassionate eye you could see great contradictory movements. Globalization was growing ever stronger. It was also fracturing, coming apart, retreating.

The high point may have been 1995, with the creation of the World Trade Organization. It replaced the old trade regulation structure of GATT. And there was every reason for everyone to be pleased that there now existed a centralized body designed to arbitrate trade issues.

What made this administrative accomplishment a major triumph for one school and a major defeat for the other was that both sides treated its creation as far more than a matter of utilitarian organization. It was as if the reconceptualization of civilization through the prism of economics had reached a critical stage. Taken in its fullest meaning, the purpose of the WTO was to ensure that any international exchange containing some commercial element could be judged through that prism. The positive implication was that no other effective system of binding arbitration existed. Trade possessed the only one. At least in that area, problems could now be dealt with. And if because of the economic prism approach other areas could be straightened out from a commercial point of view, so much the better. The negative implication was that issues that were not fundamentally commercial could now be reduced to this utilitarian system of measurement.

Culture, for example, the moment it crossed borders, could be seen as fundamentally a matter of commercial activity, subject therefore to a WTO point of view. Food could be treated as only secondarily something that goes into our stomachs. That we might wish to decide the makeup of what we eat could be dismissed as an interference with the primary question of competing agricultural industries. National health and food rules could be — and quickly were — treated as protectionist interference. All of the questions relating to labelling, sources, genetics, insecticides, herbicides and fertilizers might be of primary concern to citizens, but they would be only secondarily of concern to the WTO. Food was a matter of competition and trade.

At a time when citizens were becoming more involved in how to deal with technology gone wrong, as in mad cow disease or what conditions and prices should surround the use of pharmaceuticals, the creation of the WTO seemed to suggest that such issues should first be treated as a matter of industrial competition. Citizen involvement was therefore a form of protectionism. Unless based on hard science, citizens' desires to choose were not welcome arguments. The precautionary principle had thus been demoted, just as a growing number of public interest groups had focused on its importance.

Above all, people were disturbed by the evolution of the idea of choice. Globalization had been announced as — at least from a commercial point of view — a powerful force for increasing choice. Now it seemed that choice was not to be understood as the citizen's right to decide what she put in her stomach or what his social priorities might be. Instead, choice was to be concentrated on corporate desires and their decisions about how to seek profits. That would mean limiting the personal choices of individuals.

Alfred Eckes has said that those who got us as far as the WTO are "the real revolutionaries of the twentieth century."[3] The chairman of Ford was convinced that "we're moving toward a borderless world." International business organizations were comfortable announcing that "the private sector is the main source for the creation of added value, wealth and jobs…. Business self-regulation has proved to be the most flexible way to get results."

In this way the cheerleaders of Globalization kept urging us on. Mrs. Thatcher in the midst of yet another crisis in 1985: "The temptation of barriers to free trade is strongest when economic growth falters. But while the relief which protectionism gives is also superficial, the after effects are painful.... Modernisation is held back. So the boundaries of the open trading system must be pressed forward."[4]

This was something she said in Malaysia, where thirteen years later a sophisticated and agile leadership, caught in the middle of a meltdown, would prove the exact opposite.

But Mrs. Thatcher was not encouraging us to act in a normal or down-to-earth manner. She was evoking Herman Kahn's "ideology of progress." If you just keep moving in what you believe to be a forward direction, the world will adjust to your pace. It will all come right. Just give it a bit more time.

13

1991

That the world wouldn't or couldn't keep pace began to show in 1991 with the unexpected re-emergence of nationalism at its worst. If you mention the Balkans to almost anyone in the Western world, a facile pessimism quickly emerges. *What would you expect? The Balkans!*

This is a handy way to dismiss the possibility that what happened there was as much a failure of the West — distracted by its global economic obsession — as it was of the society that destroyed itself. After all, the basic facts are simple. Negative nationalism had reappeared with a vengeance. And it had reappeared in the most unlikely of places — within Europe itself.

The strongest political advocates of Globalization had been using a bipolar approach to public argument from the late 1970s on. They had spoken endlessly about international economic integration. At the same time, they had been pushing all the old hot buttons of nineteenth-century nationalism in order to win elections. This was obvious in Ronald Reagan and Margaret Thatcher, but you could find it in more or less subtle forms almost anywhere. In Italy, three parties expressing the most primary sort of nationalism in combination with the most primary sort of free market theory were on the rise. False populism was growing in respectability throughout the Americas.

Playing with such false populist discourse, whether in earnest or as a distraction, is dangerous. By the early 1990s, there were growing signs of people exploring their sense of alienation in a world of abstract global assumptions by falling back on old-fashioned nationalism.

I'm not suggesting that the monsters of the Yugoslav civil war were the products of Globalization. But nothing happens in isolation. You have to ask yourself why Europeans were so catastrophically unprepared for what happened in 1991, when Slovenia and Croatia decided to separate and the Yugoslav army intervened.

It wasn't simply that European leaders were mentally unprepared to take the military action necessary to prevent this human tragedy. They were ethically unprepared. Politically unprepared. They appeared unable to focus on the reality of full-blown negative nationalism at work. Perhaps it felt to them like a nightmare out of their own recent past. Perhaps they hoped to wake up and find it gone. They seemed so convinced that the world — Europe in particular — no longer acted in such a way, that they could not bring themselves to think and act.

The reality was that Europe's leadership and administration had been distracted for years, deep as they were in their well-intentioned but tech-nocratic approach to building a continental system. On a broader plane, they were convinced that the world responded above all to economic mechanisms, sometimes to administrative mechanisms or eventually to political negotiations of the most basic sort. They saw populism as just something you used to distract the population. They no longer had a feel for humanity acting at its worst.

Yugoslavia aside, it's worth remembering that after 1989 some twenty-five new countries or newly independent countries had abruptly appeared on the scene. Most of them had never been democ-racies, never had a citizen-based legal system, never had a modern free market. Their dreams — now perhaps realizable for the first time — were the different dreams of different people with different histories. Poland had centuries-old ambitions to be a major player on the conti-nent. The Czech half of Czechoslovakia had an intellectual hero for a leader and a sophisticated industrial background. Moldova was poverty-stricken and quickly became a corrupt military dictatorship involved in the drug and arms trades. And then there were all the Stans — Kurdistan, Tajikistan and the others, which stretch along the southern Islamic border of Russia and would begin nation building from scratch.

Europe had good reason to be distracted. And yet, ever since the death of Yugoslavia's long-time leader, Tito, in 1980, each European government had been receiving clear warnings from its embassy in Belgrade. I was there often during the 1980s. Everyone I saw repeated that things couldn't last, that there was a power vacuum, that something would explode. Periodically I would be witness to the sort of verbal explosions that revealed how much violence lay just below the surface. There were already riots and murders in Kosovo. In Ljubljana and Zagreb there was constant talk of rebellion. And much of that talk was about race and racial rights and the racial weaknesses of the other groups.

Throughout that long decade — years of shapeless, endless drift — Western governments were either silent or, worse still, playing little political games in the Yugoslav vacuum, old-fashioned games. Perhaps they themselves were letting off steam, given that at home and in their mainstream diplomacy they had to stay rigorously away from the traditional sorts of nationalist rivalry.

In 1988 I spent a morning in Belgrade with Vasa Cubrilovic, ninety, the last survivor of the gang that assassinated Archduke Ferdinand in Sarajevo in 1914, thus ending the nineteenth century and giving birth to the twentieth. He had survived everything: prison, death sentences, resistance, even serving as a minister. He clearly felt the world was collapsing all around him, yet again. "Countries that still go to war have not evolved."[1] Evolved from what? From fear. From nationalism based on fear.

Europe and the rest of the West were unwilling to see any of this. When the Yugoslav wars began, the various foreign ministries in the democracies pulled out their old Balkan files. As if still functioning in 1914, the French chose to support the Serbs, the Germans, the Croats. Others chose sides on the same sort of grounds. It was as if they rejected nationalism for themselves, but accepted it when *less evolved* people were involved, even if it was nationalism in its most primary form. Thus, for foreign policy purposes, each Western country reverted to the old idea of racial, nationalist-based alliances. Guns were sold or supplied. The violence grew.

Then, one day, people outside Yugoslavia seemed to wake up. They abruptly realized this wasn't a game. Negative nationalism really was back. Worse still, it was a malignancy spreading right inside Europe.

That awakening took several years and several ethnic cleansings. Meanwhile, as if in yet another black comedy, international elites, led by economists and consultants who saw themselves as the voice of the new global inevitability, flitted about from global meetings to consultancy contracts, from national capital to national capital, chatting on about how global economic forces were gradually making nation-states irrelevant. As they chatted, thousands of people were being murdered and whole areas cleansed to smooth the creation of brand-new traditional nation-states. All the while United Nations forces were struggling to make an impact, but were held back by confusing and even contradictory rules of engagement and other orders. For this the UN could be blamed, but the real problem lay with the Western governments, which were unwilling to concentrate on this return of ugly nationalism and its full implications. All of that was happening just down the road, just down the two-thousand-year-old highway that had linked the Western Roman Empire to the Eastern Roman Empire's capital in Constantinople. The road passed right through the centre of Sarajevo, which would be martyred before the business was over.

Were you to mention Yugoslavia to this chattering economic determinist elite, they would give you that *Oh, the Balkans* shrug or describe it as a hiccup or a last nationalist eruption. An anomaly. What with the global economy and interpenetration that sort of thing just wasn't realistic any more.

By the time that particular hiccupping fit was over — or almost over — in 1995, a few hundred thousand people were dead and Europe was properly awake. Europeans who wished to think about it were conscious of the fact that they had failed to respond to their own problem. It had been a nation-state problem and they had been locked up in a technocratic continental logic as well as a global economic and administrative logic. The United States had had to take the lead to save them from themselves. Most European leaders knew that they had failed, even if they couldn't bring themselves to publicly admit it. Now they began slowly preparing not to fail again.

There was one other part to their awakening. In public they were still convinced that economic forces dominated all other forces. In private they admitted that this was not true.

Bernard Kouchner, who would later administer Kosovo, talks of how when people are insecure they need to belong to a group, and how a group sees diversity as the enemy: "It is easier to use nationalism to crush diversity than it is to rely on diversity to drive back nationalism."[2] Louise Arbour, now the UN High Commissioner for Human Rights, was regularly exposed to this sort of nationalism when she was chief prosecutor of the International War Crimes Tribunal. She warns that the collective memory can confuse "factual accuracy with allegories and metaphors." That confusion justifies unacceptable acts, particularly if others pretend that they accept the confusion, which is exactly what the West did in the early days of the Yugoslav meltdown.

The point is, at the height of Globalization, the worst of negative nationalism reappeared. Yugoslavia was the vortex, but it was by no means alone. For those who watch the movement of events, the basic assumptions of the Globalist argument had begun to dissolve.

14

The Ideology of Progress

One of the signs of this disintegration was a growing disconnect between the global system and the lives people lived. In spite of the violence in Yugoslavia, the disorder in the old Soviet bloc — which was, after all, a continent and a half of people — the collapse of Africa and the sequential collapses in Latin America, there was no sign that any of this was having an effect on the dominant view that the world should be perceived through an economic prism. High unemployment and slow growth had been institutionalized. They were now permanent fixtures. Yet no one in charge seemed to see this as failure. Or more precisely, no one in charge and none of the supporting ideologues were able to see this as a failure of the Globalist theory — a theory that had growing power for two decades. That is, twice the length of Napoleon's reign, four times that of a world war.

Perhaps their perception was obscured because other indicators of global progress were seen to be positive. Corporations continued to grow. The number and size of mergers and acquisitions increased, particularly those that involved companies in several countries.[1] Both the number of deals and their size doubled in the 1990s. The biggest growth area was in services, not so much because it was a cutting-edge area as because it was the sector least dependent on geography. If the transnational was a virtual state, the service sector was a virtual industry.

This period leading up to 1995 was one of self-confidence and emotional comfort for the believers. Davos was at its height as a court in which people wished to be included. The theatrical need of any economic ideology — the willing suspension of disbelief — was highlighted there thanks to "the three unities of classical drama: place, time and action."[2] A traditional idea of class was developing in a way not seen at the international level since before 1914. Granted, this was a new class system with new players. The old subtle hints of clothing and accents and table manners were irrelevant. But the titles, the levels of power, the obsequiousness, the development of shared "consent" on how to deal with issues when on the outside — all of that was flourishing.

For example, it was considered old-fashioned — déclassé — to worry about who owned what and whether ownership respected borders. What mattered were investment, consolidation and corporate growth. The consensus was that you should act in public as if geography no longer mattered.

As so often in a class system, people at the top said things they didn't really mean, just to reassure the more junior players. And so while there was some selling off to foreigners in the larger economies, it was limited and informally discouraged. In the smaller or more peripheral economies, foreign ownership through transnationals moved up over one-third toward 50 percent. Business leaders from these places were quite proud of their ability to fit into international structures because they weren't tied to national ownership. They didn't seem to notice that in the presence of the big players, their discourse was in reality a soliloquy.

One of the signs that a country was losing standing was how high that barometer of foreign ownership went. The Australian Tax Office began to worry in the 1990s about the minimization of taxes by multinationals. Their reason was simple. Under Globalization, foreign ownership had moved from 20 to 60 percent of GDP.[3] The same sort of argument could have been made in Canada and New Zealand. Part of this passivity was tied to the nineteenth- and early-twentieth-century British theory of free trade, in which industrial countries tried to play a dominant role in commodity-based countries. As the leading nineteenth-century American economist Henry Carey put it, "England had been warring against the agricultural communities of the world, for the reduction of the prices of their rude products." The difference today is the high percentage of food and other commodity industries now organized into transnationals and owned in industrial economies. This paralleled the collapse of most commodity prices under Globalization.

The other sign had to do with senior leadership. Finland began to see its most successful companies moving head office activities abroad. Their reason was the cost of the Finnish social system. Perhaps the other, unstated reason was that international consolidation draws headquarters to a smaller number of larger places. John Ruggie: "This growing divorce between national ownership and location of production can yield entirely contradictory policy implications and potential policy paralysis."[4] If international corporations tend to consolidate their most senior management in a few places, that has serious implications for citizens elsewhere, as well as for such parallel activities as research and community support.

There was one other confused element. The deregulation of international markets made foreign investment much easier. Countries around the world said they needed foreign investment to finance the development of their economies. But they rarely differentiated between the two sorts of foreign investment: investing in order to build up something versus simply buying a fully developed corporation. The first is an investment. The second is coupon clipping for the lazy, a sophisticated form of asset stripping at the international level.

On December 3, 1984, there was an incident in India that could have been seen as a warning of the dangers implicit in long-distance ownership structures. In Bhopal, a Union Carbide plant suffered a major leak. It was engaged in chemical work under conditions that would have been illegal in the United States. Three thousand people were dead within hours, 15,000 more in the aftermath; 200,000 were seriously injured, and 500,000 still carry special health cards.

The CEO of Union Carbide flew in to sympathize. He was horrified to find himself arrested. Horrified that the profession of manager could be confused with that of ethical responsibility for the actions of corporations. The corporation got him out and he fled the country. Dubious backroom negotiations with some level of the Indian government eventually led to a tiny settlement of $470 million. And that was that.

The plant sits abandoned with twenty-five tonnes of toxic waste lying around. From the global point of view, the corporation, now part of Dow Chemical, itself seemed shocked to discover that in the real world there was a geographical reality and there was a possibility of being held responsible in a non-virtual manner.

They had forgotten, if they ever knew, the broader assumptions about free markets that were central to Adam Smith's theories and to those of nineteenth-century free traders. Smith and the free traders assumed a unity among ownership, the production location and the headquarters. Perhaps this is no longer suitable. But if not, then the other assumptions they made about markets might also be worth questioning. Perhaps they also are no longer suitable. After all, the early-nineteenth-century theories assumed that free markets and trade would create jobs, contribute to taxes, improve the social infrastructure and promote leadership within the market, but also within the community.

This brings us back to Davos and its growth as an imitation royal court. It's worth remembering that the effect of any court system has always been to alienate the aristocracy from their geographical obligations. And that is what leads, under each regime, to their downfall. As they become more sophisticated, so they become more irrelevant to the reality they benefit from, and so they are somehow replaced.

Six concrete points arise out of this ideology of progress.

First, global corporations are structures designed to consolidate what they control. They automatically empty activities out of smaller or more isolated communities, unless there is some quite remarkable reason to stay. This presents a challenge for democratic systems, which cannot function if large parts of their nation-states are abandoned economically. This is particularly awkward if the abandonment has been provoked by the application of a theory that the leaders themselves and their leading technocrats adopted. There are no forces of inevitability at play in this situation. A choice has been made by those in charge. Their problem may be that while they sold the theory to the citizenry, they never really explained it. Perhaps as believers they would not have been able to explain it.

Second, in well-organized markets there are strong rules against dumping. There is nothing new about this. It has been true for thousands of years. You can't have competition if some people can dump underpriced goods into markets in order to destroy the local structures and replace them with their own. Traditionally we think of dumping as the underpriced offloading of surplus goods. But in a consumer economy almost all goods can be seen as surplus. You could say that Globalization as a system has normalized dumping. The argument in favour is that only through dumping can the client buy the cheapest goods. This argument ignores the necessity of a stable market, which permits competition, which in turn is destroyed by such pricing. The most institutionalized and destructive form of modern dumping is industrialized agriculture. Why? Because it undermines the capacity of farmers in both the producing and the consuming societies to make enough profit to stay in farming.

Third, there is another form of post-modern dumping. The protection of the WTO permits the owners of intellectual property to overprice their goods. You might call this inverse dumping.

Fourth, and more original to our day, it could be argued that there is yet another new form of dumping. That is the sharp rise of international trade taking place within transnational corporations as a way of sourcing the least expensive parts without going into the marketplace. This is internal shipping. A few years ago it was thought to account for a third of what we call trade. I argued earlier that we may be naive to consider it in the same category as other trade. Instead of celebrating this phenomenon as a trade success story, perhaps we should call it internal dumping or structural dumping.

Curiously enough, this internal shipping system often has the effect of disassociating competitive production cost from the sales price. The gap becomes so large that the internal system both allows for this new sort of dumping and permits the corporation to hold on to larger profits. This is wealth accumulation, not economic growth. And it drives transnationals to spend this money by constant mergers and acquisitions, yet further undermining the sort of competition that produces growth.

These various forms of unfair competition or deformed competition could also be thought of as a new type of combine or price rigging. They remind us that the consolidation of transnational corporations has very little to do with open global markets in the free trade tradition and everything to do with the dark side of seventeenth- and eighteenth-century mercantilism. And that means everything to do with the old problems of oligopolies and monopolies.

Fifth, there do exist many other economic models. Whatever people think of national politics in Italy, it is a country with strong and successful regions and highly successful cities. One of the reasons is that behind the screen of the two or three giant corporations, there is a healthy world of small- and medium-sized corporations. About 23 percent of Italians work in companies with fewer than ten employees. The equivalent figure in Britain is 7 percent, in the United States 3 percent.[5] If you look at corporations with fewer than a hundred employees, the portrait of both the economy and the society is quite remarkable. Here is a country that makes things. Italy controls its own market with those goods and also sells a great number of them abroad, taking full advantage of the real purpose of free trade.

The sixth point relates to taxes. "A gentleman," Confucius argued, "helps out the necessitous; he does not make the rich richer still."[6] *The Economist* agrees that "[p]rinciples of fairness underpin the liberal state." Yet it is virtually impossible to speak of taxes today in a straightforward, honest and positive manner.

The Keynesian period had high growth, high employment and an ambition to strengthen the public good. The result was a straightforward use of taxes. By the 1970s the tax system had some of the disadvantages of the rest of the opaque mountain of intense social reforms. But the preceding quarter-century had proved that high growth and high taxes can go together.

The Globalist period has brought or has been a period of low growth and high unemployment, driven by an ambition to strengthen the marketplace. Everything possible has been done to free up market forces, the principle being that the release of new international energy will drive all the rest — growth and employment just for starters. So far, this has not worked.

One positive development is that there is some shrinkage in the statistics that count the poorest around the world. Unfortunately nobody, not even the statisticians, is clear about whether this improvement is real or statistical.

There is, however, general agreement that the gap between rich and poor has grown. And this has a direct effect on the tax system. Taxes have been brought down in the top brackets. More of the tax burden now falls on the middle and lower sections of society. This conforms to today's belief system. It also accepts the argument that there is no alternative. Why? Because corporations and people in the top bracket can move across borders easily. If you don't lower their taxes they will leave.

In spite of these major changes in rates, governments are finding it increasingly difficult to collect taxes from corporations. This suggests that part of the Globalization idea is working — as far as taxes are concerned, the nation-states seem to have weakened before the large corporations. Not surprisingly, transnational corporations are very adept at moving their money around according to tax rates. If they don't like the tax system in a place, they move their money out and run their local subsidiary on debt. These debt-friendly tax systems were created to help corporations build up their activities.

In 2004 *The Financial Times* looked at the British operations of twenty major non-oil companies with a turnover of almost £100 billion. These corporations had managed to organize a total loss of £700 million and paid taxes of £350 million.[7] Almost nothing.

Is this the inevitable outcome of an inevitable global force? Or is it a question of G7 countries being unwilling to deal with the need for an international binding agreement on taxation in order to prevent corporations acting in a legal but dishonest manner?

The failure of democratic governments to deal with international taxation has forced them into a permanent tax and poverty crisis. Their response to the tax crisis has been perfectly utilitarian. They have sought to raise taxes without seeming to do so. The result is stealth taxes. These can take many forms. Perhaps the most demeaning to the dignity of citizenship and democracy has been the decision of governments to become the largest croupiers ever known.

There is nothing wrong with gambling. It is one sort of fun among many. But there is something fundamentally wrong with democratic governments pushing gambling as a way to raise serious amounts of public funds.

There is a precise ethical point. It is reached when governments spend tens of millions of taxpayers' money on advertising to encourage citizens to gamble. In the United States alone almost $500 million is spent every year encouraging mainly less-educated, poorer people to gamble more.[8] "A million a day — Just Play." In Australia, $600 million goes to publicity.

The Globalization period has seen gambling revenues grow in Germany from 8 billion marks a year in the early 1970s to 42 billion. Everywhere the growth rate is the same: 10 to 15 percent a year. Mexico, new to the game, is aiming at US$3 billion gross. New Zealand is at $12 billion. In Britain some £25 billion. In India, $7 billion — 2 percent of GDP. Worldwide, some $900 billion is spent by citizens on gambling. Many governments could no longer survive without this income.

In 1995 in Britain the combination of government net earning from gambling and money also from gambling given to good works — in lieu of public funds — was £9.7 billion. This was more than half of what was raised in corporate taxes. It was three and a half times the combined amount of capital gains and inheritance taxes. In the energy-rich Canadian province of Alberta, government gambling revenues rival and sometimes pass oil-and-gas-tax revenues.

The justification in every one of these cases is that some percentage of the earnings is given to good works, to culture, to schools. In other words, the governments silence precisely those who would criticize the ethics of using gambling as a tax tool by addicting them to its revenues.

Normalized poverty has been the other solution to the tax crisis. Governments save money by simply letting people slip through the safety net. The logic is simple. If the rules of Globalization prevent you from looking after the citizens most in need, don't look after them. Someone is bound to pick up the slack. After all, charity was a feature of the nineteenth-century market system. Free trade, utilitarianism and charity, or philanthropy, as it came to be called — the new form of noblesse oblige indulged in by the new rich — all came together. And they came in opposition to an inclusive approach to the public good.

Now charity is a feature again. And it is perfectly adapted to the needs of the poor, because international economic consolidation is the opposite of local, while charity is almost by definition local. Many who oppose Globalization call for the revival of local structures and local solutions. They forget that there are no local solutions if there is no reliable local access to tax revenues.

It is important to remember that whatever the original free trade movement's hesitations over workers' rights, charity was not the intent. Cobden: "We often hear a great deal about charity, but what have we to do with charity in this House? The people ask for justice, and not charity. We are bound to deal out justice; how can charity be dealt out to an entire nation?"[9] The conviction that charity was not the solution to the needs of the public good had been growing since the Industrial Revolution and the creation of the poor houses. August Strindberg a century ago: "All charity is humiliation." And yet, once free trade was in place, charity seemed to grow effortlessly. And continued to grow in a destabilizing manner, until the late nineteenth century. Public policy, pushed by a broader base of voters, began to establish fair and inclusive public policies. The point is not that nineteenth-century philanthropy was all self-indulgent or inappropriate. The point is that some was and some wasn't. And none of it could address the broad needs of the disinterested public good.

Then suddenly, a century later, with the rise of Globalization, charity was back as a serious tool of public policy. There were 16 food banks in

Auckland, New Zealand, in 1990. By 1994 there were 130. In most cities around the democratic world, food banks were set up to deal with temporary emergencies in the 1980s. They have never stopped growing. Being unable to feed yourself is the basic level of poverty. As for the temporary homeless shelters, they have been rebuilt into solid dormitories. It is common that about half those who sleep in them have jobs. They earn too little to pay rent.

Am I saying that charity should have no role in a democratic society? Not at all. But for reasons of dignity and reasons of realism, charity should not and cannot fulfill the needs of a society's poor, nor can it get the mass of those affected out of poverty. As Cobden said, only the state can. The role of charity should be to fill the cracks of society, the imaginative edges, to go where the public good hasn't yet focused or can't. Dealing with poverty is the basic responsibility of the state.

That Globalization recreated this problem and has offered no solutions to it was another of those hints that it would be a short-lived ideology.

15

1995

The high point of Globalization came in 1995 with the creation of the WTO. This included a secondary triumph — the inclusion of intellectual property in the WTO's responsibilities. The collection of royalties was now to be treated as an item of trade. This inclusion of TRIPS (trade-related aspects of intellectual property rights) was a vote of confidence in the idea of transnationals as virtual states. The effect would also be to convince smaller, poorer countries that whatever its strengths, the WTO could be used to advance unfair Western advantages.

Just a few months before, in late 1994, Mexico was celebrated by the *World Competitiveness Report* as the most admirable of economic success stories. Here was proof that a developing economy could pull itself out of the old-style crises and follow the new path. Better still, the young women and men who had advised the Mexican president on how to do it were all products of the finest Western universities and experts in both modern management and the new global economics.

At the same time, international development assistance hit a new high of $61.5 billion. And in this optimistic atmosphere the Organisation for Economic Co-operation and Development (OECD) launched the negotiations to create the Multilateral Agreement on Investment (MAI). According to *The Economist*, the OECD negotiators "were oozing optimism" that within three years they could "create a set of global rules that would lock in liberalisation[.]"[1] The MAI was to be the next stage in the progress of Globalization, after the WTO.

The world, strange as it is, does have a tendency to go in opposing directions at the same time. Three months after Mexico was celebrated as a model economy, its economy collapsed. This was called the tequila crisis, and many said they had seen nothing like it since the 1930s.[2]

At the same time, world commodity prices began to drop. They kept on dropping. Coffee prices are now 32 percent of its value in 1995, cotton one-half. At the same time, development assistance began dropping. By 2000 it was down 25 percent. In the West, each new study carried disturbing news. When trends in equality and inequality were examined, it turned out that the two champions of Globalism — New Zealand and the U.K. — were at the top of the chart of countries with growing inequalities.[3]

But perhaps the single most damaging indication for Globalism lay in the Dayton Peace Agreement, which had finally in 1995 put an end to the vicious civil war in Bosnia. I have described how between 1980 and 1991 European states either did nothing or made things worse in the Balkans. Once the civil war had begun, they interfered in an even more ham-handed way, then sat back while the violence spread. The armies they sent via the UN were themselves martyred by weak and confused political leadership at home. Eventually, the United States took the lead and wrung this Dayton agreement out of the three warring groups.

But the underlying model of the peace accord was adapted from that of the local extremist nationalist leaders. About the only thing they didn't get was the right to kill each other. The painful detail of racial separation created by the war, town by town, was largely formalized. It was accepted that in order to function as a citizen or vote you had to have an identity card defining you as belonging to one of the three races. If you were Jewish, you didn't exist unless you lied. If you were of mixed blood, you had to lie and choose a pure race. It wasn't until 2002 that this racist rule was dropped.

The point is far broader. The West, launched on a global crusade that said economics could straighten us out and nationalism would shrink away, felt obliged to go along with the sort of racism it had fought against in the last world war. It went along with this for a new country within the West. Bosnia is a small place with a small and poor population of 4 million. Yet the West, unimaginably rich, with unprecedented military power and a population of 350 million in Europe and another 350 million in North America, acted as if it had no power to do more. At least there was peace. People had stopped dying. But it was an ethical humiliation for those who said they believed in a new, open world.

In that same year, Eduard Shevardnadze, former Soviet foreign minister under Mikhail Gorbachev and then the embattled leader of Georgia, went to London where he both warned and accused the West: "Enormous sums of money were spent in ending the Cold War; no similar amounts are being put towards helping to build democracy.... We do not have a triumph of Western democracy.... Regimes with markedly Fascist tendencies [have come to power. Rampant nationalism poses] threats to nuclear armageddon."[4]

In the period just before Dayton, a genocide took place in Rwanda. Half a million to a million people were killed. The developed world did not move. Gen. Roméo Dallaire, the Canadian officer sent by the United Nations to command a minute force, has said that he considers this inaction pure racism, in particular the stalling at the Security Council. The vagueness surrounding the number murdered is in itself interesting. We live in a world of statistics: measuring growth, productivity, height, longevity, money markets from every angle, increases in obesity, frequency of orgasms, divorces, vegetables eaten. Yet no one seems to know or care whether half a million Rwandans were massacred.

The Rwandan genocide rolled right on into the Congo catastrophe: 4.7 million people died between 1998 and 2003. Or was it 3.4 million? Or 5.6?

Where were all the powerful forces of economic inevitability during these disasters? Where was Western leadership? They were busy speaking with confidence about Globalization while large parts of the world were in an accelerated political meltdown marked by terrifying levels of nationalist violence.

There was a small but important initiative taken over this same period by the International Labour Organization. In 1994 it set up a Working

Party on the Social Dimensions of the Liberalization of International Trade. This group began to look at what kind of binding regulations could be installed at the international level to create some balance in world affairs — to reintroduce the idea of the public good at the global level. By 2002 this had become a World Commission and by 2003 it had produced a report. It is an extremely reasonable report, filled with ideas that could stabilize the gains made and draw our attention to a broader view of how the real world works.

There it sits. Waiting.

PART IV
THE FALL

The King's head was not taken off because he was King, nor the Lords laid aside because Lords ... but because they did not perform their trust.

— Oliver Cromwell, 1653

16

A Negative Equilibrium

As if in a great confusion, the next six years saw a tumbling-down of global expectations. The precise events were there to be noted and enumerated, forming a pattern if anyone wished to stand back and join the dots. Perhaps more important was the broader impression that the great truths of Globalization were not coming true.

Neither Globalization nor free trade was in trouble because of anyone who opposed either issue or sought to approach these issues in a down-to-earth way. They were in trouble because of the careless, romantic, ideological approach of their religious supporters. To advance a totalist theory devoid of a central role for both societal leadership and society itself could not help but provoke a crisis and a backlash. To blame those who oppose ideologies is a bit like blaming the disaster of the First World War on those who criticized messianic generals like Foch and Haig for their failure both to win battles and to win battles without massacring their troops.

Early in the twenty-first century, people would begin to focus on the growing number of failed democracies and, indeed, of failed states. It is difficult to attribute such broad problems to specific causes. But as we have seen, there is a fundamental contradiction between two promises of the Globalization movement: that there would be a decline in the power of the nation-state, along with a growth in the number of democracies and in their vibrancy. But democracy is an expression of the nation-state. It is an expression of the role and the power of individual citizens inside those states — an expression of their ability to engage in national choices; to set the direction of the nation-state on internal and external matters; to define the nature of the public good. Their power applies directly to the structures and choices of their state.

Weaken the nation-state through the idea of *inevitable* international forces and you cannot help weakening your democracy. A quarter-century of civilization being restructured through the prism of unstoppable economic forces could only undermine those nation-states and democracies that were anything other than rock solid.

Where democracy was firm, the lessons being learned were quite different. Politicians and civil servants began to notice that the specific Globalization theories guaranteed to produce healthy growth and a broadening of wealth quite simply were not.

Perhaps the simplest example was the outcome of the broad privatization of state corporations and the resulting movement of trillions of dollars. Some privatized corporations did do better, but it was by no means a majority of them. Privatization brought no pattern of success, except for a smallish group of managers who converted themselves into rich make-believe capitalists by dipping into the capital worth of large corporations. As for the vast sums injected into the public coffers around the world, they seemed to evaporate without any particular effect. There was no economic surge, no particular improvement in public economic health. Just a one-time payout in return for removing large blocks of long-term value from public wealth.

This was an illustration of something common in the new global economics: the vaporization of money. A half-century earlier it would have been described as an inflationary phenomenon. But this was a new sort of inflation, difficult to measure. Vast sums of money entered into the marketplace and just as quickly seemed to evaporate without any particular effect, as if it had been sucked up into the sky like the bodily assumption of the blessed virgin. Perhaps it was the economy's natural reaction to the disjunct between the spiralling capital markets and the stolid movement in real activity.

By the late 1990s the privatization mania had shrunk to a dribble. There was a lot more to sell off, but the politicians and civil servants had lost their enthusiasm for the game. Why? They couldn't see the purpose of it.

If privatization dribbled on at all, it was only as a way for political parties to feed large fees to a variety of professional groups. Lawyers, accountants, merchant bankers and so on would then pay smaller sums back to the parties through contributions, other forms of support and senior jobs.

Perhaps the hardest failure to admit was the disjunct between trade and growth. Trade was at the heart of the global belief system. So rather than openly debate its positive and negative specifics, the believers in Globalization let their doubts dissipate into mulish silence.

Yet the frustrating questions grew more obvious in the silence. Why did the astonishing and continuous expansion in trade not produce broad economic growth, spread wealth and reduce unemployment?

I asked earlier whether the new phenomenon of trade between subsidiaries of the same transnational should be counted as trade at all. This movement of elements probably now accounts for the majority of international trade. If it isn't trade, we shouldn't expect it to have the effect of trade. Perhaps its effect is neutral or even negative. If we don't honestly ask the question, we cannot begin to understand the disjunct between massive trade and sluggish growth.

On the surface there is nothing to ask. For the purposes of local regulations, these inner-company movements are usually accounted for as if goods were being sold and bought, as if it were a matter of classical trade. In reality, actual profits are rarely made at each stage of movement. If anything, losses are intended in order to use international movements to avoid taxes. But the fundamental absence of a desire to make a profit at each stage suggests that these goods are not trade goods. Besides, the process is unrelated to market competition.

There is nothing peculiar about the intent. Why not assemble the constituent parts at the lowest possible cost and sell the final product at the highest possible price? But if the whole process is internal, it resembles not so much market trade as the earlier mercantilist model or that of the nineteenth-century empires.

This process is able to maximize internal end profits, without being touched by market mechanisms, which include taxes.

The additional factor here is that, thanks to mass production, most of these markets are permanently in surplus production. The need is not to invest but to prop prices up.

The challenge, therefore, is to develop a corporate growth strategy that has little to do with growth in the economy outside the corporation. Part of the solution has been to funnel this wealth into mergers and acquisitions, which permit corporations to become ever larger, but to no economic purpose. This process has been explained with particular originality by Jonathan Nitzan and Shimshon Bichler: "In the late nineteenth century, there was less than one cent's worth of mergers and acquisitions for every dollar of 'real' investment. Fast forward another hundred years and for every one dollar of 'real' investment there were over two dollars put into mergers."[1] The outcome, Nitzan and Bichler argue, permits the ever larger corporations to do four things at once: avoid creating new capacity, which would drive prices down; gain more control over the market by reducing competition; reinforce earnings, again by reducing competition; and reduce risk by narrowing markets and competition. This in turn gives them greater influence, indeed power, inside the nation-state structures, which again in turn gives them a greater influence over the designing of public regulations to protect their position by reducing competition. I have already described a prime example of this — the inclusion of intellectual property — TRIPS — under the WTO umbrella.

We begin to see that much of what is justified as part of the new structures needed to support a global economy of growing exchanges does not support "real" trade. It neither increases societal wealth nor contributes to societal growth.

Global mergers and acquisitions grew to a peak of $1.2 trillion in 2000, then collapsed slowly back to $300 billion in 2001, then began expanding again. By late 2004 this phenomenon was hitting $100 billion a week. "[T]he path of least resistance" is irresistible to large techno-cratic, directionless bodies such as transnationals.

The cynic might argue that such accumulation of power through wealth demonstrates the success of Globalization and the growing weakness of the state. A more down-to-earth interpretation would be that any system that must vaporize wealth in order to consolidate power is acting in a defensive manner that makes its power fragile. The odd thing about this merger and acquisition approach is that it manages to combine a remarkable accumulation of power with an equally shocking vaporization of the paper wealth involved. In such an atmosphere, it was only a matter of time before citizens and their governments rediscovered that they were far stronger than large corpo-rations. They are stronger because they can shape events by creating policy through choice, as opposed to the transnational corporation, which accumulates power by reducing choice.

The disjunct between money and growth has spread into almost every area, as has the curious phenomenon of financial vaporization. As the 1990s wore on, the Bank for International Settlements kept warning that "our financial revolution has been accompanied by an accelerated growth in financial transactions without any detectable link with the needs of the non-financial economy."[2] It was becoming "increasingly difficult to assess the direct credit, liquidity and interest rate risks" of lenders because so much was happening in "off-balance-sheet business." Both personal and corporate debt ratios kept on growing, as if no sensible levels existed. By 2004 British personal debt hit £1 trillion, an all-time high. Paul Krugman wrote of "a new Gilded Age, as extravagant as the original" — the one that led into the collapse of 1929; the Haitian writer George Anglade had been calling for a rejection of "superfluous growth" in favour of "necessary development."

But the financial markets just kept on inventing new sorts of debt and, indeed, of privatized taxation. What are TRIPS or bank charges for basic services or credit card charges if not a privatizing of taxes in the eighteenth-century salt-tax-collector style? While central bankers remained concerned about classic monetary levels, the private sector was printing however much money it wanted through a broadening set of private mechanisms — from junk bonds to credit cards.

Western society has taken to pretending that speculation no longer has consequences for economic and political well-being. Modern methods, we tell ourselves, have made speculation useful. Then abruptly reality is reasserted and we explode with anger. Jacques Chirac, 1995: "Speculation is the AIDS of our economies."[3]

There was nothing new in the delusion that speculation and a consumption-based economy could last forever. And there was nothing new in the conviction that it would lead to disaster. Sophocles:

> Money, gentlemen, money! The virus
> That infects mankind with every sickness
> We have a name for no greater scourge
> Than that!

What was new was the effective loss of the old global trading idea that Keynes had described as "the duty of saving," a "virtue" that permitted "the growth of the cake." The myth of Globalization still includes this idea of trading to feed growth — an idea built on saving — while in reality the conversion into a speculation or consumption or vaporizing society does the exact opposite. And so the cake — particularly inside the developed economies — does not grow, because the global system does not wish it to grow.

In the mid-1980s this idea of trading to feed growth was accepted in business communities as welcome relief from the heavy hand of government. There was little questioning of how it all really worked and what its profound effects were. The world of business does not easily admire internal debate, let alone disagreement. It is a world of pyramidal order, obedience within structures and solidarity among senior figures. Received wisdom is the aristocratic code.

By the mid-1990s this belief system was breaking down. There were loud and celebrated dissenters, often from among those who had led in the creation of the received wisdom. Jimmy Goldsmith and George Soros were the most famous converts from Globalization to more careful and questioning positions. But there were dozens of other dissenting voices, each with particular concerns: the Australian merchant banker Rob Ferguson; the Canadian pulp-and-paper executive Adam Zimmerman; another Canadian, the food-business leader Jon Grant. The majority of the German and French industrial leadership had great misgivings. So did hundreds of owners and executives throughout the United States. Robert Menschel, the senior New York merchant banker, was an eloquent voice.[4] And off the record, thousands of business leaders were increasingly uncomfortable with the Globalist assumptions.

What all of them had in common was their intuition and a sum of observations that the world was adrift in passive received wisdom. In 1826, when the West was in the middle of provoking a century-long violent backlash by letting the received wisdom that profits rated above social well-being get out of hand, the Scottish writer John Galt warned against the newly established economic theory, "the theoretic beauty of which has been of late too often worshipped[.]"[5] The dissenters of the 1990s were reacting against a new atmosphere of worship. Their idea of the public good as the trump card of civilization, as well as of long-term economic success, pushed them to break the silence of corporate loyalty. This more conscious, and therefore more intelligent, face of corporate leadership was breaking with the fundamental global received wisdom that you could — indeed must — view and organize civilization through the prism of economics.

One of the most obvious factors causing them to doubt Globalization was the theory's incapacity to increase and spread wealth. Many business leaders are convinced that if wealth is not spread, all wealth is endangered. In 1999 Kofi Annan, the UN secretary general, went to Davos to send precisely this message: "History teaches us that such an imbalance between the economic, social and political realms can never be sustained for very long." What is that imbalance? Unacceptable levels of unemployment. Job insecurity. Exploitative work conditions.

The most obvious failure of Globalization has been its incapacity to maintain employment. The entire global period has been one of high unemployment, with the numbers running ahead of population growth. In 1973 the OECD had 10 million unemployed job seekers.[6] By 1979 this was 18 million. Through the 1980s the numbers ranged from 29 to 30 million. During the 1990s it was mainly in the mid-30s. Already in the new century it is rising toward 40 million.

And this is happening even though employment statistical methods have been constantly redefined since the 1970s in order to minimize the figures. Most important has been the growth in the long-term unemployed and in the number of people who do not appear in the statistics at all, because they are no longer seeking jobs or have been retired early or are struggling to survive with several minor and unsecured part-time jobs at once. The 1973 and '79 figures of 10 and 18 million were probably accurate. But an accurate figure today would be much higher than the 35 to 40 million announced — in some countries, half again as much. Altogether there are now at the very least 45 to 50 million unemployed in the OECD countries.

And while the very real rigidities of European regulations are often blamed for this, you have only to look about to notice that the situation is far more complex than the simple statistics suggest. The real wages of the lower-paid in the United States fell during the 1980s. In the early 1990s President Bill Clinton admitted with frustration that over half the American workforce was earning less than a decade before: "[T]he global village we have worked so hard to create [has produced] higher unemployment and lower wages for some of our people.... This is a powerful testament to the painful difficulty of trying to maintain a high-wage economy in a global economy where production is mobile and can quickly fly to a place with low wages."[7]

In fact, there was a steady increase in inequality in every industrialized country. The income of the richest over the poorest in the U.K. grew from four times to seven by the 1990s. The gap between the highest and lowest paid is at its highest since the 1880s.

In 1995, the year of the WTO triumph, there were 800 million unemployed or underemployed in the world — that is, according to the use of minimalist statistical methods. The International Labour Organization (ILO) said unemployment was at its worst since the 1930s. The WHO in 1995: "The speed of decline in some countries in sub-Saharan Africa really surprised us. They had made good progress till the mid-1980s."[8]

Ministers from the OECD governments had got together in 1994 to deal with the employment failure in their own countries. They announced a program aimed at nurturing entrepreneurship, easing regulations and so on. They promised they were "not talking about unraveling the welfare system, taking away the basic rights of workers or undermining long-standing collective agreements."[9]

Yet it was hard to believe any of this was more than vague technocratic tinkering in the context of a strong belief that the broad Globalist approach would eventually pay off. If it wasn't tinkering, why were — are — no questions asked about the vaporization of the new wealth that women have brought to the economy?

This is one of the most troubling outcomes of the last quarter-century. After all, women are playing a growing role everywhere, and at every level. For a century they had gradually been occupying space in the workplace — first on the factory floor as cheap labour, but then as teachers and nurses and clerks. Abruptly the pace changed, as did the proportion of higher-level jobs. That whole half of the population was injecting itself into the process of creativity, leadership, professionalism and management, beyond its obvious contributions inside the family and homemaking system. This should have produced a great shot of energy into the creation of real wealth. The full involvement of women was and is increasingly a far more important impetus for real growth than any reduction of tariffs or deregulation of markets could possibly be. Tariffs and deregulation are matters of technical adjustment. Women entering the full range of activities means a virtual doubling of the workforce and a profound restructuring of society's creativity and energy. Yet there has been no surge. And the fault is certainly not with the women.

If you were to look at a middle-class family in the 1960s, you would find that it did all right on one salary. Now two are required. The real wealth contributed by women has somehow been inflated away, while a great deal of new paper wealth has been created in such areas as money markets and mergers. In other words, real growth input has not produced growth, while inflationary input has produced not growth but artificial wealth.

Agreed, a middle-class family today now consumes more than it did forty years ago. But looked at through strict definitions of poverty — for example, the need to choose between essentials such as food and clothes — studies show that large parts of the middle class today are barely making it.

Was the inflating away of the real wealth created by women a result of reducing the central societal perception to mere economic logic with its utilitarian limitations? Was this exacerbated by the absence of counter-balancing international treaties in key areas such as taxation, work conditions, myriad legal obligations, the environment? The short answer, at least in part, is probably yes. Imbalance in public affairs will almost always rebound in two stages. First, it produces destructive situations. Then it backfires or explodes in some unexpected way.

The other obvious failure of Globalization was the reintroduction of job insecurity. Some job security systems had become overly ponderous and unnecessarily costly. The ad hoc way in which democracies make changes was responsible for much of this, particularly in Western Europe. But the solution to the problem was not to undermine social stability.

The old free trade solution to high labour costs had been to import cheap goods. That was the meaning of the revocation of the Corn Laws in nineteenth-century Britain. During the first stages of Globalization, the market solution had been to import cheap, unsecured labour, which has left today's Europe with the unresolved question of 17 million *guest workers*. The next solution — still with us today — involved a return to the nineteenth-century strategy. The growing internal structures of the transnationals have once again given the West access to cheap labour abroad.

But the existence of cheaper labour at home or abroad has never been the problem. If carefully handled, this could even be part of a positive global development strategy. The problem is the market conviction that a corporation must both maximize profits and yet offer the customer the cheapest possible goods.

The idea that the customer is always right should not be interpreted as a right to the cheapest goods. That is false populism confused with economics. It leads to overproduction and underpricing. Seven pairs of men's underwear for $10 at Wal-Mart in upstate New York, summer 2004. This cannot be good for any economy. It cannot be a growth strategy. Rather, it is a defensive approach, reducing the flexibility of every economy involved. The unstated assumption is that the workers who produce the goods and those who purchase them will — thanks to low wages and low prices — all be able to live on the marginal line of poverty.

In contrast to the production and pricing of Wal-Mart underwear are those Nike shoes produced for $1.60 in Indonesia and sold for $70 elsewhere. Both cases are the product of a market approach delinked from competition, value and need. These are the two extremes of Western consumerism: goods too unnecessarily cheap to support a growth economy; goods too artificially expensive to feed a growth economy.

Both cases relate to the return of unsecured, cheap labour, the sort of unethical use of labour Western societies debated and theoretically settled over a century ago. Britain and France led the way with child labour laws. In 1841, Paris forbade the hiring of children under five and limited the workday of those eight to twelve years old to eight hours, those twelve to sixteen years old to twelve hours. The creation of the ILO in 1919 focused on "humane conditions of labour." If one nation refused this, it was "an obstacle in the way of other nations."[10] Twenty-five years later the ILO produced the Declaration of Philadelphia. It was another one of those moments of progress generated by the Second World War, and it insisted that employment policies promote social justice.

And yet the pricing mechanism of Globalization has involved a return to child labour and unsecured labour. By the mid-1990s this was being debated everywhere, even in the most conservative of reviews. No one really accepted the old argument that children needed to work to help feed their families — 200 million of them by most accounts — when the problem could be solved as industrialized societies had solved it in the nineteenth century, by paying their parents more. And yet this is a world in which statistics suggest half the globe's children are affected by poverty, war and AIDS. Such numbers float by us. Six million children under five died in 1992 from pneumonia or diarrhea. Is this really accurate? How accurate does it need to be to suggest a failure?

Children were only a small part of the cheap labour and unsecured labour character of deregulated markets. And these in turn were only a small part of crucifixion economics. Then-president Carlos Salinas, as Mexico entered into the world of global trade, promised that "by increasing our trade we will increase our standard of living." This was shortly before Mexican incomes were halved. In such a context the $1-a-day measurement of poverty doesn't mean a great deal. And the dragging on of Third World debt becomes an obscene leftover of old-style Protestant moralizing. The debt-to-export ratios of the most indebted countries multiplied three to four times between 1970 and '90. They have just kept on multiplying, many of them ten or more times by century's end.

Again, in such a context, the idea of unregulated cheap labour as a global growth strategy made no sense at all.

And so there was growing criticism on all sides. Slowly corporations began to react to criticism from the public. Slowly governments awoke to the not-inevitable nature of a return to early-nineteenth-century standards — or lack of standards.

All of this took place in a world of accelerating violence. Most statistics on war-related deaths since 1945 total up to some 40 million.[11] If you add up the numbers from 1945 to 1970 they come to approximately 18 million. This includes the highly unstable period of the decolonization wars of independence. And yet, from 1970 to 2000 — the Globalization era — the numbers were higher: 22 million or some two thousand a day. What statisticians call *excess* deaths — that is, deaths resulting indirectly from war through such things as malnutrition and disease — are even more disturbing. In the late 1970s they were running around 12 million a year. In the early 1990s it was 14 million. In 2000 it was 18 million. In 2003, 25 million.

This does not include deaths from those epidemics that could be prevented or lessened by effective global policies. For example, over 20 million people have died of AIDS since 1981; 2.6 million in 2003 alone. The rate of infection in 2003 was at an all-time high. In Asia, where the two miracle economies of China and India grow constantly, the infection rates are hovering on the epidemic level, beyond which the effects would be hard to calculate.

Is all of this the direct fault of Globalization? No. Has Globalization succeeded as a planetary system capable of lessening or preventing deaths from violence and preventable epidemics? No. Have such things got steadily worse under the leadership of the global system? Yes. Have things begun to turn around in the new century? So far they seem to be getting worse. At some point it is no longer enough for respectable, intelligent economists like Jagdish Bhagwati to go on repeating "one can conclude that freer trade is associated with higher growth and that higher growth is associated with reduced poverty. Hence, growth reduces poverty."[12] Such reductionism is not respectable.

Leadership is not about defining your turf. It is about judging the effects of your theory and style on the broad situation. Communism must carry responsibility for death camps and failed production. The Vatican must carry responsibility for the Inquisition and the destruction of the Latin American indigenous population. Globalization must carry responsibility for the growth in violence and the ineptitude that has allowed epidemics to get out of control.

17

NGOs and God

At the beginning of the Globalist era, there were already hints of how it might end. Just as a new elite — centred on economics and management — was taking power, a rather quirky little force appeared on the horizon. It was made up of non-governmental organizations. At the time, very few people knew about the concept of NGOs or followed their expansion. To apply the word *force* to them at that time would have struck most public officials as comic. As a group, they seemed distant and irrelevant, given the fresh ideology setting up shop for eternity. But these NGO leaders and their organizations quickly began to multiply. At the same time, God, a spent force, in fact one thought to have been dead since the mid-nineteenth century, abruptly reappeared and began to win back ever larger numbers of true believers. Rather like Globalization, he was served by messianic believers, who in an earlier era would have been called disciples.

And yet, neither the leaders of the NGOs nor the disciples of God could have been further from the elite style declared necessary, if not inevitable, by the Globalist movement.

Even earlier there had been signs of what might happen. After all, free trade itself had first found power in the nineteenth century in a fervent atmosphere of what today we might call reborn Christianity. But 150 years later, the two forces seemed to have been decoupled. As for public associations unrelated to governmental, particularly democratic, structures — what we now call NGOs — they had been few and far between. If anything, they had often been suspect as the anti-democratic arms of traditional religious forces. In the early days of modern free trade, in the middle of the nineteenth century, representative democracy was itself new and still finding its way. Faced by the old class elites and the new industrial elites, citizens saw the greatest potential for their power in banding together under nation-state governments or large worker unions.

There were a handful of new-style non-governmental organizations getting under way: workers' associations, activists in the reform wing of some religious denominations, pro-education associations. Some of them, like the Red Cross, were even international. Some independent pressure groups seemed to come into being almost by accident. In our contemporary terms, Theodore Roosevelt was often more a one-man NGO than a president. He launched what we can now recognize as the environmental cause on November 11, 1907, when he wrote to governors and other U.S. leaders, convening them to a national meeting: "Facts, which I cannot gainsay, force me to believe that the conservation of our natural resources is the most weighty question now before the people of the United States."[1] That meeting encouraged a citizen-based movement to protect the environment.

The young Gandhi and the ancient Tolstoy began a detailed correspondence in which they laid down how groups working outside government might change the world. "Tolstoy and Gandhi made it their work to rediscover a negative vocabulary, to re-introduce *no* and *not* into our moral syntax."[2] They were, in today's terms, laying out the citizens' capacity to say no when faced with theoretically inevitable forces. Gandhi built his life around this idea. The NGO movement would come into being as an expression of this ability to say no.

But it was not until Globalism, seven decades later, that these non-profit and non-governmental organizations exploded. The explosion seemed to come in reaction to Globalization. More fundamentally, it may have been coming anyway. Often one fading era gives birth to several new competing forces that will create a new era. Together they represent human complexity. They must either fight each other or find a new balance. At first there were a few hundred NGOs. Now there are more than 50,000 at the international level alone. In France, between

1987 and 1994, 54,000 new associations were created. In Chile there are 27,000; in the Philippines 21,000; in the United States 1.2 million.

The OECD had registered 1600 NGOs by 1980. They were spending US$2.8 billion. By 1995 there were 3000 spending almost $6 billion. Governments have taken to spending more and more of their aid through NGOs. In many cases it is now half.

What happened? The easy answer is that the constant chorus of international economic inevitability drove people who wanted to make choices and changes away from politics and government. They discovered the non-profit organization — a form of free-floating influence, perhaps even of authority, without the inconveniences of assuming power. In other words, the NGO had the strength to free people from the forces of inevitability, but the weakness was that it cut citizens off from responsible democracy.

Some of these bodies are remarkable, some fraudulent. Some effective, some self-serving.

The model was perhaps Médecins sans frontières. A group of young doctors found themselves on the firing line in Biafra. It was 1971, the birth year of Globalization. The Nigerian civil war would go on to cost two million lives. The founder of Médecins sans frontières, Bernard Kouchner, often describes the frustration they all felt as doctors. They were supposed to be neutral, passive, to wait for the wounded to appear. That was the professional rule. And that was what international and national forces expected of them. They were to pick up the pieces of human folly, which had been dressed up as inevitable conflict. "As a good doctor, you are supposed to just wait for an opportunity to try to save your patients from death. So we decided to talk. And to talk was to say to the public that we couldn't take care of these thousands and hundreds of thousands of young patients. This situation was not our fault. The fault was political. But it was against our oath of silence to say so. And so we organized Doctors Without Borders. We discovered that we didn't have to remain neutral."[3]

Here was a perfect illustration of the Tolstoyian/Gandhian idea of action as refusal. Action as refusal soon proved to be a great force in a world where the received wisdom was to remain passive before the inevitable. In 1992 the Catholic activist NGO Sant'Egidio played the key role in negotiating peace in Mozambique. Wherever you turned, wherever there was a belief in choice, a refusal of economic inevitability, NGOs inserted themselves for better and for worse. This was a direct challenge to the dominant economic theory of leadership. More troubling, this was also a challenge to citizen-based democracy.

As democratic leaders had increasingly accepted the Giscard d'Estaing argument of the leader as castrato, so citizens had sought their inspiration elsewhere. Here was a clear sign of the citizen's desire for choice. But it was also a threat to the solid idea of elected government as the basis of responsible choice.

And then there was the matter of God and his unexpected return. The highly sophisticated, passive and fundamentally non-believing professional class that led, administered and advised in the twenty Western democracies slowly found itself surrounded by immeasurable forces of true believers.

Pentecostal, evangelical, reborn, neo-Catholics and a variety of other forces, tangentially through religion, refused the idea of economic inevitability. If there was to be an inevitability, it would be God's. Many of them seemed to come from an almost forgotten sort of right wing. Others came from a more identifiable Christian left.

Americans seemed to be the leaders in this movement, so much so that this force has been a determining factor in the last four presidential elections. The manner in which President Clinton used the Christian activists actually prepared the way for what followed. But it would be a mistake to miss the rise to power of old-fashioned Christian leaders in much of northern Europe. And the obvious rise of Muslim fundamentalism. And Jewish fundamentalism.

We don't quite know yet what the return of God will mean. We know it perplexes the classic liberal. We know the political lines remain very confused. For example, these days strong belief is often bizarrely allied with the most dubious of free market morality. And yet this does not resemble the reform Christian–free trade union of the nine-teenth century.

What we do know is that God is once again among us and available to be on our side, if we so declare it. He is an unlikely partner for the NGO. But the two have this in common: they refuse the idea of civilization viewed through the prism of economics.

18

A Chronology of Decline

1995

This was a cusp year. But it was more than that. Four specific events told us that a new trend had been set.

The tequila crisis — Mexico's collapse from international glory into a national catastrophe — was more than the economic failure I have already described. It was the signal that a quarter-century of Globalization-inspired economics had not produced a new Latin America. Already in 1982 Mexico had suspended interest payments on $85.5 billion of foreign debt, a phenomenon that would gradually spread. In 1994 there had been an old-fashioned and bloody uprising in Chiapas, in reaction to market-driven economic activity imposed from outside the province. More generally, Mexicans observed that this approach had given a new force to old-style corruption.

The Inter-American Development Bank reinforced the perception that the new economic experiment was not working. "The resumption of economic growth has been bought at a very high social price, which includes poverty, increased unemployment and income inequality, and this is leading to social problems."[1] Soon it was clear that the economic growth itself was spotty, then increasingly ephemeral.

In the middle of the year, James Wolfensohn was named president of the World Bank. He would be there a decade. He immediately began an endless battle with the Bank's bureaucracy and its culture and wrestled it away from the abstract, top-down economic-destiny idea of the world toward a more complex path relating to the realities of the non-Western world.

He quickly brought in a senior advisor, the Canadian Maurice Strong, father of the international environment movement, an out-of-the-box thinker intimately tied to the developing world. A series of other important appointments followed, all aimed at changing the direction of the Bank.

A difficult battle ensued, not only against the Bank's preconceptions but more broadly against various Globalist bureaucracies of what could be called the OECD system. By the time of Wolfensohn's departure in 2005, Washington was chomping at the bit to get one of its own back in charge but not to re-establish the old technocratic/economist view of Globalism. Its new desire was to tailor the World Bank more closely to its more nationalist view of the world.

Late in 1995, Ken Saro-Wiwa, the leading Nigerian writer and activist, was hanged, along with eight of his supporters. The underlying reason was his opposition to the activities of Shell — the energy transnational — in his country. There were seven thousand political prisoners in Nigeria. Shell itself admitted to supplying arms for the national police.[2] The nine executions began the end of the military dictatorship. But they also confirmed, in many people's minds, that transnationals were not a bright, new progressive phenomenon but were simply built on the old oligopolistic-imperial model.

And in a strange foreshadowing of future events, Timothy McVeigh blew up a federal building in Oklahoma City, killing 168 and wounding more than 800. Some might say there were no signs of the future there. This was just an American blowing up Americans. After all, there have been hundreds of internal terrorist incidents in the United States every year for many years. But what McVeigh did was splice the U.S. into the modern terrorist trend, which had been so strong in Europe in the 1970s and '80s. We still know little about this form of warfare. What we do know is that it has grown over the last 150 years as an indirect way to strike at apparently unbeatable forces. And it is dependent on the blending of a particular state of mind with a particular intuition of what might possibly be done.

1996

Suddenly it became clear for those who wished to notice that nationalism was making a strong comeback all around the world. This sort of nationalism didn't have global economic inevitability at the centre of its logic. The Chechnya uprising had become a full war. Fifty thousand died in eighteen months. It was as much about Russian nationalism as Chechnyan.

The international trend was toward more religiously based nationalism as political parties identifying themselves that way became dominant in Israel, India and Turkey and began to grow almost everywhere. Aljazeera, the Qatar-based television network, began broadcasting. The extreme fundamentalist Taliban took power in Afghanistan.

But there was also a revival of democratic nationalism, seemingly as a reaction to the sweep of global forces. And so Scotland voted to create its own Parliament after being integrated for 290 years into one of the world's most centralized states.

At the same time, irregular warfare became the dominant military strategy around the world. An outbreak of IRA bombings could be seen as joining the old-style with the new. Sri Lanka and the Sudan were the stars of this combination of bombings, incidents and unpredictable running conflicts. A bomb at the Summer Olympics in Atlanta. Five hundred hostages in Lima, Peru, an incident that would last 126 days. The beginning of terrorism in Saudi Arabia with nineteen American soldiers killed. This whole irregular approach toward destabilizing mainstream armies — with their high technology, armour, large size and clumsy, top-heavy staff structures — still confuses those who believe that highly organized and intensely managed power brings order.

Alan Greenspan, the Federal Reserve Board chairman, who always found a way to adjust his theories to the tendencies of the market, nevertheless sent up a warning about the "irrational exuberance" that had "unduly escalated asset values." In other words, the market disconnect between money markets and real activity was out of control.

At the same time there were the first signs of a new, balanced internationalism, centred on humanist principles. In Ottawa, 122 countries signed a treaty banning land mines.

1997

How out of control things were would become clear in 1997. The year began on a positive note of radical change — change by choice. James Wolfensohn named Joseph Stiglitz to be the World Bank's chief economist. Here was a clear sign that the international institutions at the core of the original Globalist argument could move to new ground.

Stiglitz's negative views of the Washington Consensus and all-purpose market-centred solutions were well known. In this pivotal position he became the key to changing the official view of how developed, developing and international structures could work together. Instead of taking for granted that all-purpose solutions would deal with society's needs, people began looking at particular needs. To varying degrees, other serious thinkers shared his views. Paul Krugman, Jagdish Bhagwati and John Williamson all had severe doubts about confusing trade with money markets. They worried about disorderly, inflated currency trading.

It was already too late. In the middle of the year, East Asia began an economic meltdown. By July Thailand felt obliged to devalue. The IMF pushed the Thais, the Malaysians and the Indonesians down the standard road of redemption through economic and social self-flagellation. They did as they were told. Indonesia closed down 220 banks, accepted an imposed package of reforms and received a loan of $23 billion from the IMF. The meltdown accelerated.

The IMF and the Western establishment turned to blaming the Asian countries for their situation. The problem, they said, was local corruption, *crony capitalism,* not *liberalizing* fast enough. In reality, the family-based systems of Asia were far closer to pure capitalism than the West's own more anonymous corporate systems of speculation. Besides, the Asian economies had long been more stable than those of most other regions. They had prospered by financing development through "their high savings rate."[3] They had no need of what we often call *foreign investment.* Their strength had come from not following the international consensus and from "the important roles that the government had played." Was there corruption? Yes. But if we ask that question, we must ask another: is there corruption in Western market systems? Yes. Which is worse? It depends on your definition of corruption.

These countries had been destabilized because they had ceded to the pressure to open themselves up to global economics. Done another way, at another speed, more carefully, with local realities in mind and better international controls on currency movements, it might have worked. Instead, the global ideal of borderless markets was allowed to dominate. Great waves of loosely defined international money swept in — five times more than ever before — distorted the economies to its own purposes and, when the collapse began, swept back out, thus further accelerating the disorder. Paul Krugman described the catastrophe as "gratuitous."[4] "[T]hat something like this could happen at all in the modern world should send chills up the spine of anyone with a sense of history."

As the autumn rolled in, the Malaysians began to tire of internationally imposed failure. Their prime minister, Mahathir Mohamad, struck out verbally in all directions, sometimes in a racist manner. But in strict economic terms he hit a real chord: hedge funds were out of control; currency trading beyond the level needed to finance trade was "unnecessary, unproductive and immoral." At that point hedge funds could invent up to US$1 trillion "to bet against currencies."[5] Why do I say *invent*? Because their capitalization was subject to no national or international asset-ratio system. Hedge fund managers acted in a way that came straight out of the nineteenth-century golden era of irresponsible speculation.

By late in the year, Malaysia was showing signs of slipping away from the global system. Its government began by slowly raising tariffs. Horror of horrors! There was more to come.

At the same time, the Multilateral Agreement on Investment negotiations, begun in 1995 with negotiators "oozing with optimism," were bogging down. A multitude of NGOs dogged the negotiators and their arguments. OECD ministers of finance were themselves increasingly skeptical about the MAI. Some saw this proposed treaty as another step toward their own castration as effective ministers. Others saw the aim, as the *Toronto Star* columnist Richard Gwyn put it, to create "a charter of rights for absentee landlords."[6] In this case the absentee landlords were the foreign investors and the transnationals.

19

A Chronology of Decline: The Malaysian Breakout

1998

And then the centrifugal forces accelerated and large pieces of global certainty began flying off. The year began as if nothing had changed. Paris saw "the first-ever international gathering of industrial ministers and the first OECD meeting to invite executives to participate" in order to suggest international policy. The result at this gathering was "strong support for private-sector, market-driven solutions to problems." David Aaron, U.S. undersecretary of commerce: "[T]hat's a big change ... likely to lead to a lighter hand [of regulation]."[1] At the same time, in Helsinki, Joseph Stiglitz was speaking out as the World Bank's chief economist. His message called for quite a different tack, as he warned us not to misinterpret the Asian crisis. Governments had made mistakes, but in South Korea, for example, they had produced "not only large increases in per capita GDP but also increases in life-expectancy, the extension of education, and a dramatic reduction in poverty." The key to the crisis had not been too much government, but too little. "[T]he government underestimated the importance of financial regulation and corporate governance."[2] In spite of Stiglitz's corrective speeches, it seemed that the international institutions were continuing on without any dramatic change.

But then the MAI negotiations began to fall apart. The first serious hint came in January, when some governments insisted that the treaty include binding rules on labour standards and the environment. The economic prism was no longer acceptable. The combination of NGO protests and ministerial doubts began to build.

On April 27, the OECD announced a suspension of the negotiations. This was a technocratic nicety. The treaty was dead. Why?

Because politicians were no longer willing to accept systems built around binding discipline for governments — that is, limitations of political and democratic power — while for the private sector there would be mere guidelines. The paragraph that killed the MAI — the key paragraph — guaranteed that foreign investors would receive "treatment no less favourable than the treatment [a country] accords its own investors and their investments with respect to the establishment, acquisition, use, enjoyment and sale or other disposition of investments." In other words, money would be perfectly global. Nation-states would not be able to get in the way. Ten years before, this sort of argument might have sailed through.

Now, abruptly, elected leaders seemed to wake up to their own reality. They realized that they wanted to keep their power to choose policy directions. After all, it was the product of democratic legitimacy. They didn't see why investment should trump considerations of the public good.

This change in direction was nevertheless filled with contradictions. There had been a great defeat for a global ideology on a matter of enormous public importance. Dominique Strauss-Kahn, the highly intelligent French minister of finance: "No one will negotiate after the MAI the way they did before…. Citizens will no longer accept that they be governed as they were in the past."[3]

And yet this defeat was greeted by the engaged technocracy and the true believers with sullen silence. It was as if they hoped to continue their logic, unchanged. How? Perhaps through discrete bilateral agreements.

After all, there would have been no public debate on MAI if the working documents hadn't been leaked. The public debate was led through the internet by NGOs. Even so, by the end of the battle only a tiny percentage of international business leadership knew anything about it. To take just one revealing example on the political front, at the time of its death the proposed treaty had still not been made available to members of the German Bundestag that they might read it and informally think about it. The idea had been to get the negotiations to the point of no return before any public debate took place.

The end of the MAI should have provoked a broad public debate involving the academic community, in particular economists, and the political leadership. Instead, where there was not only sullen silence among the elites, there was confused embarrassment.

A few months later in Africa, the unresolved divisions in the region surrounding Rwanda — those that had already killed some 800,000 people — slipped across the old colonial borders into the Congo. The result was five years of violence and over 4 million deaths, directly or indirectly caused by the war. Some of that violence still simmers on.

Surely, we assume, we had all learned from the 800,000 deaths in Rwanda. Surely we had learned that our global theories were irrelevant in large parts of the world, where political and military initiatives based on national initiatives alone could deal with crises. In reality the various international institutions and those of the West in particular did even less to stop the catastrophe in the Congo than they had in Rwanda. They — we — successfully pretended that nothing was happening until most of it was over, some four years later.

What possible relevance could this have to global economic theory? We had put so much of our international energies into market-led reforms that our political and military mechanisms had — have — not evolved, grown, been reformed to deal with reality.

And even on that economic front the global mechanisms were failing. The leaders of Malaysia had finally lost all willingness to continue down the road of Globalist masochism. For months, Jagdish Bhagwati had been calling for capital controls as the best way to stop the decline. Paul Krugman did the same. In September the Malaysian prime minister, Mahathir Mohamad, went about breaking most of the rules of Globalization and market leadership.

He pulled the Malaysian currency, the ringgit, off the world market, made it unconvertible and pegged it low enough to favour exports. He stabilized the country's economy by blocking the export of foreign capital and raised tariffs.

A tidal wave of contemptuous condemnations followed from the public and private institutions of international finance and trade. Columnists, editorialists, economists of all sorts, governments, bankers, almost all wrote off Malaysia as a basket case and Mahathir as mentally unstable. The most important Asian economic index, run by Morgan Stanley, expelled Malaysia. How could you measure an economy that refused to follow the rules of inevitability? They all averted their eyes and waited for the inevitable collapse.

It didn't come. Those who watched saw the Malaysians play the full hand of Keynesian flexibility — the way Keynes had intended it to be played, with complexity and finesse, adjusting regulations, strengthening and weakening controls. With Stiglitz's support they converted their capital controls into an exit tax.

All the while, Mahathir mocked the West's need for simple economic truths. "You must be more tolerant of the stupidity of Malaysia. Why not leave us to do the wrong things we want to do."[4]

The crisis eased. Investments grew. Production and exports strengthened. Sensible bankers began to ask why Globalists were so against local or regional controls at appropriate moments. Krugman pointed out that the rising star of international trade was Asian but had remained untouched by the crisis. Why? Because China had an old-fashioned unconvertible, pegged currency. You couldn't speculate on it. And you couldn't move currency in and out at will. And China continued to grow on this preposterously old-fashioned model. The lesson to be learned was simple. The West, ideologically obsessed, saw the Asian crisis as one of economics and therefore subject to established market rules. The Malaysians saw it as a national political crisis with economic implications. They therefore acted politically and nationally. In the process they demonstrated that the economic determinism was little more than wishful thinking. And that nation-states were capable of making their own choices and succeeding through unconventional action.

Not everyone understood this. U.S. Vice-President Al Gore went to Kuala Lumpur in November and made a fool of himself by insisting that the crisis was all about "cronyism, corruption, and social unrest — adding to the problem of attracting world investment." The officials who no doubt wrote the speech were so obsessed by theory that they couldn't see what was happening in the real world.

There were, however, signs of changing institutional attitudes. The first came in Australia, where I.J. Macfarlane, the conservative governor of the Reserve Bank, began speaking out against the global financial system. Until 1995 he had been a true believer. By October 1998 things had changed: "[M]ore and more people are asking whether the international financial system as it has operated for most of the 1990s is basically unstable. By now, I think the majority of observers have come to the conclusion that it is …" "[T]he intellectual underpinning of the free market position … — the Efficient Markets Hypothesis — is very weak. In all the exchange rate tests of which I am aware, the hypothesis has been contradicted by facts." "We need to devise a system for maximising the benefits to be gained from international capital while limiting the risks." "It is simplistic to insist on the totally free movement of capital in all countries and in all circumstances."[5]

These sorts of ideas were fair representations of what most reserve bank governors, deputy ministers of finance and even finance ministers were thinking. Few of them had Macfarlane's courage to speak out publicly. Perhaps the most active and organized questioning was taking place inside the G20, which brought together the ministers of finance of the twenty largest economies, thus linking West to East, North to South. They were no longer true believers. But, as if in the early eighteenth century, their disavowal of the received wisdom of the one great church took place in private, off the record. At the end of the G7 meeting on October 31, an effort was made to show leadership. The Western leaders promised to put in place "international principles and codes of best practice in fiscal policy, financial and monetary policy, corporate governance and accounting" to "ensure that private sector institutions comply with new standards of disclosure."

Some progress had been made. But these reforms still haven't happened. What had changed was that politicians and officials now knew that their failure to act was a failure. It was no longer the result of enthusiasm for market leadership. And in case they wanted to forget this, political leaders were reminded every time they gathered to discuss the Globalist projects, because they had to meet behind complex systems of barricades and police to separate themselves from thousands of activist citizens eager to express their opinions.

1999

By now the dominant public vocabulary when it came to Globalization was negative and defensive. Lee Kuan Yew of Singapore was warning that Globalization could "unravel age-old values that have held our country together."[6] Leaders of the IMF were astonished to find themselves — and their ideology — in the limelight as responsible for the international crisis. First Deputy Managing Director Stanley Fischer: "I feel outraged and offended to be told things that are patently untrue. It is errant nonsense to say that IMF programs didn't take the social factors into account." But of course they hadn't. The president of the Bundesbank began calling for a G7 committee at the very least to jointly watch the global economy. This committee was quite quickly formed and just as quickly became an informal policy formulation unit. Kofi Annan called for corporations to meet standards on human rights, labour and the environment. That the impact of these corporations on different societies would be positive was no longer taken for granted. Paul Krugman began to argue more aggressively that tariffs in certain circumstances were the correct solution: "Right now a tariff would increase employment in Argentina and to pretend otherwise is intellectually dishonest."[7]

Then, in November, Joseph Stiglitz resigned from the World Bank to be free to speak out against its sister organization, the IMF. The World Bank was changing, but he had joined as a non-ideological force and after only two years felt that the changes were not coming fast enough to meet the spreading failures.

The year ended with riots in the streets of Seattle over a WTO meeting. The technocrats and true believers were stunned that they could be publicly humiliated by non-professionals. Their sullen silence after the cancellation of MAI, the blame coming their way over the Asian crisis, along with contempt from Malaysia, and now the broad public belief that trade was fine, but civilization was not a servant of trade, all brought out the anger you would expect from international economic managers who had always taken for granted that their motives were morally driven.

Few people now believed their assertions that NGOs were disconnected from reality. Jim Wolfensohn went out of his way to worry publicly about those left behind by Globalization. Those in the streets of Seattle, he said, were not just a "group of radicals." In fact, they spoke for some "very legitimate" views.[8]

2000

In a last act before formally leaving the World Bank, Stiglitz stood up before the American Economic Association to attack some of the assumptions of Globalization: "Capital market liberalization has not only not brought people the prosperity they were promised, but it has also brought these crises, with wages falling 20 or 30 percent and unemployment going up by a factor of two, three, four or 10."[9] Most astonishing before such a crowd, he was given a standing ovation. At about the same time, Malaysia was readmitted to the Morgan Stanley economic index. Apparently currency controls, a pegged currency and tariffs were now acceptable in some circumstances.

Kofi Annan, in front of corporate leaders, publicly supported Wolfensohn's view on the NGOs. "The demonstration in the street [in Seattle] reflected the anxieties felt by many people faced by Globalization. You must respond to these anxieties." He put part of the blame on the egotism of the developed world.

As the year advanced, the social and economic problems in Latin America multiplied. For a decade the continent had in various ways done what the Globalists and their international institutions had ordered them to do. They had passed through the stages of crucifixion economics and many had come out the other side, apparently stronger. But their recoveries had been short-lived. Now it seemed that the purge had made them profoundly weaker, not stronger. Their evolution resembled that of people bled by pre-modern doctors.

Wolfensohn was becoming clearer by the month. South America was "no better off than ... in the 70's."[10] He said the gap between rich and poor in Latin America was the worst in the world. Forty million more people lived below the poverty line than in 1980. The global market reforms had, even in the period of apparent recovery, halved growth.

That the believing technocracy was reacting badly to this criticism could be seen in June when the World Bank's leading expert on poverty, Ravi Kanbur, was driven by outside political pressure to resign because he was suggesting that economic growth alone would not be sufficient to reduce poverty; that redistribution taxes and policies would be necessary.

2001

The events of September 11 would mark a radical reassertion of both nation-state power and the pre-eminence of politics and violence over economics. The economic prism would become a sideshow.

There were, however, a few non-9/11 details in 2001 that suggested the direction the world was taking. In May the Stockholm Convention against persistent organic pollutants added to the slowly growing set of international agreements centred on the public good, not mere economics. In July the G8 meeting was held in Genoa. The leaders were kept out on a large ship, isolated, to avoid clashes with the demonstrators. One of the demonstrators was shot dead by the police. In November there was international agreement to back off the strictness of intellectual property rules if there was a developing world crisis in question. This was a tiny, unclear retreat, but still, there was movement.

Then Joseph Stiglitz was given the Nobel Prize, agreed for a separate set of work, but nevertheless at the very height of his status as an intellectual dissident. This award had more or less belonged to the standard Globalist school, whether to disciples of Hayek or of Friedman or to highly technical market analysts — jumped-up microeconomists. They had had such a lock on the prize that for decades the academy had ostentatiously avoided giving it to the most obvious candidate, John Kenneth Galbraith, because he belonged to the Keynesian tendency.

But as the world has begun to swing away from Globalism, so the Academy has slowly changed its opinions. It had given the prize to Amartya Sen in 1998 and now to Stiglitz in 2001.

In December, in a moment of macabre comedy, Argentina collapsed yet again, crippled by the combination of debt, corruption and IMF solutions. Twenty-seven people died in the ensuing riots. The era of classic Globalism could be said to have ended with a bang in Latin America. A few days later, as if to provide a further comic footnote to the era, Enron filed for bankruptcy and the year came to a close. It was the biggest financial failure of this sort in U.S. history. It marked yet another one of those eternal definitive ends of applied economics as alchemy.

20

The End of Belief

"You ram something down your throat and you're bound to throw up."
— MARSHALL McLUHAN

Ideologies resemble not very good theatre of the romantic sort. That is why Coleridge's formula — *the willing suspension of disbelief* — applies so neatly to the natural life of any ideology.[1] In defence of the poet, he had in mind a far nobler use of the human ability to choose to suspend our disbelief — a nobler idea of theatre and of the romantic ideal. But you could argue that the more flimsy the theatrical device — a romance novel, a Schwarzenegger adventure — the greater the demonstration of our ability to suspend our critical faculties.

How we arrive at the decision to suspend our disbelief when it comes to ideologies is mysterious. Historians and social scientists spend their lives trying to explain the phenomenon. Creative writers usually do a better job at explaining this sort of politics, because in a curious way they are in the same business as the ideologues. Both are dealing with the human heart.

Less mysterious is how we decide to drop our suspension. The inevitable — and here the word is accurate — failures of any ideology gradually build up. A growing number of people notice. The propaganda of triumph evolves into one of denial. Language that was once enthusiastically received by the public is increasingly treated as the equivalent of elevator music, then as an actively annoying noise, and finally as inadvertent comedy. When the voice of power is heard by the public with irony, skepticism and, at last, as if from a farce, our willingness to suspend our disbelief has seeped fully away. The ideology may go on for a time because its advocates hold so many of the mechanisms of power. But this is simply power.

While the true believers continue to insist — sometimes enthusiastically, but more often angrily these days — on global inevitabilities, you will hear, if you listen carefully, a rising babble of contradictory sounds. A growing number of nation-state leaders, along with the more interesting businessmen, have changed their vocabulary, gradually weeding out the global assumptions. The new discourse is more complex, sibylline, less grandiose. Much of it is built around the idea of citizens and society. On the other hand, some of it suggests an accelerating political meltdown matched by rising levels of disorder. There is a growing incidence of old-style nationalist violence. Our memory has changed again. There is no longer an assumption that the years 1945 to 1973 were such an era of failure. It is accepted as normal that there were both disappointments and systemic flaws during those three decades, but it is again respectable to admit that the era preceding Globalization was one of the most successful in history for both social reform and economic growth. Why, apart from an ideological sweep, should we ever have dismissed it as a failure when we could have weeded out its weaknesses and built on its accomplishments?

The idea of failure was central to the dramatic arrival of the Globalist ideology as a rescue mission. A new willing suspension of disbelief seems to require the drama of society trapped in a burning car or caught in an undertow. The new truth rushes to the rescue.

The worst thing we could do today is attempt to sweep Globalization away as we attempted to sweep away the more humanist era that preceded it. We would be equally unwise to deny Globalization's failure and the self-destructive crisis into which it has slipped. The true believers will probably bleat on about the dangers of any criticism and how such critiques could provoke a return to the horrors of protectionism and nationalism. But if we cannot calmly cherry-pick the current system's strengths and admit its failures, we may well provoke that protectionism and the worst of nationalism.

Theseus, the king, speaking to Oedipus at Colonus, near the end of his torment:

> I've heard threats before. Noisemakers and bullies
> Are always very free with them. Very rarely
> Do they come to anything, when people calm down
> And assess the situation rationally.[2]

Have the failures of Globalization really been so numerous as to reduce its believers to threats and cause more sensible people to draw back warily?

airlines. the economic comedy of one size fits all.

Deregulation began in 1978. Since then, the airline business has been in constant crisis. You can't blame the passengers. They have continued flocking into the air. World passenger numbers have grown every year since 1945 except two: the year of the first Iraq war and the year following September 11. Global passenger kilometres multiplied forty-four times between 1950 and 1998.

Yet in 2004 European airlines were still collapsing one after the other. Alitalia was alive thanks only to government intervention — a government devoted to free markets and Globalization.

The story is the same around the world. Bankruptcy laws suspend the force of contract. Airline companies have been using them to stay alive while they were breaking employment contracts and pension plans. Some companies have already gone under several times, reorganized themselves on a global footing, re-emerged fit and lean, only to sink back into debt and despair. Other firms have been repeatedly revived by government subsidies, particularly in Europe and the United States. In spite of all this manoeuvring and help, the number of companies has shrunk by half. And most survivors are just hanging on. The president of Air France–KLM in 2004: "Air transportation is in the state of a total wreck."[3]

There have been lots of sophisticated explanations. Oil prices. But these have been low for most of the two troubled decades. Overexpansion. But freed markets were supposed to support growth. Besides, there was and there is today continuous passenger growth. Besides, competition was supposed to create a sensible balance, not permanent crisis. September 11 had led to a one-year drop of 5.7 percent in passengers. For any industry that had benefited from sixty years of strong annual consumer growth (in this case, passenger growth), a one-year blip should not have been a disaster. Not unless the business had already been put on a disastrous track for reasons of ideological blind faith.

As if living in a delusional dreamland, the expert who designed the American deregulation policy, Alfred Kahn, repeatedly insists that "most disinterested observers agree that airline deregulation has been a success." If the industry is losing billions, that's its own fault: "the industry's wounds have been largely self-inflicted."[4] So he believes in deregulation in order to free up the marketplace, but he doesn't believe in the market.

Actually, an increasing number of disinterested observers have been saying something quite different:

> [Open skies] will accelerate the process of industrial concentration.
> Average airline yields will continue to decline in real terms.
> [Global alliances are a] way of reducing or limiting competition.
> [There are] powerful pressures towards oligopolistic concentration in a deregulated airline regime.
> By the mid-1980s it had become clear that without government inter-vention the industry would eventually evolve to exhibit a high degree of market concentration.
> The eventual outcome in Europe…. An oligopoly.
> [T]he choices that consumers will be presented with will be extremely limited.

This oligopoly system reduces passenger choice in several ways. One is to prevent customers from using their tickets on their airline of choice, as they used to under regulation. What a curious observation: regulation forced choice while the deregulated system denies that the customer is right.

What about the growth in cut-rate air travel? First, this is concentrated on non-essential travel. And pleasant though these $121 beach holidays or $49 transcontinental bargains are to some of us, they are not self-financing. Most bargain-basement companies are parasites, living off the money-losing infrastructures of normally scheduled and priced travel, not to mention the very expensive safety structures, both engineering and security, that the industry requires.

And even with the success of the bargain-basement business, the reality is painful. Since deregulation, no matter how great the passenger growth, no matter how many personnel are let go, how much wages are cut, how much services to most passengers are cut, the yields per passenger just keep on dropping and the oligopoly pressures get worse.

Every indication is that a stable deregulated industry requires an oligopoly. A combine. By the early 1990s observers couldn't help noticing that the only method in the history of the business that had brought stability and competition was — God forbid — regulation.

The reasons seem to be relatively simple. All objects sold in the marketplace are not the same. All markets are not the same. An industry dependent on billion-dollar investments in large flying objects that pay out via tickets sold for a few hundred, perhaps a few thousand, dollars is fundamentally different from industries that buy and sell houses or shirts or books or computers. The airline ratios are, at best, improbable. Add deregulated instability in markets, ticket prices and routes and you have a recipe for disaster.

Add to that the reality of business cycles. Every industry has them. Those of the airline industry are naturally dysfunctional. They involve the particularly long and therefore difficult lead times necessary for designing, choosing, ordering and building new planes. You have to order them when things are going well. By the time they arrive, you are usually in a slump. The system works only if you have institutionalized stability.

All of this is a sharp reminder that the purpose of the industry is not to provide cheaper tickets to those of us who can be flexible about our holiday plans. The airline business provides an essential service — one of the essential services of communication on which our civilizations depend. Instead, failure has been snatched out of the jaws of success by restructuring the whole thing through open-market forces into an oligopoly system dependent on the bargain-basement methods of shrinking margins, short-term planning and long-term instability.

the decline in competition. the return of oligopolies.

Has Globalization in general been concerned with competition?

Competition usually involves the continuous tension of price, quality and continuity. That continuity is just one aspect of the variety of related services we expect from competition. Competition also involves short-, medium- and long-term utility; utility as a servant of society and industry; the effectiveness of industry working in balance with its efficiency. All of this should have a long-term positive effect on society. And that in turn should lead to continuous growth in well-being, education and research. And all of that should increase the economy's capacity to raise the sophistication of the tension that indicates competition.

Instead, the most common themes for a quarter-century have been cost-reduction, most often by stripping out the structures of employee stability. Both of these are about profit retention; selling at the cheapest possible price in unstable markets with the aim of destroying smaller competitors; selling at the highest possible price in other areas, where there are already the elements of oligopolistic combines in place. These approaches have almost nothing to do with quality, continuity, services, utility or societal growth as a support for further competition.

The overarching theme has been the need to increase corporate size. The most common reason given is that markets are bigger. But a large market does not require larger corporations. If what you are after is efficient competition, then highly focused medium-sized corporations, capable of moving fast in the market, would be ideal.

The last quarter-century has resembled, if anything, the mid-nineteenth century, with its drive toward monopoly and oligopoly. And in some strange way it has related to the old mercantilist approach and the idea of royally granted monopolies. None of this is about embracing competition. It is about limiting and, if possible, removing competition. None of it takes into consideration the essence of any long-term industrial structure: that it is dependent on a healthy, stable civilization.

A modern term like *convergence* is just a new word for the old-fashioned idea of vertical integration: a large organization gets control of an industry from top to bottom and so eliminates competition by defining all aspects of the market.

There has been convergence. There is continuous, remarkable growth in size. There is ongoing severe rationalization. The result has been heavily indebted giants with no particular purpose. Is it a victory for competition that 50 percent of the New Zealand dairy industry is now controlled by a single company? Or that when the Canadian beef industry fell into a mad-cow disease crisis early in the twenty-first century, the only group to benefit was a tiny handful of large middlemen? Or that the effect of a global removal of quotas on cloth and garments in 2005 is expected to be a rapid shrinking of competition in the industry? Today there are strong cloth/clothing exports coming from fifty-odd countries and the industry employs 50 million people. It is expected that this will quickly shrink to five or six countries, mainly China, India and Pakistan; that China will have 50 percent of world exports within three years. This has already happened in places like Australia, which opened its market earlier. China's advantage is size and vertical integration.

Of course, the old free trade arguments did say that everyone should specialize on the basis of comparative advantage. Our reality is quite different. What should the 3 million garment workers in Bangladesh specialize in? This is not clear. Anyway, their problem is not comparative advantage. For a start, their produce is generally cheaper than that of China. But they do not have the size and the vertical integration, two elements that reduce competition.

In other words, advantage today is size and power. This is not competition. You can see the same happening in industry after industry. Retail banking tends now to include merchant banking, insurance, other businesses. Vast newspaper chains are linked to television networks and publishing. Big-box retail chains aggressively eliminate the real competition of smaller retailers through predatory dumping. Their very size permits them to link this approach to internal or external domination of retail production. As you glance around, you find mining conglomer-ates. Pulp-and-paper conglomerates. Agro-food conglomerates.

These new oligopolies take two forms. One is attached to the combine activity of transnationals that appear to be international but usually represent a geographical base. The other involves regional monopolies or oligopolies, such as the United States for pharmaceuticals or China and India for garments and clothing.

None of this has to do with free market competition. The more accu-rate historic models are, first, the seventeenth- to eighteenth-century European trading companies, which divided up the world; and second, the nineteenth-century vertically integrated private corporations that worked in tandem with the imperial empires. The intent in both of these cases was to split markets among reasonably compliant opponents. In other words, an oligopoly combine system.

Nation-state governments and their citizenry are confused by today's unexpected outcome. They recognize the phenomenon. After all, it has been recognizable since Elizabeth I gave her Golden Speech to Parliament in 1601, following complaints from the middle class that her Royal Grants and monopolies were exploiting the people:

> Of My selfe I must say this, I never was any greedy scraping grasper….
> But that my Grants shall be made Grievance to my People, and Oppressions, to be privileged under our Patents; this our Princely Dignity shall not suffer.[5]

Some governments see these modern grants and patents as national tools and so defend the international power of these industries. However, a growing number are reacting to combines as they did a half-century ago.

In 2004 the EU condemned a price cartel created by the five biggest European copper tubing manufacturers. The fine was 222 million euros. A few governments continue to support the power of the pharmaceutical giants. But most now see them as "greedy scraping grasper[s]" who will use their *Grants* to do more grievance than good. The United States, and then more seriously the European Union, have begun to take on Microsoft.

One motivator for change is that citizens are increasingly supporting populist or false populist political parties. These parties reject the assumption that economic power should trump individual power. Moderate parties are being pushed to inescapable choices. Do they support the continued rise of oligopolies and risk losing power? Do they give way to the mixed agenda of false populism? Or do they attempt to reassert the ideas of citizen power, citizen choice and a moderate, regulated marketplace that encourages competition?

Even if the current trend to combines were to continue, it would represent both a failure of the promise of Globalization and a step backwards into a world of shrinking competition.

intellectual property. the return of the absentee landlord.

If the creation of the WTO in 1995 was the last clear victory for Globalization, the specific point of farthest advance was probably the inclusion of intellectual property inside the trade regime. No sooner was TRIPS in place than the backlash began.

The most dependable of pro-Globalization economists were horrified. Why should coupon clipping be treated as trade? Jagdish Bhagwati: "[T]he corporate lobbies in pharmaceuticals and software had distorted and deformed an important multilateral institution, turning it away from its trade mission and rationale and transforming it into a royalty collection agency."[6] The developing world saw this as an attempt to limit their progress by installing a Western-oriented international pricing system for pharmaceuticals and other high-end products that they would not be able to afford. But there was a third, even more fundamental, problem. The structure of intellectual property, now consecrated at the international level, creates cliffs of knowledge that newcomers to research are legally discouraged from scaling. This is a sign of an effective oligopoly system.

Indeed, here was a system designed for the pleasure of private sector technocrats frightened of risk. Ownership of intellectual property would give them safe, regular income. It now represents up to 5 percent of GDP. In an economic system that facilitates both capital and property accumulation, the larger groups could simply purchase the smaller corporations that did the research and took the risks. Or, through their financial influence on governments, they could encourage publicly funded R and D programs that at the last moment would convert into the private ownership of ideas.

This is particularly true of the United States. As a result, European idea-based corporations began moving their activities to take advantage of what are, in effect, public subsidies leading to private intellectual property. I regularly hear German and French executives complaining about governmental regulations and interference at home as their excuse for decamping. The reality is that they are seeking the greater public funding of private ownership that exists in the United States.

In the mid-nineteenth century there was an international political crisis provoked by the ownership of land and commodities around the world by corporations and people living elsewhere. This absentee landlord problem was made famous by the Irish famine. But it was also central to the rise of false populism in Latin America. That false populism led to a spread of populist military dictatorships throughout the continent. Today this absentee landlord problem is often described as a positive force — foreign investment. Increasingly it relates to a constant extraction of royalty payments. The populist rejection of this system is already well under way. Today's potato farms are patentable ideas, and the post-modern absentee landlord lives off the resulting income.

The problem is not only international. Governments are everywhere giving in to the owners of copyright, particularly in the communications field. The period that copyright can remain in effect has been lengthened eleven times in the United States in the last forty years. It is now ninety-five years for corporations through most of the Western democracies. In other words, a movement that describes itself as driven by market competition and contempt for nation-state regulations has staked billions of dollars of income on its ability to influence or corrupt nation-state law.

Whether through TRIPS or local copyright law, what is at stake today is market control — the elimination of competition — through a rigid architecture of access. This architecture of access has used technology as a control mechanism, size as another means of control and law as the ultimate form of control.

But all three are dependent on public compliance. And signs of public refusal to comply are growing.

There will be a restructuring of the WTO in the next few years. When it happens, the central demand will be for the removal of TRIPS. This will be broadly embraced — except by the direct beneficiaries — because the growing rebellion against these rules is making them increasingly unenforceable.

pharmaceuticals. profit through fear.

The cutting edge of public anger, when it comes to intellectual property, is focused on the pharmaceutical industry. This anger cuts across all political lines in all sorts of societies. Populations in Africa, forced to face epidemics without the necessary medical tools, are on the same side as aging Americans, who can't afford the medications they need, along with politicians everywhere caught in a permanent budgetary crisis because they cannot afford to finance public drug programs. The broad context has two implications: Western populations are aging, and epidemics in the developing world are spreading. The large pharmaceutical corporations are part of the problem in both cases.

The question is quite simple: How long will a handful of the most profitable joint stock corporations in the world, whose declared purpose is human well-being, be allowed to cause tens of thousands of premature deaths each year in the name of patent protection and stockholder interests? There are growing signs that the answer is not much longer.

The problem seems to have begun around 1980, when changes in laws — particularly in the United States — converted a healthy business into a bonanza.[7] One of the key changes allowed the private sector to get patent control over research done in universities at public expense.

The signs that the public no longer believed began in Brazil and South Africa. Brazil had chosen to treat health as a human right. From the early 1990s on, it attacked the growing AIDS crisis as Western countries had once successfully attacked polio: as a matter of public well-being, not market profitability. It distributed HIV/AIDS drugs free of charge and broke the back of the disease's growth.

In 2001 the United States government dragged Brazil before the WTO to protect corporate patents. After six months of protests around the world, Washington withdrew the complaint.

In South Africa a small citizen-based movement set out to accomplish the same thing, gradually convincing its own government to take up the cause. This provoked thirty-nine pharmaceutical companies into suing the South African government. In 2001 the corporations climbed down and withdrew their case.

These victories are never as clear as they might be. The corporations have now taken to offering cheaper drugs in needy countries; this is an attempt to hold on to their patents, avoid the use of generic drugs or, worse still, drugs given free of cost by governments. But the need is not for cheaper drugs when it comes to HIV/AIDS, malaria and tuberculosis. In May 2003 the companies agreed to cut prices in South Africa by 25 to 80 percent. This approach was supported by the EU and the United States — homes of the major corporations. Going from an expenditure of $11,500 per person per year to $2,500 is meaningless in such circumstances; $100 would be unaffordable, except to the local elite. It is difficult to avoid asking whether these corporate cuts are not precisely an attempt to buy the silence of the society's leadership. The dean of Yale's school of medicine, David Kessler, said in the same year that the companies had to wake up to the public good. "At stake is the very patent protection system that allows them to control drug prices. They want to keep the power of pricing their products, but they must bend for a true international crisis."[8]

Instead of bending, they continue to play the corners, as if this were a cynical game. They offer some cuts here and there, all the while attempting to undermine public health systems. The CEO of the largest corporation, Pfizer, moans at specialist meetings: "[T]he fact is that Europe, Canada and Japan do not pay their share of the costs of research."[9] This is not a fact.

The fact is that "research and development is a relatively small part of the budgets of the big drug companies — dwarfed by their vast expenditures for marketing and administration." In her remarkable analysis, Marcia Angell, author of *The Truth about the Drug Companies,* goes further. "The prices drug companies charge have little relationship to the cost of making the drugs and could be cut dramatically without coming anywhere close to threatening R and D." Most new drugs have been "based on taxpayer-funded research." Foreign companies are moving their R and D operations to the United States "to feed on the unparalleled research output of American universities and the National Institutes of Health. [I]t's not private enterprise that draws them here but the very opposite — our publicly sponsored research enterprise."[10]

Their obsession with their corporate rights seems to prevent them from absorbing what real people identify as reality. Seventeen hundred children infected with HIV/AIDS every day. Two million children under fourteen with AIDS in sub-Saharan Africa. India, Russia and China with infection numbers on the edge of tipping into full-blown epidemics.

People cannot believe in the seriousness of organizations that put their right to maximize profits ahead of the human right to life. In September 2004, as if to prove that they had learned nothing, the corporations provoked the U.S. trade negotiators to once again threaten Brazil over intellectual property rights, this time threatening to punish Brazil in unrelated trade areas.

Why pick on Brazil when earlier attempts have failed and the international public sees this as an expression of irresponsible self-interest? Probably because Brazil is encouraging the developing world to embrace its approach toward medicine.

It used to be that individuals, scientists, universities were terrified to say no to the pharmaceutical giants, let alone to denounce their misuse of power. Since the mid-1990s a growing flow of public denunciations and court cases suggest that Brazil is the least of the drug companies' problems. In 2004 a Spanish court ruled in favour of a pharmacologist who had published an analysis of a drug accusing one of the giants of "a scientific fraud."[11] The *Canadian Medical Association Journal* revealed how another of the giants "sought to manipulate the results of published research," endangering the lives of children, rather than risk the yearly $5 billion sales of this particular drug. Much of the problem in these sorts of cases goes back to the corporations' contractual right to prevent scientists from discussing or disclosing the negative outcomes of their tests. Dr. Nancy Olivieri set the example on this front in the 1990s in Toronto when, at first almost alone, she stood up to a pharmaceutical giant and the hospital and university structures, asserting her ethical obligation to speak publicly whenever she — the researcher — felt the public good required it. A sizable part of the Canadian, and then international, research community came to her support. Increasingly scientists everywhere have begun slowly to place ethics ahead of corporate contractual rights.

All the same, the whole area of corporate power via the contract and patent system remains highly controversial. In a case involving the breadth of a drug patent defined and held by Amgen, the world's largest biotechnology company, the courts of different countries have ruled differently. An American court has come down on the company's side, while the House of Lords' Law Lords — the highest British court — has revoked the patent, saying its claims were too broad. This refusal of a patent monopoly will now reverberate through the European system. The withdrawal of a painkiller — Vioxx — from the American market provoked the revelation from senior scientists at the Food and Drug Administration that this was not an isolated case, that the public evaluation systems "are broken." The suggestion was that "the FDA has become too chummy with the industry it regulates." The point is that an industry that benefited greatly from our willing suspension of disbelief is now broadly distrusted. The Vioxx hearings involved industry's having to explain itself. According to *The Economist,* when the head of Merck was called to testify, he "looked terrified."[12] It was yet another of those tiny moments when the nation-state reminds itself of its power, and the virtual power of the transnational is revealed as furtive, fragile and above all undefendable once brought into the light of day.

the ethical slide of the market.

When the public in any Western democracy are asked in the proverbial opinion poll whom they trust, whom they respect, who contributes to the advancement of the public good, private sector leaders and elected leaders compete for the two bottom spots. It can't be an accident that they find themselves so closely and unhappily linked.[13]

In both cases this is a new phenomenon. And in both cases it is tied to a marginalization of ethics, marginalized by a rise of corruption not seen in such intensity since the glory days of the nineteenth-century robber barons. Early in the twentieth century, Theodore Roosevelt led a "campaign against privilege," which he saw as "fundamentally an ethical movement."[14] His definition of privilege was unregulated financial power with its panoply of speculation and lobbying. His target was "men of wealth, who find in the purchased politician the most efficient instrument of corruption."

In the early 1990s Spain's socialist government was overwhelmed by financial scandals. Modernization, opening up to the world, seemed to have gone hand in hand with private sector–political corruption. Italy's prime minister has been under siege by the court system for alleged corruption. The United States has increasingly built in indirect corruption through the election campaign funding system. In 2004 it emerged that German politicians quite commonly received salaries from large corporations. The BAST chemical group topped up the public salaries of 235 former employees now in elected office. Volkswagen has paid salaries to elected former employees since 1990. "The system has developed an extraordinary vulnerability to corruption, influence-peddling, cronyism and the violation of democratic principles."[15] The corruption in France is considered to be less formalized, more endemic. A hint of this came in 2004 when the former prime minister and mayor of Bordeaux, Alain Juppé, was condemned on specific issues and banned from public office for a fixed period of time.

Elected leaders and private sector leaders seem to have been tied together by the politicians' acceptance of the ideology that the world must be dealt with through the prism of the market. The politicians, in their willingness to accept the ideology of the inevitable, forgot the perpetual warning tied to the public good and succinctly put by Aristotle: "wealth is desirable, but not as the price of treason."[16]

There has been a subtle side to this corruption — subtle, yet understood by the citizenry. The normalization of influence peddling through the registration of lobbyists is the most obvious. The use of consultants has developed into a slightly more sophisticated way to broaden influence peddling. Under the appearance of seeking independent outside advice, public officials have created a *modernization* process for privatizing the public service psyche and distributing large amounts of public monies to friends and supporters.

Much less subtle has been the use of deregulation and the establishment of self-serving corporate regulations to normalize the most basic forms of corruption. An obvious example is the explosion in the use of share options by executives. But even elements as basic as executive salaries and benefits have been swollen in a manner unrelated to services given. The vast majority of people in the private sector do not benefit from these arrangements. But enough do — particularly the technocracy that manages the largest corporations — to destroy the confidence the public might wish to have in their leadership. This corporate ineptitude and feeding at the trough have been intense enough to make our brilliant leaders appear not so much craven calculators as somewhat ridiculous, rather like spoiled children.

The results are now well known, as are the various statistics. The assets of the 358 richest people in the world exceed the combined annual incomes of countries containing 45 percent of the world population. Under Globalization, the ratio of the share of global income controlled by the richest 20 percent versus the poorest 20 percent has doubled from 30 to 1 to 61 to 1.[17] Every statistic shows the income of the richest leaping up, the middle class scarcely moving, the poorest at best stagnating. Suddenly, after 1971, it was all right to serve yourself and not worry about the *other*.

It isn't surprising that such an atmosphere has spilled over into straight fraud. Some, like Enron's, have been massive. But the publicity surrounding Enron has drawn attention away from Parmalat in Italy. Ten billion euros were missing from the company's accounts — almost 1 percent of the country's GDP. Even among the most venerable of corporations, some were giving in to temptation. Shell had been habitually exaggerating its reserves for almost a decade to keep its share price up. The Dutch head of exploration finally wrote to the chair, "I am becoming sick and tired about lying about the extent of our reserves."[18]

But these criminal cases are perhaps less serious than the general atmosphere of self-service. The British car manufacturer Rover was in financial trouble and was taken over by something called Phoenix Consortium. Its four owners — theoretically saving the company — took the opportunity to scoop out £31 million for themselves. One of the most admired executives of the Globalization era, Jack Welch of General Electric, wasn't satisfied with the almost $1 billion he had personally accumulated as a mere manager — not a risk capitalist. He organized a retirement package for himself covering everything from meals and servants to sports tickets, as well as $10 million a year for the rest of his life.

Perhaps the darkly comic height to all of this came in 2004 with the accusations against Conrad Black and his management of the Hollinger newspaper business. *The New York Times* editorial on the matter was titled "Corporate Kleptocracy" and referred to a report accusing Mr. Black and his CEO of "helping themselves to some $400 million of Hollinger Funds from 1996 to 2003. That's roughly 95 percent of the company's net income for the period." The *Times* put this in the context of "other recent tales of corporate thievery."[19]

The backlash against this culture of corporate leadership began in the mid-1990s. It involved a gradual reassertion of public authority. In 1998 the annual G7 communiqué included a "commit[ment] to develop and implement international principles and codes of best practice on fiscal policy, financial and monetary policy, corporate governance and accounting; and to work to ensure that private sector institutions comply with new standards of disclosure."[20]

The leaders did not follow up on much of that, which is why they are rated by the public as partners of the offenders. But at least there was the sense that the old Globalization assertions of inevitability and automatic shared benefit were no longer credible. In the same year, the EU, the United States and Canada agreed to coordinate their efforts against illegal cartels and the "abusive dominant positions by multinational companies."[21]

In 2001 the European official responsible for competition policy went out of his way to accompany an £822 million fine against eight pharmaceutical companies with the strongest possible statement against their conspiracy on vitamin pricing: "the most damaging series of cartels the [European Commission] has ever investigated." This had been "a strategic plan conceived at the highest possible levels to control the world market in vitamins by illegal means."[22]

He was speaking up in the great tradition of public ethics as first formulated for our democratic age in an early modern mercantilist/trade crisis — the 1788 trial by the House of Lords of Warren Hastings for his actions in India. Hastings, seen in today's context, was a remarkably modern man — virtually like the CEO of a large transnational. Against great elite opposition, the philosopher and parliamentarian Edmund Burke had led the long fight to ensure that there would be a trial. The establishment argued that the East India Company was so central to English national and economic interests that patriotism demanded silence. Burke argued that public ethics trumped the *realpolitik* of both national interests and the marketplace. "My Lords, the business of this day is not the business of this man, it is not solely whether the prisoner at the bar be found innocent or guilty, but whether millions of mankind shall be made miserable or happy."[23] Hastings was accused of high-handed, corrupt and violent leadership. Seven years later, with Hastings's acquittal, *realpolitik* and the establishment seemed to have triumphed. But the long-term effect was to clarify the idea of public ethics and the need to constantly defend them.

The year 2004 was filled with a constant public harping on the failures of corporate leadership. It was noticed that from the second half of the 1990s on, two-thirds of American corporations paid no federal income tax. Yet corporate profits were soaring. Ninety percent of companies paid under 5 percent of their total income. In Equatorial Guinea, newly rich in oil, the national income is statistically sixth in the world. In reality the money goes elsewhere and the multinationals involved are complicit in its disappearance. William Donaldson, chair of the U.S. Securities and Exchange Commission, publicly accused the business leadership of "failing to provide 'ethical' leadership."[24] "The tone is set at the top. You must have an internal code of ethics that goes beyond the letter of the law to also encompass the spirit of the law."

Early in the twenty-first century, the Davos organization began to suffer from its overt use of the organization to advance global policies aimed at serving the specific interests of its effective owners. They began to back off their open manipulation of the organization and instead couched their statements in what *The Wall Street Journal* called "touchy-feely concepts." German authorities began insisting on the public disclosure of the remuneration of top managers. If they didn't comply voluntarily, legislation would be introduced to force them. Real owners, like Warren Buffett, began complaining that U.S. chief executives "don't care whether their boards are diverse or not diverse — they care about how much money they make." He claimed "there had been more misdirected compensation in corporate America in the past five years than in the previous century." I have said several times that our era has come to resemble the late nineteenth century. The literary references can't help being to Émile Zola's novel on market manipulation, *L'Argent*, or to Joseph Conrad's *The Arrow of Gold* — "They weren't poor, you know, therefore it wasn't incumbent on them to be honest."

The pessimist might point out that all of these complaints have had little effect. For example, a comparison between the two Iraq conflicts shows that complaints about governments' privatizing warfare during the first war had no effect on the second. From a 50 to 1 ratio of military versus contracted employees and mercenaries during the first war to a 10 to 1 ratio today, the trend simply continued. One company alone — Halliburton — has earned over $10 billion from the second war. By privatizing war, the democratic mechanisms of transparency are cut back. Public regulations are avoided. Contractors can be paid "at least double" what the military are paid,[25] while the public justification is that money is being saved.

In comparison with twenty or even ten years ago, the public no longer believe that this sort of activity is inevitable or acceptable. They see it as simple corruption and as a deformation of the public good.

transnational loss of direction.

There are those metaphysical moments in the life of empires when their sheer size and their overwhelming power become the reason for their loss of purpose, direction, flexibility. What follows is a gradual loss of public respect and — often long before their collapse — a loss of power. How? Well, the process is deceptively simple: millions of people who must believe, if such dominance is to function, emotionally disengage.

Today the opposite might appear to be the case. Of the thirty largest revenues in the world, a majority belong to corporations, not countries.[26] In 1990 there were 3000 transnationals. Today there are over 40,000. There were 63,000 subsidiaries. Today there are over 820,000. Altogether these structures produce a quarter of the world's GDP.

What the numbers miss, however, is that a corporation is only two-dimensional. Nation-states are three-dimensional. In fact, they are multi-dimensional. Revenue is an indicator of moderate consequence when it comes to judging their power and importance. The purpose of a corporation may be its revenue. The purpose of 58 million Italians or 82 million Germans is not their revenue, neither as individuals nor as a nation-state. Only childish obsession with economics could produce such a narrow comparison of power as if it meant something.

As for the growth in the number of transnationals, that confuses apples and oranges. A small number of them will be the gigantic, form-less technocratic bodies we associate with the word. The overwhelming majority will be smaller, agile, nation-state-based operations involved in a nineteenth-century approach to production and trading on world markets. These represent a triumph for national and regional development and international cooperation. Their success does not require a trumping of national power.

The technocratic, non-competitive nature of the classic transnational has become ever clearer as it has slipped gradually away from risk and creative development. Instead, transnationals buy up smaller, more creative companies; concentrate on capital accumulation; clip the coupons of intellectual property; and lobby elected officials and civil servants into adjusting the public good to encourage private complacency. In spite of all these advantages, they often find their enormous mergers impossible to digest, their unprecedented debts impossible to service. Among the major players, the number of failed mergers and — as in the airline industry — of bankruptcies was so high during the 1980s and '90s as to be disturbing. Billions were theoretically invested, only to evaporate in the marketplace. This was part of the continuing hidden inflation — the continuing vaporization of money, which somehow did not even meet the standards of imagined reality that sensible monetary systems require.

This romance of gigantism was beginning to look pretty silly. Size seemed to have replaced thought. As if it were a male thing.

The thinker and British diplomat Robert Cooper has captured today's situation perfectly with his formula: "[I]t was not the empires but the small states that proved to be a dynamic force in the world. Empires are ill-designed for promoting change."[27] At least political empires have pockets of flexibility within their complex multi-dimensional nature. The two-dimensional transnationals become sclerotic frighteningly fast. Their obsession with constant growth in revenue merely masks their weakness.

As they have fallen back on a sort of passive-aggressive reliance on capital and power accumulation and on eliminating competition, any widespread belief in their capacities has seeped away along with most public sympathy.

The very real power of citizens to limit these groups is being rediscovered, just as it was in the early twentieth century, when trusts, combines and public corruption dominated. One of the most eloquent contemporary examples has been the decision of a growing number of municipalities in North America to refuse the world's largest corporation, Wal-Mart, permission to build one of its stores. Often this refusal comes via a referendum. When Inglewood near Los Angeles rejected a gigantic Wal-Mart by a vote of 60 percent, one of the organizers said, "The question was whether the wealthiest company in the world could circumvent the law. The answer was no."[28]

The more basic question was whether the cheapness of goods trumped societal well-being. Or inversely, in developing countries suffering from epidemics, whether expensive goods trump social well-being. The answer in both cases is no. The fundamental question is whether citizens are more powerful than corporations, if they take the trouble to try. The answer is yes.

Perhaps the clearest hint of the weakness deep within these large private bureaucracies is the extent to which their executives seek to create new versions of old class systems to solidify their social positions. A great deal has been said about the pretensions of the technocracy — their jets, their clubs, their stock options, their feeding at the shareholders' capital trough as if by right. Recent studies have begun to reveal something more serious: a decline in social mobility in the developed countries; a decline in inverse order, as the United States has become more stratified than Canada or Europe. Even Europe, having increased mobility after the last war up into the 1980s, now seems to be slipping back in imitation of the new American class-based dream.

The corporations' responses to growing accusations of self-indulgent waste through the 1980s and '90s have simply made them more of an obstacle to mobility. They began to slim down first their employment structures, then their guarantees of employment, moving at all levels toward more part-time, occasional and contract relationships. As a result they cut back on their role in apprenticeship, training and professional education, throwing all of that back on the nation-states, to whom in turn they did everything they could to deny the tax revenues necessary to finance such programs. The precise effect was to weaken the transnationals' role as agents of societal change, whether on the shop floor or in the executive offices.[29]

In *The Economist*'s words, "You can see elites mastering the art of perpetuating themselves."[30] This is a classic failure of an empire structure. But the fragile inflationary nature of today's transnationals can be seen in the rapidity with which they have converted the meritocracy model — still visible in the large corporations of newer economies — into an autocratic self-protective system.

privatization. it all depends.

A trillion dollars worth of real assets launched into the marketplace around the world ought to have made some impact. In some cases, government is leaner, the public better served and the market healthier. In others, billions have evaporated to no effect except personal gain for a few.

The result does not resemble so much a principle applied as the sort of mixed bag you would expect in the real world. In Britain some numbers show the privatized companies outperforming the market average.[31] Some credit privatization with the revolution in communications. Others point out that the revolution happened everywhere in the world. It was the result of new technology and this boosted the privatized corporations, just as elsewhere it boosted the public corporations.

What is widely agreed on is that technocrats and middlemen profited everywhere from these sell-offs. A new monied class was created out of selling public property. This was widely seen as *sleeze* and profiteering, while, curiously enough, the official economic theme had been to make the newly private companies efficient. And one of the key methods had been to fire thousands of employees. Since this slimming-down was handled by managers, the tendency was to get rid of people who provided services or, in some way, actually did things.[32] The example of the British Rail breakup and sell-off has marked people's imagination. Eight people were killed in the five years before privatization, fifty-nine in the five years after. There was also a drop in punctuality, cleanliness and service. Yet the companies responsible for such mismanagement make record profits. In another sector — energy — fifteen years after privatization, *The Financial Times* found that the dream of competition had produced market concentration — twenty companies *consolidating* into six. The government watchdog complained in 2005 of continually rising rates, "powerful industry oligopolies" and "the potential for collusion and market manipulation." And yet, it could also be said that other parts of the economy were much more energetic.

The story in New Zealand was among the least happy. The government sold off some 80 percent of its assets, mostly to foreign interests. Yet the country's foreign debt more than doubled.[33] As the economist Gareth Morgan points out, "You have to make sure that you have the capacity for fair competition.... That there *is* a market place" before you privatize. Otherwise "the privilege of a state monopoly was simply transferred." And then you had created in Stiglitz's words "a private, unregulated monopoly [that] will likely result in even higher prices for consumers."

What most clearly hasn't worked, therefore, is shoving utilities into the marketplace. Why? Because in most cases there isn't a marketplace in what they deliver. Instead there is a natural monopoly, at best an oligopoly. And what is being delivered is not a market product. It is a slice of the public good. The British complaints about water systems going wrong in the hands of technocrats looking for profits, avoiding the heavy infrastructure investments, unreliable on quality control, is a story that is being repeated around the world — from South Australia to Latin America.

In some places governments are actually starting over again by recreating industries they sold off a few years before. In Argentina they are recreating their national oil company, first set up in 1922 as an anti-trust mechanism. It was sold off in the 1990s, then bought up by Spanish interests. Why is the Argentine government getting back into the energy business? Because energy is a strategic need and, like other commodities, it is difficult to regulate. So sophisticated governments feel they need a window into the machinations of the market. Unsophisticated governments don't seem to mind not knowing.

In general, has privatization worked? That depended on whether there was a real market and whether the sector was of strategic importance. If it was done judiciously, with these two factors in mind, the effect might well have been positive. If it was done in an ideological — that is, blunt and heavy-handed — manner, as it often was, the result was more likely to be harmful. And then there is one of those paradoxes produced by ideology: the less there was a real market, the more tough new regulations were needed. So privatization has tended to force even reluctant governments back into the private sector as ever more severe regulators. Today the global story is the gradual advance of binding international regulations aimed at giving back to individuals and individual governments the power they need to shape the public good.

expert confusion.

If these cycles I have been describing are so obvious, why does a civilization dominated by experts find it so difficult to respond to reality rather than to ideology?

The simple answer is that specialists, consultants and technocrats, whether running transnationals or government departments, are not natural leaders. They are not meant to be. Their methodology tends to be narrow and linear. Globalization, in the name of the marketplace, has pushed to the fore people who are frightened by the complexity of that market, and indeed of broad reality. The kind of lateral thinking and open communication that dealing with reality requires tends to strike them as unprofessional and disloyal. And so a quarter-century centred on an ideology devoted to opening up society has curiously led to an epidemic of secrecy and a chronic lack of communication.

If you follow the mad-cow story as it moved from country to country, you find identical patterns of secrecy and denial. In each case, in the name of saving the market, the market was destroyed. If you follow the recurring drama of the international fisheries, you find the same combination of panic and denial. Some 90 percent of the stocks of ocean fish over thirty centimetres long have disappeared in the last half-century.[34] Central to this decline is a linear obsession with technical detail and a fear of looking at the broader situation.

These stories of agricultural industrialization are emblematic of the management idea of Globalization. They are all about grabbing hold of dozy old regionally based sectors and turning them into efficient international industries driven by technology and management. These industries are to be based on a model of permanent growth.

What is it that prevents sensible people from identifying problems, then solving them? First, it is the unshakeable belief in market imperatives. Second, there is a specialist and managerial self-pride common to today's economic ideology. The result is the incapacity of true believers — in this case, managers and specialists — simply to admit error.

If you can admit error, you can get on with fixing the problem. But the managerial ethos is wedded to the idea that problems are not solved. They are managed. And so tens of billions of dollars were lost in the newly modernized cattle industry with its dependency on international trade. And people were killed. Farms and ranches are still being destroyed. And the resources of the oceans, which have always existed, have been so destabilized and undermined that we do not know what will happen next.

Call it the sin of self-pride, if you wish. I would rather call it the mystification of civilizational structures. The purpose of mystification is to make it seem that there are no choices. There is only the inevitability of economics. Sensible people are deprived of their self-confidence and left reliant on the sophisticated exercise of power by leaders intent on riding the wave of global economic and technological forces.

Put another way, a growing number of people have noticed that a global ideology, which declared itself the force of capitalism and risk, was spoken for largely by tenured professors of economics and management while being led by technocrats — that is, private sector bureaucrats — working for large joint stock companies that were rarely owned by blocks of active shareholders. And most of the changes they sought were aimed at reducing competition.

money markets. the reregulation shift.

Malaysia remained a pariah for about twelve months. Sometime in 1999 its pegged currency, tariffs and capital controls metamorphosed into normalcy for most bankers and bureaucrats. How? Why? Because regulations had worked. The country's foreign reserves had begun to grow. Soon *The Wall Street Journal* was describing the situation with confused semi-approval.[35] By 2002 Mahathir was lecturing the world on the need for "a proper International Financial System" and describing the seven steps of global financial decline, which had led to the crisis, ending with "the rampage of the currency traders."

In 2003 he was received as a hero at Davos. At about the same time the International Institute of Management and Development rated Malaysia fourth among larger countries on its chart of world competitiveness. At last even the IMF leadership put their seal of approval on his policies.

By 2004 they "saw no convincing case to reconsider the peg [of the Malaysian currency] at this time." Of course, the IMF has never admitted that it was part of the problem.

The principle and the reality of reregulation had thus been demonstrated. How would it be applied elsewhere?

Part of the answer was the speed with which those few respectable voices calling for "a better system in the long run" had multiplied into a common sound.[36] I.J. Macfarlane, the governor of the Reserve Bank of Australia, focused attention on the future problems for everyone in a deregulated world: "[H]edge funds have become the privileged children of the international financial scene, being entitled to the benefits of free markets without any of the responsibilities. Our reconstruction of the transactions that hedge funds undertook in Australia in June suggests that they could engage in almost infinite leverage in their off-balance sheet transactions if they so chose." He warned that if there was no action at the international level, such a vacuum would provoke inward-looking national regulations. Harold James, who compares the trends leading to the 1930s Depression with those of today in a book called *The End of Globalization,* warns that while the massive growth in financial movements has increased instability, world crises can be precipitated by flows of as little as 4 percent of GDP (Germany 1931) or 3 percent of GDP (U.S. 1971). The 1997 Asian crisis, with its unregulated system, involved a flow of 10 percent of GDP.[37] That is a lot. But it isn't a quarter or a half of GDP. His point is that you don't need a general meltdown to produce a general meltdown. Any shift toward normalizing instability therefore carries exponential dangers. For several years there had been warnings from some international institutions of "the increasing opaqueness of the financial system." Some economists had been pointing out the return of "the tension experienced in the 1920s between global finance and democratic governance."

And yet, after the Asian crisis had given us such a dramatic near-death experience for global well-being, the regulators moved with excruciating slowness. By 2004, seven years later, nothing much seemed to have changed. Mainstream commentators like Fareed Zakaria were predicting a "need for new regulation and a renewed appreciation of the role of government in capitalism."[38] Pension funds were expressing their distrust of market transparency. The IMF and G7 ministers of finance were busy blaming the hedge funds yet again, this time for oil price manipulations.

Why were governments moving so slowly? Partly because the Asian crisis had taken place in Asia. Leaders in the West somehow couldn't quite relate it to their own situation. Some of them even believed the IMF's gambit to shift blame to *local crony capitalism*.

The broader explanation is that the received wisdom of the day remained global. But real reactions were determindly national, at best regional. And political leaders were only slowly rediscovering their power. They couldn't yet quite believe they had the power to shape events. And their technocracies either were committed to the received wisdom of Globalization or, rightfully, did not have the political power to take the lead. Besides, everyone in power — except a few non-conformists like Mahathir — was still terrified of the criticism that would crash down upon them from a highly organized Globalist network if they dared to show any real doubt in the established received wisdom.

On top of that, the corruption of formal democratic structures by lobbyists and consultants, who had penetrated to the heart of policy making, made it very difficult for ministers, let alone deputy ministers, to generate arguments critical of Globalist assumptions. If they asked their officials for advice or action, they received reassurance, suggestions for patience, or at best, for minimalist movement.

And yet. And yet much more had already been done than was generally boasted of. The most obvious change was the launch of the euro in 1999. This created a working system for an initial twelve economies, which was also a protective wall from the speculative world. What transformed the euro from a distant plan to reality was Europe's aggressive reaction to the battering of the pound, the franc and other national currencies had taken in the unregulated money markets of 1992. Michel Sapin, the French finance minister of the day: "During the French Revolution, such people were known as speculators and they were beheaded." "France and Germany will fight this speculation, which is based on no economic fundamentals."[39] The individual nations had been defeated in that international battle. But their defeat had pushed them to focus on highly regulated cooperation as their future goal. The irresponsible victory of the speculators led within seven years to their exclusion from the world's largest market.

And then, also in 1999, there was the call of the president of the German Bundesbank for an international financial monitoring system. Two months later, it was in place. On the surface the Financial Stability Forum has no regulatory power. And its members continue to protest that it has none. But it pulls together senior representatives from twenty-six national and international financial authorities. They have a clear program to establish at least administrative transparency. And their purpose is to identify where and what regulation is needed.

It is assumed within this continual work that the Globalist belief in taking down the financial walls around every sort of economy as fast as possible was quite simply wrong. The IMF was wrong. The economic prism believers were wrong. They caused the crises of 1992 and 1997.

Of course, no one in a position of authority will actually say this. In a world of specialists and technocratic calm, no one is ever publicly wrong, let alone held responsible for errors, even if they have damaged the lives of real people. Professionalism is all about smooth waters and the appearance of continuity. And so the public power structures of the financial world have set about slowly getting control over the marketplace, without ever saying there has been a change of direction.

Underlying this return of regulation is a simple discovery. The Globalist argument had been that markets open twenty-four hours around the world, linked by permanently vibrant technology, meant that trading took place with such complexity and speed that regulators were obsolete. It turns out that the opposite was true. Until all of this remarkable technology came along, markets were semi-oral and relatively isolated one from the other, thus very hard to regulate. Now, thanks to the written and integrated nature of modern technology, nations as well as international regulators responsible to nations can control financial markets in detail. That is, if they decide to do so.

On a more basic level, Western governments, in cooperation with one another, are slowly tightening their regulations around tax havens. This activity is increasingly driven by the knowledge that such places are used by both organized crime and terrorists to launder and move their money — that is, on top of the habitual tax evaders resident inside the democracies. Why have our governments not simply rendered such places irrelevant by shutting them out of our economies? Nothing could be more easily done. The answer takes us back to the deep penetration of corrupting forces into our democratic structures during the Globalist era.

And yet. And yet there was California in 2002 banning all state government business with corporations located in offshore tax havens. Twenty-two corporations were immediately named. The state treasurer, Phil Angleides: "Corporations hiding behind a mailbox in Bermuda are shirking their duty as Americans."[40] There are two messages here. Governments, even mere state governments, have real power in the international economy. Second, nationalism is on the way back as a real force in setting economic policy.

Everywhere you look there are quiet, discreet signs of reregulation. Under the wings of the Bank for International Settlements, banking supervisors from around the world are working to set global rules for bank capital. One of the key *uncounted, unregulated* new tools for printing money — credit cards — will in some way be included. There will be dozens of exceptions to these Basel Rules. And again, the reach of speculators into the heart of government means that constant roadblocks mysteriously appear to slow the process. And yet, there is already some agreement.

On August 2, 2004, the world's largest bank, Citigroup, ran an old-fashioned Globalist speculation gambit. It sold enough European bonds all at once to collapse the market. Thanks to our remarkable technology it was able to sell €11 billion worth in two minutes. Then it bought them back at the depressed price and made a nice little profit of €15 million. It was the sort of thing that used to happen in a smaller way with penny mining stocks on the Vancouver Stock Exchange. But this was a gigantic and sophisticated exploitation of electronic global markets.

The public regulatory system reacted with speed and authority. Two days later, temporary limits had been put in place on trading volumes in the MTS electronic system Citigroup had manipulated. Within two weeks, the bank was under investigation by British regulators. European authorities then began to devise a regulatory regime to prevent such speculation. One of the central ideas was to slow down the trading process! In other words, artificial speed, made possible by technology, was recognized to be irrelevant to real market values, not inevitable and not necessary. That a lot of young traders, overburdened with gonadal energy, like to blend their emotional state of being with an idea of spinning global markets is beside the point. It has nothing to do with economics, let alone with civilization.

Rape is illegal. Speculation as social rape is equally easy to forbid through regulation.

the new idea of regulation.

There is nothing magical or ideological about good regulation. It works when it is appropriate to the system, so it needs constant reinvention. That the rules put in place in an ad hoc manner between 1930 and 1971 had become increasingly cumbersome and some even inappropriate is hardly surprising. Times change. Regulations need to change with them. Every few decades that will cause a little crisis, because what has been put in place in an ethical manner may take on a self-interested logic; or in a utilitarian manner will take on a self-indulgent life of its own.

By late in the 1990s, our crude and rather child-like slippage into a Manichean argument pitting regulation against deregulation for a quarter-century was being looked on by sensible people with some embarrassment. The waves of financial crises, corporate scandals and executive self-indulgence at both taxpayer and shareholder expense have pushed us gradually into a reregulation phase.

In the global theory, financial markets were a brand-new reality in which currency was transformed into a trade good. But the abstract nature of these virtual trade goods theoretically made them the least likely to respond to regulation. The resulting deregulation has now been proven to be dangerous and unnecessary. But if money markets can be shaped, other areas will be much easier to give shape to.

That is why Fareed Zakaria felt comfortable assuming there "will be need for new regulation."[41] Kofi Annan warned transnationals that they must pay attention to human rights, labour and environmental standards for the same reason. And he did this at the 1999 Davos gathering, where the widely shared assumption had changed from earlier years. Suddenly people believed that free trade and capital flows were having a negative effect on many developing countries. The gathering's overall theme was "managing the impact of globalization."

In such an international atmosphere, it was not surprising that regulators at the European level were willing to take on Microsoft. Acting for all the nation-states of the continent, they eventually ruled that the company was abusing its "near monopoly," trying to "squeeze out rivals."[42] They ordered the company to alter its product and disclose information about it. Faced by the world's largest software company, European regulators simply told it what behaviour was unacceptable and regulated it into acceptable behaviour.

Some might say, *that's all very well for Europe. But a mere nation-state no longer has that power.* Paul Keating, the former prime minister of Australia, pointed out in late 2004 that the ratio of government outlays to GDP and the ratio of government revenue to GDP have in most cases not shrunk under Globalization. Government power in the economy remains the same. "What has changed is the nature of the regulation. Today governments are more interested in what I have often termed *steering the boat* rather than *rowing the boat.*"[43]

globalization. a regional belief system.

The promise of Globalization was that a rising tide would carry all boats. But a rising tide is a dangerous thing. From dories to liners, vessels left to the vagaries of rising waters are dashed onto rocks, beached, swamped, overturned, carried out to sea. A rising tide requires careful captains, clever crews, anchors, lines, every form of organized flexibility and control. Nothing is more regulated than a vessel on a moving sea.

In a startling, yet obvious observation, the economist Martin Wolf pointed out that while most people believe the importance of nations is on the decline, in reality borders have never mattered so much.[44] International investment in high-income countries is some $6000 per person; in the middle-income countries $1350; in low-income countries $400; the first category covers 900 million people, the other two 5.2 billion people. The borders within which you are born will determine your life. The outcome will be partly economic. The original cause of that outcome, however, will have been the social structure of your nation-state.

South America tried Globalization for a decade, and it led to collapse. For true believers, the continent just hadn't tried hard enough; there had been too much nepotism and corruption; unions had been too strong. But real economic policies aren't dependent on perfect conditions. Perfect conditions don't exist in the real world. After all, Western democracy emerged slowly out of highly imperfect conditions. Today Peru and Bolivia are on a precipice, as is Ecuador. Venezuela is led by a nationalist populist. Argentina is picking itself up yet again and this time searching for a route particular to its needs. In the process it has aggressively negotiated the largest ever regularization of a financial default — some $80 billion. Here is yet another hint, if one were needed, that the Third World debt crisis could be solved instead of managed. Brazil is further along on its national re-examination. It is cherry-picking global opportunities to suit its vision of its own choices.

In the first half-decade of the twenty-first century, six South American countries chose moderate left governments opposed to neo-liberal economics. They are focused on egalitarian, anti-poverty policies, reticent about global trade theories, particularly if encouraged by the United States, and they are especially interested in regional cooperation. Brazil seems to be the lodestar for this expanding group. Meanwhile, Chile, stable and increasingly prosperous since the exclusion of General Pinochet, has developed a particular model that is both nationalist and attached to free trade. In other words, the continent is no longer caught up in the Globalist experiment.

And if South America no longer believes, what is the mindset of Africa after a quarter-century of collapsing growth and wealth, epidemics left to run wild and millions of deaths through war? If Africa has been a party to Globalization, it represents the most eloquent statement of an ideological failure.

As for South Asia, after the crisis of 1997, it also began cherry-picking its international positions. Asian-centred political and economic groupings are not merely strengthening. They are focused on a pragmatic view of markets in which powerful government involvement, family systems and market competition are balanced to meet the Asian view of how a society should work.

None of this means that the global economy is coming to an end. What it does mean is that the Globalization model of the 1970s and '80s has faded away. It is now, at best, a regional project — that region being the West. But even there, the moves to reregulation and the return of nationalism are carrying the twenty or so old democracies in quite unexpected directions. It could be said that American nationalism is the primary force in undermining the old Global project. Washington's lead role in inserting TRIPS into the WTO, then defending the power of pharmaceutical transnationals over the desperate needs of poorer countries caught in epidemics, then devaluing its dollar to try to solve national problems whatever the effect on other countries, have all demonstrated to weaker countries that nation-states and their own view of their national interest are still far more important than any international economic theory.

21

India and China

Globalization isn't in trouble. India and China are there to prove it. Two gigantic developing countries — one socialist and bureaucratic, the other communist — have embraced the theories of liberal economics and trade. What's more, it is bringing them happiness. So much so that their exports are exploding, high-tech jobs are flowing their way, poverty is shrinking and the middle class growing.

All of this is in some ways true. The question is whether their success is about Globalism or something quite different. Take the 1997 Asian meltdown. Neither India nor China melted. In fact, they did better than average during the crisis. Why? They had capital controls and various other limitations on movements and investments. In general, they have done well out of economic modernization by not following the economic principles of Globalization.[1] Whatever market reforms there have been, they have come in the context of nation-state interests.

Part of the explanation is that both countries do see modernization from a national — indeed, nationalist — point of view. The Chinese government still controls half the country's industrial assets. It invests heavily in infrastructure, shapes much of the development. The Indian government does less, but it is still very much involved.

The principal Chinese obsession is neither free trade nor free markets. It is dealing with internal poverty, which is a political time bomb. We hear a great deal about new model cities built around high-technology factories. But China also has the most dangerous mining industry in the world, with some five thousand accidental deaths a year. These are real challenges for a gigantic and contradictory economy. In such a context, global theories of economics are quite silly. India has the same tensions and complexity, and an identical poverty time bomb. China's view of economics "is flexible enough that it is barely classifiable as a doctrine.... [P]ragmatic and ideological at the same time, a reflection of an ancient Chinese philosophical outlook that makes little distinction between theory and practice. *[G]roping for stones to cross the river*."[2]

The Indian government defeated at the polls in 2004 had tried to embrace much of the global economic ideology. The result was a sharp increase in the tension between rich and poor. When the elections came, the rural poor threw them out. The new government, although led by a modern, efficiency-minded, market-reform technocrat, is clearly driven by the central national question. Prime Minister Manmohan Singh: "Economic growth is not an end in itself. It is a way to create employment, to banish poverty, hunger and homelessness, to improve the lives of most of our people. [The direction] is equality and social justice."[3]

These two approaches come out of extremely experienced civilizations. India is not, as some English are fond of saying, an invention of the British Empire. In the sixteenth century, two Mogul emperors, Babur and in particular Akbar, created and administered highly sophisticated systems that dealt with productivity, commodity pricing and balanced taxation. By the time the British began to take over, this system had been radically decentralized and regional princes had become dominant.

This rich and complex culture in good part explains how India was able, following its independence in 1947, to resist the pressures to follow Western methods. Natwar Singh, writing before he became Indian foreign minister in 2004: "India never subscribed to the assumptions of the cold war. India was not interested in either the theory of balance of power or the domino theory, which became a part of American diplomatic mythology during the 1960s and early 1970s. We have never believed in spheres of influence, nor have we subscribed to any other concept so dear to European and American thinkers and intellectuals."[4]

As for China, it was experimenting with its own market approaches long before the Europeans knew there was something to experiment with.

These two countries have two of the world's most powerful armed forces and armaments industries. India is the world's third importer of arms. China is number one. They both believe in a "rigid defense of the Westphalian system of national sovereignty."

And their capacity to combine size, government support and a broad range of low costs renders irrelevant the simplistic Globalist idea of international competition leading to efficient markets. The United States and international economic institutions have been badgering the Chinese to float the yuan, or at least to peg it higher. The Chinese change the subject.

But the growing success of these two countries makes nonsense of large swaths of Globalist received wisdom.

And the nationalist context in which it is taking place in both countries is particularly important. The new government of India has a strong, non-sectarian core and is concentrated on an egalitarian, inclusive nationalism. But the just-defeated Hindu nationalist movement, the Bharatiya Janata Party or BJP, remains very much the largest opposition group and the only national alternative to the Congress Party.

It's worth remembering just how nationalist and sectarian the last fifteen years have been in India. The BJP's deputy leader, L.K. Advani, headed a Hindu crusade across the country riding a motorized chariot of religious figures. It ended with the destruction of the Babri Masjid (mosque) in Ayodhya in 1992. That in turn led to riots across much of India in 1993. A good thousand people were murdered. On the basis of this false populist agitation, the BJP won power at the national level and held it until 2004. Indeed, it was a classic case of false populism in which reality is swept aside and replaced by a sort of dream world — or night-mare world — in which 82 percent of the population are meant to be frightened by 12 percent.

The racial instability continued throughout this period. In Gujarat in 2002 the BJP — the ruling party — created the atmosphere of fear that led to the massacre of thousands of civilians. At the national level this same party led the government in converting India to Globalization-style development. The high-tech business in particular went into high-gear growth. So global theory was successfully applied through a sectarian prism. But as I've noted, the new government has a strong, non-sectarian core and is concentrated on an egalitarian, inclusive nationalism.

China does not believe that there is any relationship between democracy and efficient, liberalized industrial markets and massive amounts of trade. It does not believe that a particular style of economics leads to greater democracy. So far the Communist Party is doing a very convincing job of leading a traditional nationalist and non-democratic economic and trade revolution.

One of the unexpected comic turns that began to develop in the early twenty-first century was an uncontrollable fear among Western market leaders of the Chinese capacity, and eventually the Indian capacity, to buy large chunks of Western industry. For a quarter-century the same Western business leaders and economists had assured citizens and governments that the geographic location of ownership was unimportant. To worry about it was old-fashioned economic nationalism. Suddenly it appears that they meant it didn't matter inside the West. Their intent was that Western investors should be able to buy and sell anywhere in the world. Seen in that way, their Globalism has its roots in the old trading and industrial-trading models of the sort that led to the limiting of movement for Indian cloth from the eighteenth century on and the *obligation to buy* theory that led to the Opium Wars against China. Globalization, looked at from a Chinese or Indian perspective, was always about Western-centred regionalism.

It is important to focus on the extent to which China in particular, but India also, sees its growing international success as producing an increasing political, even military, threat from outside. According to Joshua Ramo, an expert on China, "[T]here is a sharp debate inside Chinese policy circles about whether or not the U.S. will *allow* China to rise."[5] In 2004, Beijing introduced its New Security Concept: "*No* hegemonism, *no* power politics, *no* alliances and *no* arms races." It is a formula designed neither for a global, shapeless world nor a U.S.-led world. It is all about the traditional Chinese view of regionalism based on geography, combined with China's contemporary view of shared concepts with different regions of the world. For example, while Washington is pushing Tokyo to play a military role in protecting

Taiwan, China and Japan are busy developing an increasingly strong and more important civil relationship and important investment patterns.

Meanwhile, the two new economic stars of Asia — India and China — are being presented in the West as rivals. Looked at from an Asian point of view, they are building a complex economic relationship based on large and relatively equal capital flows. Their mutual trade is soaring. China is now India's second-largest trading partner.

Perhaps most important, this relationship is being developed without reference to Western concepts and within the context of the Asian region. The West's projection of rivalry onto these two countries may be more wishful thinking than anything else.

There is one further element. China's growing relationships with countries such as Brazil are about more than economics. They are also about a conceptualization of the world not based on a Western economic prism.

In the first days of Globalism, in the first publication of Davos, it was declared that "Nationalism is economically indefensible."[6] Now the two leaders of global economics — a new sort, apparently — are strong, classic nationalists.

22

New Zealand Flips Again

In December 1999, while Seattle was being overwhelmed by riots and the WTO was slinking away and Stiglitz was resigning from the World Bank, one other thing happened. The only Western democracy to have formally embraced the full ideology of Globalization reversed direction.

In 1984 and 1990 governments had been elected in New Zealand on rather neutral programs, only to undertake radical Globalist and neo-liberal changes. The government produced from the 1999 election was quite different. It set about doing precisely what it had been elected to do. Interestingly enough, the reversal was pragmatic, not ideological. Helen Clark, the new prime minister: "New Zealanders have voted for a change but are weary of radical restructuring."[1]

What happened? Why did the voters change their minds about where they wanted to take their country? And how could such a small population — much smaller than that of Malaysia — take the risk of rejecting the international status quo? Surely the forces of inevitability would turn such local non-conformism into a great crisis and sweep away the offending voices.

The answer to the last question has two parts. New Zealand is an old democracy with a strong idea of itself and a habit of setting its own policy directions.

The answer to all three questions is quite simple. The Globalist neo-liberal experiment hadn't worked. It had been tried for fifteen years — the length of three world wars — and the results were clear. Most of its national industries had been sold off to foreigners, creating a constant drain of money abroad. The standard of living had been stagnant for all fifteen years. The economy was in decline. Young people were emigrating so fast that the national population was dropping. In areas as straightforward as research and development, a new, theoretically free market model had simply led to a shrinking of R and D.[2]

The emergence of an accelerating rich-poor divide, so common around the world under Globalization, took on particularly dramatic proportions in New Zealand, a country long used to being middle class. John Gray called this development "richly ironic."[3] In Globalist theory, "the underclass are products of the disincentive effects of welfare, not of the free market."

This new poverty clashed with the atmosphere of global inevitability. The result was two unexpected psychological effects. Public figures with their ears to the ground, like Graham Kelly, could sense that such radical contradictions must produce some sort of explosion. "Alienation, hopelessness and powerlessness is just as dangerous" as poverty. The leading historian Michael King put it this way: politicians became distrusted as a result of "successive governments of different colours enact[ing] controversial policies for which they had neither sought nor obtained a mandate."

As if from nowhere, a citizen-driven movement appeared. It drove a process of democratic reform that led to a nuanced electoral system resembling that of Germany. This new complexity removed from elected politicians the ability to create the kind of majorities that in turn would allow them to risk the public good, as had been done with Globalization. The new electoral system was in place by 1996, and Ruth Richardson, the outgoing minister of finance — a true believer in Globalization — understood that the game was up. "The wimps have won."[4] In the world of ideologies, moderates are always wimps, wet, soft. The definition of manhood is extreme romanticism about the belief system's power to shape the world to its purposes. Put another way, for an ideologue, the definition of manhood is aggressivity, but of a particular kind: aggressive passivity before the inevitable.

The second psychological effect was more of an undercurrent that New Zealand shared increasingly with other countries around the world.

In this case, the combination of alienation, powerlessness and anger gave birth to a false populist movement. It seemed to appear in reaction to the global atmosphere of abstract economic inevitability. But after 1996, when the Globalists were slipping out of power in Wellington, they allied themselves with the false populists — nationalistic and anti-immigrant. This made no sense. Yet the link in India between Hindu nationalism and Globalization also made no sense. And an almost identical evolution would take place in other countries. It was as if Globalism first provoked false populism, then married it in a strange Manichean relationship, perhaps because of the two's shared romantic foundation.

After 1995 Ruth Richardson's sort of anger could increasingly be felt among true believers around the world. New Zealand had been the poster boy of their movement. *The Economist* ranted on about the return of the old "hidebound economies" versus the brand-new "best monetary and fiscal-policy frameworks of any country in the world."[5] The reality was much less straightforward. Real wages were lower in the late 1990s than in the mid-'70s. Public services were in decline. In 1997 the governor of the Reserve Bank expressed his relief that the government now understood "that fiscal policy does not require unreasonable tight monetary policy."[6] New Zealand was struggling with an international deficit caused in part by the new heavy foreign ownership.

There was a third, more positive and unrelated, undercurrent. Gradually over the post-war period, the Maori had begun to reassert themselves and their culture. It was eventually accepted by the interlopers — the immigrants — that "Maori is the foundation human culture of the land." And that "what was true of Maori culture was also true of that of the country as a whole."[7] The immigrants — the Pakeha — began to think of themselves as of the place, with the Maori; and so they could more easily explain their commitment to a non-European idea of egalitarianism and inclusivity. This is a very difficult evolution for old colonial societies that have tied so much of their new societies to what they had theoretically brought with them. There are still a multitude of contradictions and tensions. In different ways you can find this same almost animist identification with place growing in Canada and Australia and other countries where there is a living tension between Aboriginal and immigrant societies. One effect has been to separate these populations from an idea of Globalism that denies the power of place, which in democratic terms is the power of choice based on local needs.

Each society has to find the strength to say no from within its own experience. The New Zealanders' growing integration with their place, tied to the Aboriginal idea of an eternal, natural presence, was perhaps the foundation for the self-confidence that would help them to change direction.

As that moment of choice approached, the situation became increasingly clear. Under Globalism the country had been through two full business cycles without escaping the boom-and-bust cycles, without finding a natural balance. Most of the privatized companies "went on being cot cases."[8] Eleven thousand people were leaving the country every year. There were low levels of savings.

In Helen Clark's first speech as prime minister in December 1999, she said the country had "one of the highest levels of national debt in the developed world ... one of the lowest levels of private sector R and D [and] faster growth in inequality than most other countries in the developed world."[9] Perhaps most disturbing after fifteen years of what the Globalists called modernization, the country was as dependent as ever on commodity exports.

Of course, the ideological position was that things would have come right given just a little more time. That is the classic romantic fixation on tomorrow. Let's just say that it represents the opposite of Seneca's more down-to-earth position *On the Shortness of Life — Vita Brevis:* "[L]ife ceases just when we are getting ready for it."[10] Put the other way around, "Life is long if you know how to use it." There is a second ideological argument based on urgency. Had they not done what they did, the country would have collapsed. There was a crisis. Action had to be taken. They had no choice.

The concept of imminent crisis is central to such situations. It erases the possibility of measured action built on citizen support.

Paul Dalziel, an economist at Lincoln University on the South Island, has compared New Zealand and Australia over the same fifteen years.

Australia faced similar problems but addressed them in a careful, moderate manner. New Zealand could just as easily have taken that moderate route. Instead, the Australian GDP gradually pulled ahead. If New Zealand had followed the Australian pattern, the output would be a third higher than it is now.

The question in 1999 was dramatic. What would happen if a small country with a developed economy withdrew from the Globalization project? Helen Clark's government answered the question by acting carefully. It re-established Air New Zealand and the rail track, created Kiwibank, brought in a constantly growing apprenticeship program, renationalized workers' compensation, removed an Employment Relations Act that had been central to the neo-liberal approach, and put a heavy emphasis on culture. "A creative nation releases energy."[11] Its aim was to "re-regulate where deregulation had gone too far." "[T]o reassert traditional New Zealand values of fairness, security and opportunity in public policy."

A little time has gone by now. What has happened?

There is a net growth in population. Unemployment is halved, down to its lowest in sixteen years. Nobody denies that this is a favourable moment in the economic cycle. But the Globalist period had stretched over two full business cycles without ever being able to take advantage of the upswings.

In any case, the change has only partially been about economics. If you elevate such a secondary factor up to the state of a religion, you invite blinders, halters, limitations. You deny your complexity. What the New Zealanders reasserted at the end of the century has a larger shape, one in which economics is an important servant, not the purpose, of society.

PART V

AND WHERE ARE WE GOING NOW?

The old is dying, the new struggles to be born, and in the interregnum there are many morbid symptoms.

— Antonio Gramsci, *Quaderni del carcere,* 1930

23

The New Vacuum:
An Interregnum of Morbid Symptoms

Vladimir: What do we do now?
Estragon: Wait.
Vladimir: Yes, but while waiting.
Estragon: What about hanging ourselves?
Vladimir: Hmm. It'd give us an erection.
Estragon: An erection!
Vladimir: With all that follows.

— SAMUEL BECKETT, *WAITING FOR GODOT*

It is hard for any society that slips into a vacuum to admit that it is no longer advancing in any particular direction. This is particularly difficult for those individuals who hold power. Their vocabulary, their image of themselves, even their skills have all been honed to fit the certainty of a direction that no longer prevails.

The sign of mediocre leaders is that they believe things will continue as they have. Why do they insist on believing this? Because they compensate for their lack of talent or ethical centre or intelligence or courage with a conviction that the forces of inevitability are at work. These forces may be said to be divine or they may be something else treated as a divinity — rationality, for example, or technology or market forces.

But even a strong leader is hampered, in dealing with the reality of a vacuum, by the received wisdom in place. We function through organized habit, particularly when it comes to language. We change it with difficulty. Vocabulary, phrases, arguments can become like prisons. They can prevent us from getting to the next stage — what the philosopher Richard Rorty calls "acquiring habits of action for coping with reality."[1]

How can we tailor our actions to reality if we can't recognize the extent to which the reality and therefore the language of Globalization have been confused — intentionally mixed — with that of neo-liberalism? There are many reformers who would like to humanize Globalization. How could that be done if the ideology is constructed in part on assumptions such as minimizing the role of government, subjecting non-economic policies to the economy, weakening competition out of a belief in size, turning a blind eye to tax avoidance, strengthening the power of private sector technocracy over the risk takers? These internal contradictions, along with dozens more, accentuate the atmosphere of disorder normal to this sort of vacuum.

The danger in such a situation is that people begin seeking sensationalist ways out of the confusion — Beckett's progress through *hanging* and *erection* — instead of trying to cope with reality. The habitual tools of public sensationalism include false populism, war, encouraging divisions between civilizations, racism, calling God in as the ultimate consultant to justify your actions.

Today the structures of power remain aligned with the methodology of a three-decade-old project known in sweeping terms as Globalization. Yet in society there is no widespread, let alone deep, belief or trust in its aims. The ILO talks of a "morally unacceptable and politically unsustainable" imbalance in its nevertheless "great productive capacity." "Seen through the eyes of the vast majority of women and men, globalization has not met their simple and legitimate aspirations for decent jobs and a better future for their children."[2] At one extreme, experts think the "modern world system is approaching its end." At the other, they are still convinced that "the process of globalization is not reversible," even if it is in good part more about "chaos than conspiracy." And after a good decade of accumulating disappointments and failures, the movement is strategically on the defensive. But its opponents also remain largely in a defensive mode.

The NGOs, in spite of holding the sort of organizational and popular power that is the envy of any political party in the West, have scarcely moved toward seeking real levers of power with the legal support of real citizens in real nation-states. They remain either on the metaphorical streets or are largely satisfied by invitations to consult, advise and argue with the power structures. This is oddly reminiscent of the Christian reformers in the early days of the Reformation, before it declined into a European civil war.

As for governments, only a handful — in New Zealand, Malaysia, Brazil — have organized themselves in clear language around recon- ceived intellectual concepts and publicly said they would lead their countries in another direction. A few others speak out, but in the old style. Jacques Chirac: "The world is not only a market, our societies need rules, the economy must be in the service of man and not the reverse. The freedom of exchange must not impose itself when the public well- being is in question."[3]

In general, a sullen public silence continues, in particular among elected authorities. Discreetly, in private conversations all over the developed world, government leaders and ministers are complaining bitterly about the assumptions of Globalization. They have been complaining for a good decade. They were frustrated by the endlessly repeated assumption that their powers had been limited by non-democratic, non-political market forces. Little by little, they have become dismissive of this assumption.

Surprisingly enough, it is the finance ministers of the G8 and the G20 who have been most openly arguing that nation-states could and eventually would again alter the direction of world events.

But this regaining of public courage remains a slow process. And the conviction widely spread among officials of all kinds — that Globalization has not really worked out or is in steep decline or radical mutation — has been kept out of their public debate by the *professional* managerial creed insisting that everyone must pretend to still believe in order to avoid even greater disorder.

Henry Kissinger warned during the previous vacuum, thirty years before, that the greatest danger of such disorders was "the erosion of people's confidence in their society's future and a resulting loss of faith in democratic means — in governmental institutions and leaders."[4] That loss of confidence is what encourages the rise of false populism, a taste for war, divisions between civilizations, racism and the misuse of gods. All of this could be summarized as the rise of fear, or what Camus called the "technique" of fear.

The USSR and its Bloc fell at the height of Globalist self-confidence. The Soviet diplomat Georgi Arbatov warned, "We are going to do something terrible to you. You will no longer have an enemy."[5] And indeed, once Globalism began unravelling, the positive advantages of no major conflict became part of the confusion of the growing vacuum. The American Samuel Huntington set the tone by lowering himself to encourage the most basic of fears with his declaration of a Clash of Civilizations. Following the collapse of the Soviet Bloc,

> the most important distinctions among people are not ideological, political, or economic. They are cultural. Peoples and nations are attempting to answer the most basic questions humans can face: Who are we …? People define themselves in terms of ancestry, religion, language, history, values, customs, and institutions. They identify with cultural groups: tribes, ethnic groups, religious communities, nations, and, at the broadest level, civilizations.

At first glance, this may seem innocuous enough. Written in 1996, it is another sign that the idea of economic inevitability is finished; that nation-states are back; that old-fashioned nationalism is back. But his argument is really all about the technique of fear. He describes civilizations in the manner that in the past produced religious wars and racial wars. And if there were any doubt, a few lines further on he identifies the preferred new generic enemy: Communists are to be replaced by Muslims. According to Huntington, the division between civilizations, which the Iron Curtain once represented, has now shifted east. Not far. Just a few hundred kilo-metres. "It is now the line separating the peoples of Western Christianity, on the one hand, from Muslim and Orthodox peoples on the other."[6]

Compare this fear-mongering to the sophistication with which the Aga Khan responds to such arguments: "It's as if I said 'what is Christianity doing with regard to Northern Ireland?' You would say to me 'what's Christianity got to do with the Protestant/Catholic relations in Northern Ireland?' You see, that's not a reflection of Christianity."[7]

This technique of fear had been let loose in people's veins well before September 11. For example, military spending and the pressures for more military spending had already started building. While the return of God to formal politics is often attributed to the current American president, the way had been prepared by Bill Clinton, who built the new waves of Christianity into his governance system. Anti-immigrant movements in Europe were already strong.

But the description of the world, how it worked and where it was going changed radically after the New York attacks. Suddenly economics and Globalism were consciously put in the back seat. Sensible people like the Dutch prime minister Jan Peter Balkenende, when his country took over the European presidency in 2004, defined "the major global issues of our time" as "combating terrorism, furthering human rights and democracy, economic development and action against poverty."[8] Our attention has clearly moved, even if it is not yet focused.

a de-castration process.

The year 2001 marked a major step in the rebuilding of public courage, but not for the reasons normally given. The first part of the year was filled with news of economic collapse. The high-tech business around the world had been in sharp decline since the year before. The chip sector was in the worst shape of its short life. The airline business, even by the disastrous standards of its deregulated existence, was firing staff in all directions. Governments were propping up companies.

Then came September 11. The effect was to push national economies and the international economy from a pattern of decline into a nosedive. Corporate leaders around the world did what they always do in a period of dangerous uncertainty. They cut back on investments and whatever else they could as fast as they could. The effect was, as it always is, to accelerate the general nosedive.

But what about the Globalist arguments that transnationals were the new nation-states, that the old nation-states, being increasingly powerless, followed the lead of the market? The CEOs were nowhere to be found. They were hunkered down in their offices doing what they were paid to do — looking after their shareholders' interests.

And yet we are not today in a depression. How were we saved?

The presidents, prime ministers, ministers of finance, governors of reserve banks and an army of their senior civil servants had rolled into action. They travelled everywhere, talked to everyone they could, spent enormous amounts of money and managed to stabilize the situation. In other words, there was a brutal reversal in mythological roles. The governments of the nation-states had taken back their full power to act. They were not castrati, after all. They were not dependent on inevitable economic forces, if they didn't wish to be. And the CEOs had retreated into their historic reactive role. That doesn't mean their enormous power had been lessened. Or that the lobbying system had changed. But the question of leadership and the ability of elected leaders to act as the primary leaders on behalf of the public good had been re-established. Leaders once again would be judged by their citizens by their ability to do this well.

the declared end of globalism.

That something had happened could be seen through the ongoing Versailles-like activities at Davos. As its size had grown over the years, so had the security bill. The idea of a club of global leaders could not survive if they were not in a secure and calm atmosphere. Already there was the problem of the growing number of demonstrators clamouring at its doors, a bit like the Paris mob at Versailles. September 11 brought the whole risk of terrorism. Somehow in this atmosphere of heightened uncertainty, the leaders of Davos couldn't negotiate their security arrangements in time. The Swiss authorities weren't sure that they wanted to take on the responsibility and the cost of such a risky business.[9] So Davos fled to New York. In an embarrassing attempt to dress up reality, this was presented as an act of solidarity with New Yorkers.

By 2003 the Swiss government had decided that it did want Davos back in Davos. And it was this session that produced such a dramatic illustration of the post-Globalist world. I have already mentioned the triumphant appearance of Mahathir Mohamad as the opening speaker of 2003. He excoriated global and economic policies, rightly boasted of Malaysia's success following a national regulated model and received a rapturous standing ovation. The message the courtiers were applauding was quite straightforward — medium-size nation-states have the power to craft their own economic models based on their particular social and economic needs, providing they do it intelligently. The unspoken admission of the listeners was that the theories of Globalization have turned out to be neither absolute truths nor inevitable. If anything, these theories seemed to have been dependent on rather tired moralism and desperate conformity.

A few days later, Luiz Inácio Lula da Silva, the new president of Brazil, received an equivalent reception. His message was that of a new sort of nation-state–based populism. Again it was a rejection of Globalist received wisdom. Again it was all about particular policies being developed for particular needs. The confused but fascinating implications for everything, from epidemics and intellectual property to new regional alliances involving a Chinese/Brazilian approach, would reveal themselves quickly over the next two years.

Close behind Lula came U.S. Secretary of State Colin Powell. He was caught up in the last complex manoeuvres before the U.S. invasion of Iraq — the manoeuvres to build an alliance, given that the traditional sixty-year-old Western alliance had split apart over the question.

With a single sentence, Powell declared Globalization dead. "We will act even if others are not prepared to join us."[10]

In other words, the model modern democracy declared that nation-states rule; economics do not. He declared that the United States would act alone (in this case to invade Iraq), according to its national understanding of its national interest, if it so wished. That he spoke for the most powerful nation in the world merely highlighted the message that other countries were free to act on their own if they so wished. Examined from a distance, Powell, Lula and Mahathir said exactly the same thing: nation-states, national interest, particular versus global approaches were all back as the prism of international action.

For his own reasons, each leader had overstated this change. The world was still very much struggling in the confusion of a vacuum.

There were a few other things to observe in the evolution of Davos as a mirror of Globalization. The atmosphere was no longer one of political leaders coming on bended knee to gain the attention of the new economic princes. Suddenly it was just another one of those big fair-ground-like gatherings where political leaders try to get across their messages. The CEOs, when they were not selling their products — after all, once you strip away the glitz, Davos is really a salesmen's trade fair — were there to listen. And, as in any overblown court, they were there to be courtiers.

Second, many of the CEOs picked out in earlier years by Davos as the "young global leaders" of the future had been eliminated by the reality of politics, economics and the new vacuum.[11]

Third, given the general loss of belief in predestined corporate leadership and the return of politics to fill the vacuum led to what you would expect in a courtier-like atmosphere: the arrival of the celebrities.

By 2005 they were there in force. The old regal assumption of economic inevitability had been reduced to stargazing. The actress Sharon Stone, for example, could be seen jumping to her feet and calling on CEOs to give money to combat malaria in Tanzania.[12] Her church charity intervention produced pledges of $1 million. This sort of emotive star turn may make everyone present feel good. Some might argue that it attracts attention to a problem. More realistically, it distracts people from the reality of government and business responsibility to organize the hundreds of millions, often billions, of dollars necessary to actually deal with Third World debt, epidemics and other major problems. The point here is the decline of Davos from temple of Globalization to circus, open to whatever fashion can capture fifteen minutes' worth of attention, whether for a good cause or self-promotion.

economists at each other's throat at last.

The other sign of a vacuum was the growing division around the world among economists, and for that matter among other believers. For decades, the very idea of a mainstream disagreement about Globalization had been impossible. Now contradictory ideas were popping up on all sides. The true believers often reacted with uncontrolled anger. The air was filled with the accusations they aimed at non-believers — *absurdity, diatribes, empty rhetoric, hysteria, nonsense.* Even when demonstrators were taken seriously by Globalists, there was no sign of respect for intellectual debate. Joseph Nye, dean of the John F. Kennedy School of Government, Harvard: "International institutions are too important to be left to demagogues, no matter how well-meaning."[13] This sort of anger among the believers often comes close to what Joseph Conrad called "the sombre imbecility of political fanaticism" or what Aristotle would have described as a lack of prudence: "[T]he man who is capable of deliberation will be prudent. But nobody deliberates about things that are invariable."[14] Gouverneur Morris, American representative in France, July 14, 1789: "Yesterday it was the fashion at Versailles not to believe that there were any disturbances in Paris."

In truth there are signs everywhere of intellectual and ethical disturbance.

Just think of the major economic questions. The vast majority of thinking macroeconomists are against the deregulation of international money markets, as are most reserve bankers. And yet the institutional economists hang on to this disorder. Why? No one knows. They use every bit of their influence on political leaders, again making it difficult for leaders to get pro-regulatory advice from their administrative structures. So at the 2004 G8 meeting on Sea Island in the American South, the whole subject was ostentatiously ignored. Added to this is constant Western political pressure on China to weaken its economic position by deregulating its currency and capital markets.

There are equivalent radical disagreements over treating intellectual property as a matter of trade, over the role of privatization, over the size and role of government, over public debt.

A fascinating example is German social system reforms. A good half of the economists and business leaders of the West are convinced that the German economy is stalling because of heavy and inflexible labour laws and social protection. They focus on the reform of these laws to release German energies. And because Germany is so powerful, they believe this is the explanation for European sluggishness. And they are not entirely wrong.

But they carefully avoid acknowledging what the other half of the experts point out. West Germany has poured well over €1.25 trillion into East Germany since 1980. The government sends €90 billion a year to the east. Could any government in the world continue to function more or less well while pouring out that amount of money each year? The economies of most countries wouldn't become sluggish. They would collapse. To be merely sluggish under such conditions is proof of the strength of the German system. Whether the money has been well spent in the east and whether some reforms are necessary to lighten the whole social system are separate issues. Klaus von Dohnanyi, chair of a panel of experts examining the country's problems: "Rebuilding the east is responsible for at least two-thirds of Germany's weak growth."[15] Yet day after day, the international advocates of the Globalist neo-liberal truth simply ignore this.

One of the most fundamental divisions is between those who do and those who do not believe that the economic prism approach is necessary for the whole world, even though a good billion and a half people lag farther and farther behind in measurements of rich and poor. Martin Wolf speculates that that split, which a century ago was 10 to 1 and today is 75 to 1, could soon be 150 to 1.[16] The division is over what kind of public intervention could reverse this trend, both internationally and nationally. Instead of entering into such a debate, a large part of the economist community lives in a state of denial that amounts to intellectual violence. You could see this in the way the market-oriented side drove Ravi Kanbur, its leading poverty expert, out of the World Bank because he was suggesting that economic growth alone would not be sufficient to reduce poverty; that redistribution taxes and policies would be necessary.

This conviction that *taxes as a tool of social redistribution must not be mentioned because it endangers the principles of global competitiveness* is increasingly tenuous. Fewer and fewer economists believe it is true. They see Sweden, an economic and social success story, with the highest tax burden. When Sweden in 2005 suggested it might raise taxes a bit higher, there was some indignation and fear-mongering, but not a great deal.

In general, OECD average tax levels are now inching up. And even though current U.S. politics is all about cutting taxes at the top, there is profound division within the world of economists as to whether this works. In 2004, 150 of the leading U.S. economists wrote to their government urging a reversal of the policy.

One of the most unexpected developments has been the growing confusion among many neo-liberal apostles when it comes to the balance between low taxes and the public debt. They had always seen low taxes as a great good and public debt as a great evil. Suddenly, many of them are leaning so heavily to the low tax side that they cannot help being acquiescent in the rise of public debt. It is as if they have forgotten about their idea of evil. Even the chairman of the board of governors of the Federal Reserve, Alan Greenspan, has adjusted his ideas about taxes and debt in order not to criticize the mounting American deficit.

Meanwhile, in places like China the discourse is all about the necessity of massive redistribution efforts through tax-funded public policy balanced with market success and regulated oversight. "China's problems are so massive that only exponential improvements in health care, economics and governance can hold China together."[17] The aim is "sustainable and equitable" development.

In the world of monetary experts, an almost irreconcilable division is growing. In spite of the near-death experience of the world economy in 1997–98, thanks in good part to unregulated, non-transparent financial groups, little has been done to control them. Hedge funds have never been so powerful and out of control. *The Economist* calls them "Capitalism's new kings."[18]

At the same time, the dominant business discourse these days is all about job creation, transparency, social responsibility and, where there is no regulation, applying self-regulation. But you can't have a private sector that is led by hedge funds yet believes in social responsibility.

Equally, we are entering into a new era of radically rising military expenditures, sold publicly in part as an economic growth strategy, while at the same time large numbers of economists and leaders are buying into an opposing theory of social development as the key to economic development. Amartya Sen, Nobel economist: "The contribution of the market mechanism to economic growth is, of course, important, but this comes only after the direct significance of the freedom to interchange — words, goods, gifts — has been acknowledged."[19] The idea of military expenditure as economic policy lies at the exact opposite end of the theoretical spectrum, beyond even pure neo-liberalism.

But perhaps the area of fastest-growing confusion lies in the sacred domain of trade and international competition. Many experts remain convinced by the classic trade argument. But an increasing number are troubled by the international anomalies. The advantages of cheap labour last for only short periods of time. There is always someone cheaper around the corner, so it is a theory that encourages boom-and-bust cycles. And international competitiveness may increasingly come down not to competitive advantage but to the size of the production system and its vertical integration — a combine approach. You may be the cheapest and the most efficient and still lose out.

The result is a growing protectionist discourse. But there is also a fresh, highly sophisticated discourse that says the primary need has never been for international trade. That it is a distraction from the real problem, which is an unsophisticated approach toward internal markets. Stiglitz: "It was the failure to create competition internally, more than protection from abroad, that was the cause of stagnation." "Trade liberalization is thus neither necessary nor sufficient for creating a competitive and innovative economy."[20] Economist Tim Hazeldine, New Zealand: "The salvation-by-exports approach has been oversold.... [W]e'd do much better to export less (and get a better price for it) and turn our attention more to supplying the domestic market."

What lies under this more complex approach to production, trade and competition is a developing understanding that the current international trade model is based upon a rather coarse idea of mass production aimed at an oligopolistic — anti-choice — marketplace. This is an almost schematic approach to commerce, rather than one in which real consumers play a real role in choosing what they really wish to consume.

Surrounding all of this is a renewed disagreement over where leadership lies — with political or economic leaders. And most surprising, there is even the beginning of a debate over ownership. After a thirty-year lapse, serious economists and leaders are suddenly asking whether too much foreign ownership is an impediment to a balanced economy and a stable democracy. Those asking the questions tend to come, of all places, out of the old Globalist school.

unnecessary crises.

Two precise issues highlight the general state of confusion. The first has to do with the role of the managers in our society — that is, managers of any sort, whether they run government departments, large corporations or institutions. It seems that their increasingly shared methodology and their subtle or not so subtle confusion of private sector money with public sector service — once known as corruption, but now buried in consultancy, lobbying and contracting out systems — has turned the technocracy into an obstacle to renewed public thought, debate and action.

The obsession of the modern manager with structure and expertise and control — usually disguised as due process — is often taken to extremes. This prevents democracy and the creative marketplace from functioning. The most common outcome is short-term, highly utilitarian actions. But this applied doctrine of form over content also favours an obsession with minutiae on the one hand and large, lazy organizations on the other. Increasingly, these organizations are the directionless transnationals. You have only to look at the West's painful approach to global warming to see what this can mean. The whole debate has been bogged down by the unreality of favouring technical detail over the real world.

Critics of this managerial approach talk of the absence of the precautionary principle — a utilitarian way to limit risk by imagining the unproven possibilities that lie ahead and that may represent irreversible tendencies if left too long. But looked at from the Aristotelian principle of prudence — a far broader approach to reality — this managerial obsession with creating its own reality becomes positively reckless. Prudence means the capacity to live in reality. The technocratic approach to global warming simply ignores reality and replaces it with competing interests and an idea of proof that, because it is projected toward the past and not the future, denies the central human capacity of prudence.

On a less grandiose scale, you can see the destructive effect of managerial dominance in the gradual growth of detail as the mainstay of the employee's life. The effect of new technology has been to draw even senior managers into minutiae. People paid to think and lead now spend much of their time typing and responding to or sending an endless stream of unnecessary messages, simply because communications technology invades every second and every corner of their lives. This bureaucratization of both the leadership and the creative process makes thought seem irresponsible and clear action seem unprofessional. It provides a sensation of activity while creating a broader sense of powerlessness. This is what used to be called *being nibbled to death by ducks*.

The second key issue is perhaps the ultimate illustration of this process. Twenty-five years after it began, the Third World debt crisis continues to grow. The technocratic obsession with the imaginary reality of detail — in this case, contractual obligation — and the fear of admitting error or failure, spins the crisis on and on. George Bernard Shaw: "When a stupid man is doing something he is ashamed of, he always declares that it is his duty."

In November 2001, Anne Krueger, number two at the IMF and a neoconservative, made a courageous attempt to finally end the crisis. She announced a simple and brilliant solution. A bankruptcy procedure equivalent to that applicable to the private sector — the American Chapter 11 phenomenon — would be created for nation-states. If in dire need, they could be freed of the contractual obligations in return for reorganizing themselves. Central bankers around the world bought in. So did many economists, both reformers and conservatives. But then the counterattack began, led by those who make money out of reselling discounted unpayable debts. A year later, with the help of the technocracy, the plan had been ground down, then kicked aside.

In January 2005, yet another attempt was made. The British had an idea that involved selling revalued IMF gold. Others opposed this, fearful for the gold market. Washington called for a straight 100 percent write-off. But when more closely examined, this wonderful proposal was hedged in with plans to micromanage who would benefit, under what conditions, given what promises. By the end of the G7 finance ministers' meeting a month later, there were seven separate positions.

Nevertheless, there had been progress. For the first time ever, all seven countries had admitted that a resolution was necessary. This was probably the result of Nelson Mandela's cry before the cameras of the world and a crowd of twenty thousand on Trafalgar Square the day before the ministers of finance met in London:

> Massive poverty and obscene inequality are such terrible scourges of our times — times in which the world boasts breathtaking advances in science, technology, industry and wealth accumulation — they have to rank alongside slavery and apartheid as social evils.

> [O]vercoming poverty is not a gesture of charity. It is an act of justice. It is the protection of a fundamental human right, the right to dignity and a decent life.[21]

The leaders all know that Mandela's inspirational power can reach into their own constituencies. And so they made their promise to resolve the problem and then dispersed.

The point is this: after a quarter-century, a crisis that kills people and continues to destroy a continent simply floats on. What remains of Globalization, of global economic theory and of the reigning technocracy are all still blocked by a problem that could have been solved overnight at any time. This is perhaps the signal problem that will tell us when we have emerged from the vacuum. If the governments of the West find the clarity of mind and the courage simply to erase the debt, we will be clearly on to a new era.

24

The New Vacuum:
Is the Nation-State Back?

If the confusion in the world were limited to differences between north and south, it might be possible to say that that was the shape of the new era. But there is just as much confusion around the revival of the nation-state.

Most people are surprised by the resurgence of this theoretically old-fashioned institution inside the West. But harder for Westerners to fully understand is its blossoming elsewhere. In their imaginations the modern nation-state is a European invention of the late eighteenth century and the early nineteenth. Its formal invention is even tied to a single treaty in a particular place on a given date. The Treaty of Westphalia in 1648 ended the Thirty Years' War and officially acknowledged the existence of the United Provinces — today the Netherlands — and the Swiss Confederation. But it did this in a way that recognized what the West would come to call a nation-state. That other parts of the world have this organizational methodology at all is surely thanks to those formal and informal empires that began to spread out from the West as of the eighteenth century. And when those empires were abandoned a half-century ago, the West created international organizations like the IMF to monitor a continued evolution along the same path among non-Western countries.

What, then, is to be made of gigantic powers like China, India and Brazil emerging on the global scene as nation-state projects that seem to

have their own logic — not the Westphalian *truth*. Everywhere I hear
Westerners referring to this phenomenon as *dangerous*. Is it dangerous
because these countries escape Western logic? The example of China's
dominating in a growing number of markets, but not by price or even
competitive advantage, is frightening for Western-centred Globalists.
Brazil, solving its problems by ignoring the Western-centred idea of
global intellectual property, is equally disturbing. And, as if in a great
school of fish, these whales are accompanied by a growing number of
smaller non-Western nation-states.

Put that aside for the moment. Westerners are having enough trouble
re-editing their received wisdom to account for the revival of the classic
Westphalian nation-state inside the West. The founders of what is now
called the European Union had the willpower coming out of the last
world war to want to change political models. And they set about doing
it with great success. But there was a latent contradiction. Europe has
always had several internal frontiers. And once you cross one of those
frontiers, the historical experience, the expectations, the tensions change.

On November 2, 1959, General Charles de Gaulle, newly elected
president of France, went to Strasbourg, a city straddling one of the
frontiers that the new Europe had successfully crossed. There he gave a
prophetic speech on a subject he understood. "Oui, c'est l'Europe,
depuis l'Atlantique jusqu'à l'Oural, c'est l'Europe. C'est toute l'Europe
qui décidera du destin du monde."[1] Europe from the Atlantic to the
Urals — that was the future. He was staring through history past and
future to imagine what would happen when the Iron Curtain was raised
and Europe could look out at its natural borders. De Gaulle thought the
natural border to the east was the Urals. On the west side of those
mountains lay European Russia. On the east side, facing the opposite
way, lay Asian Russia. Between 1959 and 1989, Europe crossed a few
difficult borders, but the dominant view remained continental and
post-nation-state, because no one had yet had to face de Gaulle's reality.
The original dream of an integrated continent persisted.

Perhaps most important, through forty-four years of internal debate,
from 1945 to 1989, West Germany had solidified its continental and
deeply democratic integration into the project. As the German historian

Heinrich Winkler explained it, the Germans also had been liberated in 1945 — from a mythology that for centuries had kept them apart from the Western evolution.[2] In 1986 the philosopher Jürgen Habermas described the "'Federal Republic's unreserved acceptance of the political culture of the West' as the greatest intellectual achievement of the postwar period in West Germany."[3] Then came 1989, the collapse of the Soviet Bloc and the opening of a very different quality of frontier. Or was it a chasm? On November 10, the day after the Berlin Wall fell, the great Willy Brandt, long in retirement and one of the architects of this revolutionary change: "What belongs together, is now growing together."

But what was happening was not so easy to seize hold of. Within a few months, twenty-five new nation-states had been created. Some had had no expectation of this ever happening. Some had been struggling toward independence for centuries; since U.S. president Woodrow Wilson's promises of 1918–19, they had been waiting for their legitimate national moment. Wilson's formulas were as confusing as they were optimistic: "self determination is not a mere phrase. It is an imperative principle of action." But what was the principle? "[A] race, a territorial area or a community?" His own secretary of state thought the promise would "raise hopes that can never be realized. It will, I fear, cost thousands of lives."[4]

From 1919 to 1989 there had been some short-lived experiments and not thousands but millions of lives lost. In general, these places had been put on hold — from Poland to Ukraine, Latvia to Slovenia, Czechoslavakia to Bulgaria. They had been frustrated, martyred, cut up, pushed about. And then suddenly, overnight, it happened. In the midst of a world devoted to overriding the nation-state, tens of millions of people appeared on the international scene embracing their first — or at best, second — chance at building their own nation-state. After forty-four years of communism, they were also interested in the market. Many of them, through lack of both experience and regulations, quickly plunged into the worst of market corruption.

And if there was one thing they were not interested in, it was melting their new nation-states into continental or global systems that might weaken, as opposed to strengthen, their national authority. What is more, they did not see themselves as coming in from the margins. In de Gaulle's formula, they were in the centre of Europe. Or as the thinker Aurel Kolnai put it, they were "the real Europe; its quintessence."[5] They therefore had long meditated views on how the continent should be organized.

This attitude could be seen a few years later when in 2004 many were eager to send troops to Iraq. It was their first-ever opportunity to be independent actors on the world scene. In historic terms, *independent* meant separate from Russia, Germany and Austria, even from France. And so sending troops to Iraq was a highly public declaration of independence. They know today that they must work with Russia and Germany, but are also quick, as Vaclav Havel was in 2004, to warn of "worrying signs of authoritarianism" in Russia.[6] Poland is quick to warn Germany if there is any action that the Poles would consider slippage. In 2004, the organization representing the Germans expelled from Poland in 1945 used that country's entry into the European Union as an opportunity to claim reparations for property lost. The Polish parliament immediately checkmated this by passing a motion making far larger claims on Germany. There have already been several other incidents due to the newcomers' stretching and flexing of their muscles, while the historic powers lean over in a paternalistic way.

What makes this return of the nation-state in the heart of Europe so complicated is that you cannot leap from dictatorship and no experience of arm's-length administration, through the corruption that almost automatically follows, and on into a moderately flawed democracy, and do all of that overnight. The process was long for the West. It will be long for the Centre. And so they are caught up in dramas that many middle-class countries put behind them a half-century ago.

What we are now experiencing is not, therefore, a little blip of nationalism or a deathbed revival. This is twenty-five separate attempts at the full process. Some like Romania and Bulgaria are rushing to fulfill enough of the characteristics of a functioning democracy to be treated as full European nation-states. Others like Belarus or Tajikistan have a very long way to go. A few, like Turkmenistan, are going in the opposite direction.

For those of us who are not part of Middle Europe, it is hard to feel the depth of emotion that these twenty-five experiments provoke inside each country. The night before the ceremony marking the sixtieth anniversary of the liberation of Auschwitz-Birkenau, there was a dinner in Cracow for the visiting heads of state or government. It was dominated by the large number of those from the twenty-five newly free countries. There was a heavy snowstorm that complicated the leaders' arrivals from across the continent, and so they filtered in, one by one, as the evening wore on. Late in the evening, Viktor Yushchenko, freshly sworn in as president of Ukraine, appeared, his face black from the attempt to poison him. The whole room rose with the sort of warmth and sympathy not habitual in political circles. It was like a family dispersed by a catastrophe but now slowly coming back together, and here was one of the last lost sons to reappear. They all know Yushchenko has a hard road ahead. But you could feel an edge of revolutionary fervour. The revolution in Ukraine, with the citizenry's going into the streets and staying there until democracy prevailed, was all about nation-state strength and independence with, hopefully, a successful growth of democracy.

Whatever continental or global arrangements these countries make, they are and will be centred on the further strengthening of that independence. A few days before, Yushchenko had spoken to the people of Ukraine in Kiev's Independence Square: "Our culture will force the world to see our uniqueness." And yet, "Our future is the future of a united Europe. Our place is in the United Europe. We are not on the edge of Europe anymore. We are in the centre of Europe."

And then there is Russia itself, bereft of an empire, bereft now even of its eighteenth-century borders following the real departure of Ukraine. Russia must now look at itself in the fullest sense as the nation Russia. That has massive mythological implications. And it must do this while healing the wounds of territorial loss and absorbing the lessons of new, untried systems. All of this is being done with little sympathy from outside. Few excuses are entertained when an ex-empire is in question. All of which can only reinforce the nation-state impetus among citizens.

When in September 2004 Vladimir Putin put an end to the election process for Russia's eighty-nine regional governors and took on the direct power of recommending candidates to regional parliaments, there was criticism and anxiety in the West. Yet the general atmosphere inside Russia — including among the governors — seemed to be one of relief. They saw this as a move to reinforce the legitimacy of the nation-state. And the rule of law.

europe changes direction.

In 2004 the European Union gave membership to ten countries, including a first group of eight Central European nations from the former Soviet Bloc. The old members quickly discovered that the frontier they had crossed was more of a chasm. The Union had become a different place. The dream of Europe as a federal project seemed to have melted away overnight. The integrationist founders appeared to have lost. The new intergovernmentalist coalition appeared strong enough to reorient the project.

Countries like Britain felt they had won in their struggle to slow down Europeanization. The British chancellor of the Exchequer talked of how "the old integrationist project is fatally undermined."[7] But once the British lay aside their rhetoric, they may discover that they are more integrationist than they have realized, that their desires lie somewhere in between those of Western and Central Europe. They may even come to regret their derailing of the broader, more serious European project and the possible weakening of the Union on the international scene.

But for once the problem is as simple as it appears. Eight of the ten most recent members joined for precisely the opposite reason that the founders did. They joined to protect the independence of their nation-states. More specifically, they want long-term protection from Russia and Germany. Their second reason was simple economics. On the other hand, the last thing they would permit is a two-speed Europe with an integrated core and an intergovernmental periphery. If they are, as they say, Central Europe, they will not allow any system that puts them back on the periphery.[8]

And so Robert Cooper may have been overly optimistic when he said that "Europe, perhaps for the first time in 300 years, is no longer a zone of competing truths." The Dutch prime minister may have come closer to some truth — "It is becoming increasingly clear that such cooperation and such a feeling of solidarity are no longer obvious to many people. We seem to be finding it more and more difficult to identify our common ground, as if we have lost sight of what connects us at the deepest level."

The new members will remain different and apart from the old members for a long time.[9] Perhaps the most pessimistic view I have heard is that all those years the Central Europeans were protesting that they belonged to Europe, not the Soviet Bloc, they were actually dreaming not of Europe but of the United States.[10] Reality is gradually making itself felt; that is, you may dream as you like, but geography has its truths. Now they are in Europe and they must work out their contradictory mythology.

The entry of the ten showed the return not only of the nation-state but of basic nationalism at its least interesting. For example, how could a body as powerful as the European Union have permitted Cyprus to join without first solving the racial division of that small island? How could they have allowed the simple transfer of this sort of snake fight inside the Union?

The answer is that Cyprus is only the first in a series of fights of this sort. Already a more profound argument has begun over the possible entry of Turkey. On one side you have a continent confused by how to handle the relatively simple normalization of the presence of a mere 17 million Muslims already long established among the 450 million non-Muslim Europeans. That same continent is now processing the entry of a country of some 70 million. The point here is merely to highlight the confusion inside Europe, caused in good part by the absence of a serious cultural conversation at a continental level.

The conscious redirecting of Europe away from its integrationist project seemed to happen over a dinner on June 17, 2004, when the leaders, having come together for a summit, fought in a very unpleasant way over who should be the new European president. The outcome was the choice of José Manuel Barroso, a former Portuguese prime minister, who quickly made it clear that he believed in intergovernmental relations. He went out of his way to declare publicly that he was not one of the "naive federalists."

What any of this may mean in five or ten years is perfectly unclear. We are in a vacuum. The strong structures of Europe may simply go on integrating the continent. Or the nationalist tendencies may strengthen. Or the continent may head to some new view of itself, resembling the old medieval view: a view of multiple interpenetrating borders within a single continent; layered, built around diversity.

a confused empire.

Europe's confusion is matched by that of the United States. It is now received wisdom in governmental circles in Washington to talk of empire. But the purpose of their empire is remarkably unclear. Or rather, its tactics are clear, its strategy unclear.

For example, by the opening of the new century there were some 725 U.S. military installations abroad.[11] What are they for? To be so broadly present when your armed forces represent half the military in the world seems at first glance an unambiguous statement. But spread everywhere around the globe in a terrestrial version of the old British Empire naval presence puts you in a static position, on the defensive — a highly visible target without an obvious purpose. The old British military tactics were tied to colonies, a light, flexible strike capacity often called gunboat diplomacy, and a clear international industrial and trade policy. The colonies produced raw material for British industry. The same is not so obvious for the United States because there is a deep theoretical confusion between that country's alliance with transnationals, which may or may not be serving American interests, and the need to make the internal American economy function.

There is an illusion now that Washington's military presence around the world is somehow related to September 11. But it existed long before the attack. And the dozen years between the fall of the Iron Curtain and September 11 were particularly violent on the international stage. So the tactics were tried and found wanting — yet they persist.

Parallel to this was the very odd decision of the United States to devalue its dollar in 2004. The technocrats of monetary policy can't bring themselves to put it so baldly, but everyone else can. *The*

Economist says that if the fall were to continue it could "amount to the biggest default in history."[12] Nothing like this has been seen since 1971, when Nixon devalued for equivalent reasons: removing the value of foreign debt, making exports cheaper and imports more expensive. The Europeans and others immediately began complaining that they should not be carrying the U.S. deficit through the foreign exchange market.[13]

Both the military positioning and the devaluation are defensive. The military interventions about which so much is said have the disadvantage of being particular, swamped in a general situation. At the same time, the world seems to be slipping into national and regional groups. The empire is ill-suited to deal with either. In the American writer Michael Lind's formula: "A new world order is indeed emerging — but its architecture is being drafted in Asia and Europe at meetings to which Americans have not been invited." Put another way, an empire is never international. It is always an extension of the nationalism of the core. Washington's far-flung system is well suited to being influential everywhere, but it is almost powerless to manage regional situations on a longer term, institutionalized basis.

a maze of factors.

These specific Western situations draw us away from a multitude of social and technological confusions that have taken on major proportions over the same period. They have no particular shape and we cannot know their impact. Some would have happened with or without Globalization, some are a product of it, all have an effect on it by their simple existence.

For example, the African borders drawn to suit the European empires a century to a century and a half ago seem increasingly to get in the way. As if out of nowhere, Kenya, Tanzania, Uganda, Rwanda and Burundi are in serious talks about folding their countries together. There you have three from the British Empire, two from the French, trying to escape the political and cultural prism — or is it prison? — imposed upon them. They are tired of the artificial divisions that contribute to their dysfunctional situation. This is the sort of restructuring that could radically change the African situation.

What is driving them, apart from crisis? Perhaps the international vacuum provides enough confusion and obscurity for them to get past the perpetual Western projections of perfect solutions. Once past, they may rediscover historic habits that worked for them in the past. Perhaps they are responding in part to the arguments coming out of China and India and Brazil, which offer a more sensible approach for developing economies by setting the contextual, humanist idea of Quality of Life against the more linear and abstract approach of GDP measurements.

But there are other, broader factors at work.

Look at the religious changes on the African continent. In a hundred years the Pentecostal, charismatic, evangelical and other related movements have gone from zero to a half billion believing members. Their growth is also exponential, driven on probably by the continent's accumulating problems. Suddenly the religion of Globalization is caught up with a seriously revived belief system involving older, more experienced gods. Which is most likely to dominate?

Look at the continuing urbanization trend around the world. In fifty years the twenty largest cities have gone from 50 million people to 200 million. In some cases the change is far more dramatic: Istanbul from 1 million to 12 million; Mumbai 1.5 million to 12.5 million; São Paulo 1.3 million to 10 million. Soon 60 percent of the world's population will be urban.

The implications could not be less apparent. They are now playing themselves out in every aspect of our lives — everything from mass production to the continued growth of the already massive slums in the developing world. Security controls, a probable strengthening of false populism, more growth of industrialized agriculture with serious implications for the environment — any one of these can shape our civilizations as powerfully as an economic theory.

Thirty years into an ideology of deregulation, the move to reregulation grows stronger every day. The leading conservative economist Samuel Brittan writes of the "danger [of] the upward creep of regulation."

"[P]rofessional advice on how to cope with the regulators could well be the most rapidly growing industry."[14]

In the evolution of technology, there are far more mysteries than answers. Open-source computer systems manufacturers are in the early stages of a battle against the monopolistic Microsoft. The outcome will have real implications for governmental powers and personal freedoms. Governments here and there are beginning to make choices against the closed system. Will they persist or lose courage?

There are early suggestions that a sort of technological sales tax — an automatic tax on each digital *bit* of information that moves — could radically change governments' ability to raise funds. But it would also suggest increased nation-state powers to administer technology and its owners. After all, the owners today are using international freedom both to be free and to create monopolies — that is, dictatorships that, although commercially driven, have serious political implications.

The extent of the societal confusion surrounding all of us can be seen in the political movements that have recently come to power with the express purpose of cutting back on government's influence over human lives. Many of them are now leading a charge for greater surveillance of citizens than has ever been seen before: from fingerprinting anyone who crosses a border to overriding individual legal rights.

Apparently panicked by terrorism, governments are looking to high technology for new, invasive monitoring powers. The banal security cameras, which now seem to exist everywhere in cities, are gradually evolving into cameras with computer programs that can theoretically interpret human movement as normal or abnormal. This *aberrant-pattern recognition system* is already in use outside some banks, particularly in Britain, which is the leader in the field. Bank robbers apparently have patterns of behaviour just before they strike. Security experts say that terrorists do, too. And so the millions of cameras on streets throughout most of the Western democracies could rapidly be adapted to this idea of aberrant-pattern recognition. On the other hand, the idea that we all act normally unless we are bank robbers or terrorists is a profoundly controlling idea of individualism and society. It is a reminder of the way in which societies were once dominated by a monolithic religious code.

Do lovers betray aberrant behaviour when they meet? What about someone attempting to avoid a person she doesn't like? Or an employee seeking a moment away from his tasks? A discreet snooze on the job? A hidden smoke? A private expression of anger or dissatisfaction?

This example may at first glance seem marginal when compared with the enlargement of Europe or the role of transnationals. But societies do not evolve in a linear manner. And civilizations stumbling through a vacuum are often reshaped by the most unexpected of forces. The disappearance of public privacy is a profound change for Western society.

Who in the second half of the nineteenth century, amid the roar of industrial and political change, would have picked false populism and jingoism as forces that would help drag Western civilization into the suicidal bloodbath of the European trenches? Look today at an apparently minor phenomenon — the evolution of video games — and you will see how far they have gone beyond mere distraction. Suddenly, for better and for worse, they have become a training mechanism for everything from cooking to assassination. Here is a wonderful tool for reviving minority languages. But the same method is a highly effective and hard-to-control tool for the revival of nationalism — jingoism — at its worst. At almost no cost, these games can reach hundreds of thousands of people, particularly the young, carrying messages that effortlessly blend fantasy with the cheapest sort of nationalist strutting.

The point is that the same facile tool that has a simple utilitarian role, may become a wonderful support for weaker cultures seeking some nationalist expression or may be the most effective tool yet seen for a populist manipulation of propaganda.

nationalism.

By the end of the twentieth century, nationalism and the nation-states were stronger than they had been when Globalization began. This remains an overriding element as we stumble about in our vacuum. Belief in global economic truths has shrunk away. There are growing signs of international economic disorder. Admiration for the designated leaders of the Globalist project has evaporated. The NGOs and their leaders remain largely stuck on the defensive because they tend to imagine themselves as specialists and as opponents of those who hold power.

As if to fill the vacuum created by these failures, nationalism has reappeared. That is the way history moves. It is neither kind nor unkind. Merely present. And there being no such thing as a prolonged vacuum, all vacuums are eventually filled. In this case, nationalism of both the best and the worst sort has made a remarkable recovery.

Few people saw it coming because the fatal error had been made of sweeping nationalism behind us. Or rather, we assumed that we had swept it behind us. West Germany, for obvious reasons, had been in the vanguard of those declaring the state — their state — to be *post-national*. And Germany, after all, was at the core of the European integrist project.[15] In 1988 one of its leading politicians, Oskar Lafontaine, wrote about "Moving beyond the National State." That was just three years before Yugoslavia exploded into ethnic nationalist strife and Germany, along with other theoretically post-national democracies, tried to intervene by backing one particular ethnic group against the others. How was it that sophisticated post-national states reacted to an initially minor European crisis by reaching into their 1914 memory bank? To be precise, each backed the same racial groups it had backed during the wars of the twentieth century.

A few years later, after his experience as chief administrator of a Kosovo still racially divided, Bernard Kouchner reminded us that nationalism — even of the worst sort — was an unsurprising reaction to disastrous circumstances. "The first thing a poor population, suffering from years and years under oppression, is waiting for is security. Security and security. The second is more important than the first, but it comes after. This is dignity."[16] How do they get security and dignity? By belonging to a group. A national group.

Yugoslavia was an extreme case of nationalism. But there are signs everywhere of its return. A quarter of English youth, when asked, say they think of themselves as English, not British.[17] This is double the percentage among their teachers. In Germany, public discussions on the question of *place* are now inhabited by the concept of *Leitkultur* — the guiding sense we must find in the dominant culture. Put another way, *Leitkultur* is the dominant culture's set of values. In the United States, the eminently sensible philosopher Richard Rorty as early as 1998 was criticizing the American left for thinking "of national pride as appropriate only for chauvinists." "They begin to think of themselves as a saving remnant — as the happy few who have the insight to see through nationalist rhetoric to the ghastly reality of contemporary America. But this insight does not move them to formulate a legislative program, to join a political movement, or to share in a national hope."[18]

Rorty's point has been laid out carefully by the historian Liah Greenfeld in a rare contemporary examination of nationalism in its fullest sense. She reminds us that its meaning has changed over time, but that it can still mean the best in our societies or the worst: "Nationalism was the form in which democracy appeared in the world ... The national principle was collectivistic."[19] Yet in its ethnic form, it was also the driving force of war and racial murder.

You could say that all nationalism is about belonging, about place and about imagining the *other*. It can take a positive, civic form, one in which belonging brings the obligation to reach out and to imagine the *other* in an inclusive, multiple way. It can also take a negative form, above all ethnic, dedicated to belonging as an expression of privilege and exclusion.

The positive form of nationalism is tied to self-confidence and openness and to a concept of the public good. Negative nationalism is dependent on fear and anger and a desperate conviction that one nation's rights exist by comparison with those of another nation, as if in a competition that produces winners and losers.

From 1995 on, it was easy to follow the rise of these two nationalisms as the most obvious growing force within the vacuum provoked by the decline of Globalization. Does that mean we are entering into a new nationalist era during which the two forms — positive and negative — must once again fight it out? The answer is, we don't yet know. What we do know is that the forces most likely to form that new era seem to be visible and still malleable enough to be shaped.

25

Negative Nationalism

> We don't want to fight
> But, by Jingo, if we do,
> We've got the ships,
> We've got the men,
> We've got the money, too.

— "MACDERMOTT'S WAR SONG," SUNG AT THE LONDON PAVILION, 1878

Negative nationalism reached a hillock of intellectual clarity in 1878 during yet another one of those Russian-Turkish crises that London tried to mediate to its own benefit. This popular music-hall song fixed the concept of *jingoism* as the expression of a certain nationalist assertion — brash, self-interested, indifferent to or ignorant of the interests of others, politically helpful at home and often, at some unconscious level, an expression of fear. In other countries there were other words. The United States had its *spread-eagleism* — a ten-thousand-mile wingspan of influence from Manila to Puerto Rico.

Insecurity, poverty, ambition are three of the roots of this destructive nationalism. Its expression is often dependent on ethnic loyalty, an appropriation of God to one's side, a certain pride in ignorance, and a conviction that you have been permanently wounded — that is, an active mythology of having been irreparably wronged. On key subjects, ignorance is often encouraged. Sometimes this is more a pretence than a reality. Such wilful ignorance allows highly sophisticated societies to remain fixated on specific wounds. At its worst this can become psychotic cynicism. Giambattista Vico, the great Italian philosopher, was denouncing this in the eighteenth century just before the modern nationalist movement got off the ground: "[W]here ever the human mind is lost in ignorance man makes himself the measure of all things.... [R]umor grows in its course... [T]he unknown is always magnified.... [W]henever men can form no idea of distant and unknown things, they judge them by what is familiar and at hand."[1]

What is closest at hand will most likely be family or race. Speaker after speaker at the 2004 Republican Convention in the United States invoked the family because, they said, family comes first and is the measure of a society. Of course, family is central to human life and to our emotional life in all its complexity. But family as the measure or structure of society is a mafia argument or an argument of the extreme right, for whom there are only two possible choices: either the sacred family or the sacred nation. In either case, loyalty is measured according to how successfully it represents a closed situation. Thus the democratic and humanist ideas of civilization, society and community, which are all dependent on our ability to imagine the *other* — the one who is not close — are expelled to the margins.

Such nationalism of proximity is dependent on fear. The psycho-analyst Erich Fromm once put its existence down to an incapacity to recover from the loss of our pre-modern social structures. And so we embraced "a new idolatry of blood and soil."[2] This is nationalism as a culture of belonging, rather than nationalism as a civilization of culture. Thus, ignorance becomes a protection from the fear within us. Ignorance, often presented with the charm of innocence, becomes a state of sanctity. Erasmus warned against this almost before it existed: "lack of culture is not holiness, nor cleverness impiety." And of course, this is nationalism in which "*nationality* becomes a synonym of *ethnicity*." Finally it is nationalism as belief, as religion.

After 1945 such misuse of the phenomenon was supposed to wither away in the absence of a vine. Over the next quarter-century there was a gradual move toward a civic model of nationalism. At least inside the democracies, nationalism as an expression of the public good grew and left the negative sort to superficial expressions of enthusiasm and emotion. Sports, public celebrations, more innocent effusions of belonging replaced what might have been negative. Then came the Globalist period, and the concept of nationalism was swept right out of sight. To mention it in Canada was to be simplistic, protectionist and out of step with the inevitable times. In Europe it belonged to an unhappy past. What mattered was a specialist concentration on the economic, administrative and political reorganization of Europe. For sixty years there was literally no discussion of European culture, of citizenship, of how this large variety of Europeans was actually going to live together. In the United States, while the nationalism was palpable, the discourse was economic.

Then, as if from nowhere, it began to re-emerge. Perhaps because there had been such denial of the positive possibilities of nationalism — such a denial of society as a humanist project — what now came out into the light was largely negative. It was closely linked to the old demons of fear, ethnicity, cultural alienation and misappropriated religion. Looking at this from the American perspective, Richard Rorty believes that it is the "distrust of humanism, with its retreat from practice to theory [that produces] the sort of failure of nerve which leads people to abandon secularism for a belief in sin[.]"[3] Whether his analysis is right or wrong, can be generalized or not, he is certainly right about sin. The rising negative nationalism has been filled with all the old shibboleths of belief, loyalty, fear and guilt.

What are the signs? In 1994 a coalition of three Italian parties, each one representing a facet of old-style negative nationalism, almost captured power. The leader of one of the parties, Gianfranco Fini, from the ex-fascists, gave a magazine interview calling Mussolini "the greatest statesman of the century."[4] Since then the coalition has come to power and Signor Fini has worked hard to distance himself from his fascist past. He has been deputy prime minister, then foreign minister and, many feel, will soon be prime minister. If this happens, the general atmosphere in Europe has so shifted that his arrival in power will be treated there and around the world as a normal event.

Over the same period Jörg Haider, who has softened none of his opinions on immigrants and on the nature of race in Austria, gained enough power to put his party into a coalition government, then lost his popularity, then in 2004 began climbing back up again. There are similar patterns in the most unlikely of places, where people have nothing to fear — in Norway, Switzerland, Denmark, the Czech Republic. In France, the one openly racist party has almost a quarter of the population in agreement with its ideas.[5] Even in Northern Ireland, where every effort has been made to soften the situation, the extremists on both sides keep winning enough votes to block long-term progress.

In Germany there are over a thousand anti-Semitic attacks and incidents each year. Chancellor Gerhardt Schröder used the sixtieth anniversary in 2005 of the liberation of Auschwitz-Birkenau to try to wake people up to the dangers and to speak about the continuing life of anti-Semitism: "It is up to all of us, together, to politically confront the neo-Nazis and the old Nazis."[6] A few weeks before, the neo-Nazi party had won seats in the assembly of Saxony.

None of this is to say that Nazism or fascism is on the edge of gaining power in the West. Far from it. But the societal atmosphere surrounding their arguments has radically changed. And it has changed on a broad front regarding people who aren't of the same colour or religion. Many mainstream political parties have adjusted their policies to occupy, for example, the anti-immigrant political space of the negative nationalist parties. The chair of the World Jewish Congress, Israel Singer, chose the same Auschwitz-Birkenau liberation anniversary to link our need to remember the Holocaust with "Rwanda's recent past, Sudan's present and Nigeria's future. Europe's governments, religions and institutions must summon the will to confront history and use it to protect the future."[7] Kjell Bondevik, the Norwegian prime minister: "I am very worried by the current tendency toward polarization and extremism. This is linked with the problem of exclusion, and often carries with it elements of scapegoat thinking."

A recent U.S. State Department report estimates that the number of skinheads spread around the West grew from a very small number in 1992 to at least fifty thousand in 2004. In Russia, extreme nationalist parties hold almost a quarter of the votes. Their positions now have mainstream respectability. When asked, over half the Russians agree with the idea of "Russia for Russians" and almost half think Jews have too much influence and the movement of people from the Caucasus should be limited.[8]

If you look around the world, there is the same slippage almost everywhere: a more nationalist government in South Korea; a classic nationalist governor of Tokyo; the rise of the UK Independence Party, winning 16 percent of the votes in the 2004 European elections. In China, the official interpretation of history is that "the Chinese people must never again be humiliated by foreign aggressors. Only a great and strong nation will guarantee the survival of the Chinese race." The writer Ian Buruma says this patriotism is "based on a sense of collective victimhood" and "has come to replace Marxism-Leninism and Mao Zedong Thought as the official ideology of the People's Republic of China."[9] In India, there is an unbroken nationalist line from 1947 to today, but the rise of the BJP, even if it is now in opposition, is a sign of growing negative nationalism. In Latin America, most studies seem to show that about half the population feel liberal democracy — the handmaiden of Globalization — has been such a failure that they would prefer authoritarian rule.[10]

As for the United States, the general atmosphere seems to be, in historian Simon Schama's phrase, a "Manichean struggle between good and evil, freedom and terror." Why would such a complex and rich society fall into the simplicities of a Manichean view? Rorty's guess is that the Globalization of the labour market without the protections of a welfare state leaves Americans "much more vulnerable to right-wing populism than are most European countries."[11]

In any case, the Manichean view is the way in which almost every senior American official presents her view of the world. Francis Fukuyama, one of the reliable road signs for received wisdom in Washington, rushed a pamphlet into print in 2004 to announce the need for a reversal of directions.[12] He admitted up front that his position might surprise: "The idea that state-building, as opposed to limiting or cutting back the state, should be at the top of our agenda may strike some people as perverse." But his message is perfectly logical if you have a Manichean mindset. Nation-states should be strengthened in order to deal with "conflict-ridden or war-torn societies," "to eliminate spawning grounds for terrorism," "out of a hope that poor countries will have a chance to develop economically." "What only states and states alone are able to do is aggregate and purposefully deploy legitimate power. This power is necessary to enforce a rule of law domestically, and it is necessary to preserve world order internationally." This intervention coincides neatly with Milton Friedman's recent admission that he regretted advising countries released from the Soviet Bloc to "privatise, privatise, privatise." "I was wrong. It turns out that the rule of law is probably more basic than privatization."

The reign of the Globalist idea being over, the dominant political message coming from those who once argued for it is that things have changed. Today's military and political crisis requires the re-establishment of the authority aspect of the nation-state. But these people who once argued for economic determinism over the conscious will of a nation-state remain silent, or continue to be negative on the positive role of the nation-state in changing the conditions that might have created the crisis in the first place. They don't mention the concept of the public good. Again, Fukuyama is a road sign for their attempt to create a new received wisdom. And what he is calling for is an energetic re-establishment of that half of nationalism that quickly becomes negative if it is not accompanied by the societal half with its concentration on the public good, justice and inclusion.

Meanwhile, there are parts of the world in which Islam is being continuously radicalized. But in the rest of the complex Islamic civilizations — the vast majority of the whole — Muslims are subjected on a daily basis to persistent ignorance from most of the West. Whenever, in a university, I come across a broad humanist program, I ask the professors what they teach about Islam or, indeed, anything outside the Greek-Roman-Judeo Christian-Western canon. The answer is almost always nothing. Among a narrow slice of specialists, there has been some reaction to this crisis of understanding. In the broader world of learning, I can detect almost no move to try to understand what this other religion might be, what these other cultures are.

What is not taught tells us a great deal about how quickly negative nationalism has risen. There are a variety of other small signs, most of them limited to false populism, a handmaiden of negative nationalism. For example, throughout the West, the organized structures of dissent remain in crisis, although there is a great deal of dissent. The unions are heavy and inflexible; the NGOs remain on the defensive. Yet there is growing participation in and seeming respect for radio talk shows, PR campaigns, polling, all of which are short term, based on reaction, highly emotional and user-friendly for anyone seeking to get things off her chest anonymously.

The pattern of public funding throughout the democracies is related to this. The effective level of corporate taxes keeps falling. They are structured to permit well-organized companies to minimize what they pay, if they pay at all. The theory is that the corporations will invest their tax savings and so provoke a rise in societal economic growth. So far this has worked nowhere. In terms of public funding, their missing contributions have to be replaced by a wide variety of stealth taxes, from sales taxes to state-run gambling. The growing absence of an openness about taxes has created an alienation of citizens from their governmental structures. And the reality of democratic governments spending tens of millions of dollars and euros and pounds on slick advertising to get citizens from the bottom end of the income stream to pay taxes by gambling is particularly demeaning for both governed and governor.

This is all the more demeaning for the governing elites when incomes in the bottom half of our societies have been blocked for some time or are shrinking. Average American wages in 1999 were 10 percent lower than in 1973. The situation is similar, although not so extreme, in most OECD countries. This is all part of the false populist conundrum that contributes to negative nationalism.

One of the least explored areas is that of the effect of an overempha-sis on consumerism in a solid democracy. It was the fascists who believed that a society addicted to consumerism was susceptible to their taking power. They thought the same about societies that had fallen into the hands of what we call transnationals. Mussolini: "When does a capitalis-tic business cease to be an economic phenomenon? When its size trans-forms it into a social phenomenon."[13]

One other tiny observation: Erasmus was the great force of humanism in the last years before the Reformation. In 2004 a popular edition of his letters was reissued in Holland, where there are eleven thousand libraries. Ten ordered the book. The general atmosphere is one of false populism, which in turn feeds into negative nationalism.

Most important, in this confused atmosphere with negative nationalism's growing, we have seen the return of the idea of race as a quality of belong-ing. It is as if the world were dividing into two groups, not necessarily organized geographically. There are those who are more colour-blind and religion-blind than any modern society has ever been. There are countries or whole slices of countries that are now able to act as if the division of races did not exist. And in those countries there are schools where this positive confusion is allowed to become a creative human force.

But there is another trend underway — one in which the Northern League, which does govern, "still believe[s] in a mythical *white* Italy called La Padania, where immigration would be forbidden."[14] One of the most open of countries, Denmark, has a law preventing citizens under twenty-four from marrying a foreigner and living in the country. European countries that had long ago separated religion from their poli-tics are suddenly describing European culture as fundamentally a child of Greece, Rome and Christianity. I have mentioned the difficulty they are having imagining how to make 17 million Muslims into real Europeans, even though they have been there for a long time — often several generations — and represent a small percentage of the population of 450 million. The solutions they do manage to produce — such as the gradual softening of immigration laws — come a particle at a time, grudgingly. There is no enthusiastic embracing of inclusive citizenship, which is the only way to make an inclusive idea of belonging work.

The problem does not lie in the details. Bit by bit the racial obstacles in democracies can be worked out. The problem lies in the return of the myth of race and racial division. Louise Arbour, after her experiences prosecuting the war criminals of the former Yugoslavia at the International Criminal Court, warned of "the numerous myths and legends, undeniable because unverifiable … these myths that feed the extremist discourse that leads not only to war, but to genocide, extermination, murder, rape, torture, enslavement, deportation and persecution on ethnic, racial or religious grounds."[15] We tell ourselves that all of that is behind us. But Yugoslavia was just yesterday. The Danish law is today, as is Gianfranco Fini, as are the French intellectuals who see an Islamic girl wearing a headscarf and call it a veil, as is the constant profiling of Muslims in a frightened United States, as is the reappearance of torture, largely based on racial fear, as are those madrasas that confuse Islam with racial difference, as is the chipping-away at civil rights in the democracies that first wrote down many of those rights as law. Just below the surface of that chipping-away are the fears that over much of modern time have risen out of an obsession with the idea that human difference is a negative.

Robert Cooper quite rightly points out that "today the primacy of the domestic sphere is evident in almost all countries. What keeps governments in power is politics at home, not foreign relations."[16] That the domestic prevails over the global tells you to what extent we have left the Globalist ideology behind us and are now coming around a blind corner in the vacuum. Shapes are emerging in the obscurity. But the point is very precise. Why would the domestic prevail over the international unless citizens feel the Globalist experiment had not so much failed as failed them?

There is nothing intrinsically negative about the dominance of domestic affairs. But negative nationalism is one of the very real, nonexclusive outcomes.

How serious is that negative?

Anyone in the West in any position of authority need only reach back into the 1990s in such places as Rwanda and to little more than yesterday in the Congo to find that millions died in two countries with hardly a peep from Western civilization. As General Dallaire, the UN commander in Rwanda, has pointed out, it is hard to find a cause for this silence, except race.

If any confirmation were needed, we need only go back to Huntington's 1996 analysis of the world as a clash of civilizations. In large numbers, the disciples of Globalization read his book and raised their voices in agreement with his argument that societies were driven and held together by shared cultures, not economies. They now understood what was happening around them, why things were not working out as expected. As for the specific case of the United States, its survival was dependent upon "Americans reaffirming their Western identity."[17] The broad welcome this argument received throughout the West revealed how confused and obscure the vacuum is. But it also told us how people have become frightened in the growing disorder of the Globalist era, how uncomfortable they are with the broad global sweeps of inevitability. After all, only a few years ago economic inevitability was on every tongue. Abruptly, the same people or their friends are insisting that exclusive culture is the key.

Father Andrea Riccardi of the Sant'Egidio movement, someone who shows no signs of fear, simply noted that Huntington, in his dividing up of cultures into exclusive groups that should hang out together, hadn't bothered to assign Africa a civilization. Suddenly you realize how crudely racial his theoretically sophisticated argument is. The Aga Khan wasted even less time: "The clash, if there is such a broad civilizational collision, *is not of cultures but of ignorance.*"[18] In this case, it cannot be plain ignorance and must therefore either be wilful or the product of fear.

The least expected and most obvious manifestation of negative nationalism has been God's willingness to make regular appearances on the side of various participants in these new civilizational clashes. This return of the deity surely cannot have been intended by the believers in Globalism.

Whether intended or not, God is clearly back in his old public, but non-religious, role, as a political sidekick, ready to justify whatever is required.

His fading participation — bored perhaps — in wars that drag on, such as in Northern Ireland, has been succeeded by star appearances in massacres all over Africa. He has been wandering the Afghan mountains with Taliban and Al Qaeda guerrillas. He has broken down temples and led riots in India. He has supported anti-immigrant campaigns in Europe. In his spare time, he inspires the rhetoric of those who want more of the death penalty, and more virgin brides, more flags of specific colours flown. He accompanies American presidents, and for that matter most American elected representatives, on all public appearances. In the 2003 State of the Union speech, there were twenty-two religious references.

This is very much in the style of the times. A series of novels with God as the active hero — the *Left Behind* series — is now the best-selling American fiction of all time: twelve volumes, fifty-eight million copies.[19] Almost more important than God in the books is Satan, who can be recognized because he speaks more than one language, is noticeably urbane and wants to unite the world. To be perfectly clear: the anti-nationalist position is presented as satanic.

As a perfect illustration of the Manichean model, both the United States and its worst enemies feel they have direct access to the divine. That is the context in which to understand the statement in 2004 by then attorney general of the United States, John Ashcroft, that his country had been spared a second attack since September 11, 2001, because the government had been assisting "the hand of Providence." There was a competitive air to his claim.[20] The point is that in most of the world the political God is back — in Africa, in South America, in South Asia.

It must also be said that in many places, God takes on a very different voice. This is a voice that can be heard via people organizing slums in Bangkok or Nairobi. These people are often the driving forces behind hospitals and schools. They speak for the God who never went away —

the force of love working for the common good, quite a different divinity from the one leading armies in the name of political inevitabilities.

There is nothing new about the political God now so actively supporting the nationalist cause. He has been active throughout the post-Napoleonic period. In the first half of the nineteenth century, the Russian czar Alexander I was in direct contact with him and received instructions to shut down most political and social reforms in favour of clear monarchical authority. God convinced him to act as he did because his enemies were driven "by the genius evil."[21]

Some kings heard a very different voice. In 1599 Henri IV of France signed the Edict of Nantes to try to deal with the Catholic-Protestant divide. He wanted "to remove the cause of evil and of the troubles that can appear because the religious slope is always the slipperiest and can penetrate all the others." The purpose of the Edict was to remove religion, and God with it, from the political debate. When the Edict was revoked eighty-six years later, God reappeared in politics and created uncertainty of a destructive sort. It seems that when it comes to politics, divine contributions tend to be negative.

26

The Normalization of Irregular Warfare

Between negative nationalism and positive nationalism lies the eternal possibility of war. Its presence tells us a great deal about how any ideology is doing and where it might be headed. Conflict is one of the ultimate measures for the state of any system.

The questions we might ask ourselves today are surprisingly simple. Are we really at war? If so, have we correctly identified the nature of the conflict? What is the purpose of the war?

The answers should tell us whether the war would have happened anyway, is a product of Globalization's failure or of the confusion during the prolonged vacuum or both. Finally, if we can answer these questions, we should begin to understand how best to deal with the conflict so that we don't simply generate more violence.

After all, our histories are full of accidental wars fought in an inappropriate manner or brutal victories that confirm the prejudices and complaints of the losers. In both cases the outcome of peace is more bitterness and conflict.

These days people in the West rarely know whether they are at war, because their idea of what serious conflict looks like has scarcely moved since 1945. Conflict, on the other hand, has been evolving since the early days of the Western empires. If you step back, you can see that the importance today of irregular warfare is not an accident. The whole evolution of conflict over two centuries has been moving toward today's confusion. On the most visible level, large formal armies have nevertheless gone on clashing until their question of power is resolved. But even within those forces, the winner is usually the one that acted in a flexible, sometimes irregular, manner.

Formal armies aside, there has been a very real expansion in the role of irregular warfare itself. As the big armies become ever more invincible in open combat, because of their remarkable equipment, so those who are smaller or too small or too poor to have the same equipment disappear into the shadows in order to strike out in an irregular, unexpected manner. This tells you that modern war is not about two roughly equal nation-states clashing. Nor is it about big states defeating small states in the field. It is about fundamentally weak forces — whether part of a nation-state or not — learning how to fight the strong. This may well involve ignoring serious ethical issues, but the history of warfare is filled with formal armies doing the same thing. The point is that unethical behaviour is not proper to any particular form of warfare. To approach irregular warfare as if it were unethical is to deny yourself the ability to deal with it.

Most of the 40 million war deaths since 1945, including the 22 million since 1970, died not in formal battle but in irregular warfare or as a result of it.

From the 1960s on, one particular aspect of irregular warfare — terrorism — began to bloom throughout the West. Over 800 people have already died in Spain as a result of Basque terrorists. The myth of the Baader-Meinhof Gang in Germany still divides the country. Several thousand have died in Ireland. In 1978 alone there were 2498 terrorist attacks in Italy. Oklahoma City in 1995: 165 dead, 850 wounded. From 1968 to 2000 there were 14,000 terrorist attacks in the world, leading to 10,000 dead. In the United States from 1980 to 1999, there were 457 terrorist attacks, mainly by Americans on Americans.

These are all very low numbers, leaving out areas with no counting or reporting systems.

And all of this could be traced in a direct line from the early anarchist attacks of the nineteenth century. The year 1881 marked their first real success, modern-style, when Czar Alexander II was assassinated.

Are we at war? There are a good five hundred terrorist attacks every year and have been for decades. And terrorism is only a small branch of irregular warfare, which includes guerrilla warfare, asymmetric warfare, insurgency, counterinsurgency, espionage, resistance forces, wars of liberation, jungle warfare, underground forces, special forces. All of this combined, plus the occasional traditional military clash of two formal armies, produces the very vague statistic of two thousand war-related dead per day.

So, yes, we are at war, but this does not mean there is a particular enemy. According to the British foreign minister Jack Straw, only 10 of 120 wars in the 1990s were between states.[1] So far I've given Western examples of these conflicts, but the same phenomenon exists in Nepal, Indonesia, Sri Lanka, India, Mexico, a good part of Latin America, Chechnya and so on. Some are Islamic, but by no means do they represent the dominant group. And even among the conflicts involving Muslims, there are myriad causes.

They do not form a pattern, except perhaps that the tendency is a war of outsiders versus insiders. That doesn't mean all the outsiders are suffering or virtuous. Some of them are monsters and their causes monstrous. Others are much put upon minorities. Irregular warfare, they feel, is their only possible public mechanism. Others still are somewhere in-between. In some cases the cause is good, but the leaders are exploitative.

What binds all of this together? The methodology, perhaps. Outside of the West, you could say that the pattern is a spreading reaction to established power. What power? Probably a prolongation of Western interests, reformulated after the collapse of their empires into abstract theories of administration, development and economics. The pattern of power in that case is the West's ability to maintain its influence by projecting a way of life and the full methodology needed to support it.

In any case, the greatest surprise is the difficulty Western military institutions are having adjusting to this new but obvious normalization of the irregular. They insist on using all of their machinery to rush across countries, defeating enemies who can't even put a fighter airplane in the sky. And once the easy war is over, the local irregular forces appear in a shadowy manner and the real war — the irregular war — begins.

General Michael Rose, who commanded Britain's SAS before leading the UN forces in Bosnia, put the situation this way: "The Clausewitzian approach to war that underpins U.S. and British military strategy urgently needs to be replaced by that of counterrevolutionary warfare."[2] Depressingly enough, that is just what the French general Gambiez said a half-century before about the British during the Boer War in South Africa: "The Boers, not having read Clausewitz, tried all the indirect methods." And the British, having read Clausewitz, lost most of the war. Yet the purpose of this type of war was clear enough then and is perfectly clear now. It is to so destabilize your enemy that they do foolish things and thus make more enemies and thus themselves further destabilize their own regime. Mahathir Mohamad made fun of how amateurishly the West fell into this trap:

> We now live in fear, every one of us. We fear the terrorists and the terrorists, their supporters or alleged supporters fear us. We fear flying. We fear traveling to certain countries, we fear nightclubs, we fear letters, parcels and cargo containers, we fear white powder, shoes, Muslims, penknives, metal cutlery, etc. etc. They, the other side, fear sanctions, starvation, shortage of medicine. They fear military invasion, being bombed and rocketed, being captured and detained.[3]

The point is the inability of the industrialized democracies to imagine this other kind of war, one that is not regular. For years various Western governments would declare a war on drugs. None of these campaigns had any effect, because drug trafficking is based on the same strategic principles as irregular warfare. There is no real structure to attack. You may spend a year discovering how to uncover and destroy a trafficker's cell. It can be rebuilt in a day. Now, in place of drugs, Western governments declare wars on terrorism. The terrorists are thrilled. That is exactly what they want — to draw large, structured, laden-down organizations into treating them as if they were just as important and just as slow.

In other words, the purpose of such wars is hard to keep track of. Think of the British war against the Mahdi, which began with London's desire to remove regimes in Egypt and the Sudan in 1874. This in turn produced a messianic guerrilla leader — the Mahdi. He led a successful uprising in 1884 and took Khartoum the next year, killing the famous English general, Gordon, an early media star. Much as many wanted to, the British felt they couldn't give up. Their prestige was on the line. And they didn't like the Mahdi's religious fanaticism. The whole business dragged on until 1898 and the Battle of Omdurman, which included the famous cavalry charge in which the young Winston Churchill took part. The result was a few British casualties and a massacre of the other side. It had taken seventeen years to get to this concluding point, but in a day it was all over, just as the rivalry with Saddam Hussein had gone on for years and then, with almost no real opposing army, it was all over.

Except it was not over. In the Sudan the outcome was the opposite of general expectations. Omdurman marked not the end but the beginning of modern Arab and Islamic nationalism: the dream of Islamic nations not to be dependent on Western nations. It also set the pattern for modern Western democracies finding themselves on the wrong side of Islam. Success in this sort of conflict can easily be the same thing as failure.

The Crimean War of the 1850s is another example. It is often presented as a tragicomedy, what with its peculiar military commanders and the Charge of the Light Brigade. But the central point was tied to the four-country alliance that had been formalized after the defeat of Napoleon forty years before. Abruptly, with the Crimean adventure, Britain was going off in a temporary alliance with France, and just as abruptly the other three allies felt freed. The war brought not a technical end to their alliance, but an effective one. Britain, Russia, Austria and Prussia had stood together for all that time, even though the British often found the others too conservative and the others found Britain too liberal.

This almost accidental liberation caused each country to examine its own ambitions. It wasn't that now they chose to become enemies. They simply discovered the pleasures of an open dance card. It was the beginning of an unruly nationalistic period that would last until the First World War.

The myriad political and diplomatic meetings leading up to the 2003 Iraq war and continuing on afterwards to today, as if the strategic implications will never go away, are all virtual replays of the 1850s. As with the post-Napoleonic pact, nations that had thought for forty years they had to act in a certain way on the international stage and do so together are now out wandering about to see if there are other ways they'd like to act and perhaps with other people. In the midst of these arguments inside the West, Pascal Lamy, the European trade commissioner, threw himself into the fray: "Stop pretending that the United States and Europe share a common view of the world, recognize that we have different world views and interests, and then manage our relations."[4]

As with Britain's ex-allies following the Crimean War, the task was to find out if you did share common cause with your old allies. From September 11 on, well before the American-led invasion of Iraq, the then national security advisor Condoleezza Rice had made it clear that her people would deal with alliances from within their own logic: "The President of the United States was not elected to sign treaties that are not in America's interest." The other allies have therefore increasingly spoken out about how they see their own interests. Even the British, so closely linked to Washington on Iraq, have made a point of placing themselves clearly in other camps over the development of a European quick-reaction force, global warming and the International Criminal Court.

Washington has never been so powerful, and yet other democracies have not felt so free to go their own way since the end of the last world war. This paradox was highlighted in 2005, when Washington named John Bolton as its ambassador to the United Nations — the flawed but still key multilateral body. Bolton is best known as an opponent of the organization and a strong believer in unilateralism, which is another way of saying old-fashioned nationalism. This nomination was followed by that of Paul Wolfowitz to replace James Wolfensohn at the World Bank. He was put forward without consultation with the other key players in the Bank. The key point here is not whether he would do a good job, but Washington's nationalist approach to multilateral affairs.

To the question about the purpose of the most recent irregular wars, the answer on the irregular side is to destabilize the West, to make those societies targeted look over their shoulders with fear and chronic uncertainty until they start removing legally guaranteed individual rights and discouraging debate as unpatriotic. The old Scarlet Pimpernel musical had it exactly right:

> They seek him here,
> They seek him there,
> Those Frenchies seek him everywhere,
> Is he in heaven, or is he in hell?
> That damned elusive Pimpernel!

On the other side, the purpose has to be very clear. The tough, conservative Athenian, Xenophon, put it perfectly. "For violence, by making its victims sensible of loss, rouses their hatred: but persuasion, by seeming to confer a favour, wins good will."[5] The purpose must be to change the context from one of hatred to one of goodwill.

Many of the causes for warfare, as seen from the irregular side, are depressingly obvious. We can linger over the names of dictators and blame them, or we can take a broader view that in part links the rise of irregular warfare back to the colonial logic of the last century. The machine guns that mowed down the Mahdi's men at Omdurman made it unsurprising that weaker forces would begin to attack the mechanized and then high-tech West in another way. The long history weaving together the West and the oil trade has marked every instant of global evolution over the last century, deforming, as only a strategic commodity can, what normal people might have wished to do.

Since September 11 there has been a sterile argument about *root causes* versus the middle-class leaders of terrorist groups. The argument is that irregular warfare cannot be taken as a serious expression of poverty or exclusion if its leaders are middle class and well educated. But there is nothing surprising here. Leaders of every sort find causes and vice versa. From its very beginnings, irregular warfare has been conceived by the middle- and the upper-middle classes. This is central to its nature. Go back and look at the nineteenth-century anarchists or the dozens of colonial independence movements. Irregular warfare may vary from courageous to monstrous, but it is almost always sophisticated.

As for Globalism, it has not been very sophisticated in the developing world. It is an ideology that has subjected troubled areas of the world to a quarter-century of favouring broad, blunt economic mechanisms, abstract monetary theories and bogus technocratic measurement over humanism. In some cases this has actually worked and people are better off. But even then, this prosperity may have been divisive for the society in which it occurs. Sometimes the prosperity comes at the expense of destabilizing the society as a whole. This is not surprising. Most Western countries went through instability and violence as an interim outcome of industrialization. But sometimes that interim lasted half a century and cost millions of lives.

The social and economic questions that all of this raises are complicated. The military implications are quite simple. Applied to the developing world in the modern context, this whole economic approach has been a generous gift to, or provocation of, any number of groups prepared to engage in irregular warfare.

Sometimes the sources of misunderstanding run very deep, even within the West itself. For example, Robert McNamara, then secretary of defence, appeared at a NATO meeting in 1961 and presented Washington's decision that nuclear strategy must change from Massive to Flexible Response. Massive Response was an all-or-nothing approach. The United States wanted to develop a variety of sizes of nuclear bombs in order to be able to actually use them. McNamara saw this as rendering nuclear warfare rational. The Europeans — particularly the Germans — were deeply upset. The rational chessboard for this nuclear warfare was set on their land. At that point in history, West Germany was so dependent on American protection that it relied on France to speak for both of the European countries.

The direct outcome of Washington's imposition of Flexible Response was a sudden surge in a wide variety of nationalisms. France ended up withdrawing from much of NATO, for this and other reasons. Other smaller, more informal coalitions were struck, and they often opposed American policies. The development of the European Union shot forward, much more focused on its needs and interests.

Interestingly enough, the key thinker and inspiration for Flexible Response was Albert Wohlstetter, who was also one of two father figures — along with Allan Bloom — for the cabinet members and advisors who after the first Bush election in 2000 created Washington's unprecedented rearmament strategy. The two strategies, separated by forty years, resemble each other. Both involve a strong two-pronged belief system. First, there is a conviction that high-tech weaponry will trump all other military strategies. Second, there is the happy, perhaps divinely inspired, coincidence that spending billions of dollars on this high-tech weaponry will make a particular group of people very rich. And they in turn will happen to be major supporters of those elected officials who advance the strategy.

The decision by the United States and France in the early 1960s, followed by Britain, and then the Soviet Union, to convert arms production into a major export industry laid the groundwork for much of the violence and insecurity that has appeared since then. There was a bit of an arms production lull after 1989, but in the late twentieth century production began to build up again with some urgency. By 2003 the world was officially spending $1 trillion on arms, half of that coming from the United States.

When thinking about the normalization of irregular warfare over the last few decades, it is important to think about this international inflation in weaponry. To that we must add the collapse of growth in Africa during the Globalist period. And the mishandling of the developing world's debt. And a multitude of unresolved issues in countries often constructed within borders that suited colonial interests.

The overall result has been the steady growth in irregular warfare, so steady that it is now the dominant strategy of our time. Meanwhile, the majority of Western forces are still arming and training to charge across the Polish plains. It is fascinating how little strategic thought has been given to dealing with irregular warfare. There has been even less consideration of what it means if this is the new mainstream of conflict. The grand, global atmosphere proper to Globalization has perhaps contributed to Westerners' unwillingness to think seriously about a type of warfare that is dangerous precisely because it isn't grand, global or high tech. It is local and almost homemade.

How irregular warfare can be dealt with is not particularly mysterious. Only the most dysfunctional of ideologues don't believe that you must concentrate on the realities of social disorder and poverty. This was the solution to the *gin ally* phenomenon of the British Industrial Revolution, when community and family structures broke down in the new working-class slums.[6] It was the solution to the social violence so prevalent in North America and Europe in the late nineteenth century. By concentrating on the public good, governments were able to build far less divided and far less violent societies.

On the purely military side, much of the solution, it turns out, is tied to speed. The industrialized democracies moved not at all in Rwanda, very slowly in Bosnia, fairly fast in Kosovo and now, once again, painfully slow in Darfur. If an arm's-length international force can move quickly, lives are saved.

Since Canada's invention of the idea of peacekeeping in 1957 to deal with the Suez crisis, armies have gradually moved from their original passive role, standing between the belligerents, to a much more sophisticated role, massaging, soldiering, rebuilding, fighting if necessary. It is in this area of managing irregular warfare that a critical mass of people need to understand how warfare has transmogrified into something not instantly recognizable to a classic soldier as warfare. And yet this is one of the key areas in which the transition from Globalization, through the vacuum, into something else is being played out.

It is on these battlefields of social disorder that the tensions of our failing system are most obvious. What we know for the moment is that the events of the early twenty-first century have given great impetus to both negative and positive nationalism. We have seen how a few errors or moments of misapprehension can give terrorists a good deal of what they want, how if Western governments are not careful, the world could slide into a dreary, violent return of the nineteenth-century cycles of irregular nationalist wars with Joseph Conrad's proverbial gunboat firing into the jungle replaced by today's high-tech equivalent.

Ten years ago there was still a conviction that Globalization would lift people out of poverty. That was one of the automatic sidebars of international commerce. In the last four years, even the most convinced have been obliged to notice the return of widespread war linked to a phenomenon of poverty, alienation, dysfunctional nation-states and disastrous leadership.

The appearance of irregular warfare as a mainstream feature of our life is a pretty clear hint that the Globalization idea has not worked out. After a few years of agonizing over this, the intelligent believers in Globalization have now focused on the billion or more of the very poor and the problems that need to be tackled if the world is not to slide back into a closed world of negative borders and yet more war. When others look back on all of this in a few years, it may be with an unpleasant historical comment on our lack of imagination and sophistication. They may point out that it took the normalization of war to solve problems as simple as Third World debt.

27

Positive Nationalism

We are caught up in a human game that is by no means played out.

In some ways, the situation is worse than we are willing to admit. The signs of negative nationalism are all around us, in our own communities, yet we are careful to recognize them only on a one-by-one basis to avoid the sensation of any general evolution. We minimize in our imaginations the levels of organized violence around the world. How? By following Huntington's advice. We really only count the dead who come from our own community, or at most from what he characterized as our particular civilization.

As for the profound instability of the financial markets, the sudden dependence of the Western middle classes on two incomes per household, the uncertainties surrounding how to raise enough taxes or how to define what a trade good is or how to support real competition, not flabby transnationals using their simple weight to control markets — all of this floats about us in microscopic pieces. It never seems to come together in a shape that might permit us to evaluate how well or badly the reigning ideology and its elites have done.

We actually know the answer as to how things are going because of our personal experiences, observations and intuition. But a false air of complicity with the way our societies are run is maintained through an atmosphere of busy managers, swirling markets, specialist reassurances and floods of shapeless information. Not only do we know, but the very disorder reassures us, because we are no longer being victimized or saved by a monolithic certainty.

At least this confusion has a certain human reality about it. We are used to finding our way across such obscure terrain.

At the most basic level of societal knowledge, we do know that Globalization — as announced, promised and asserted to be inevitable in the 1970s, '80s and much of the '90s — has now petered out. Bits and pieces continue. Other bits have collapsed or are collapsing. Some are blocked. And a flood of other forces have come into play, dragging us in a multitude of directions.

Many professional commentators and senior administrators in charge of economic questions tend to wrestle what is happening into their own terminology. Thus China and India are presented as success stories of Globalization, when their situations actually represent a quite different theory of how the world works. Economists who have tied their careers to the Globalist truth are quite protected from reality by their tendency to talk mainly to each other and to do so in bullet-proof dialects that force what is happening in the world through their narrow methods of analysis. And so they remain convinced that it is all a matter of definitions or technical adjustments or the freeing-up of those markets.

Of course academics should keep themselves busy with definitions. And there is much to be done with adjustments and market forces. But the central challenges are elsewhere. There is a need to understand what is now in play and what our choices are.

Pitt the Younger once said that the excuse for every tyranny was necessity. That is just another way of saying inevitability. Inevitabilities are felt to be tyrannies, whether they are military, political or economic. Now the idea of choice is back. Much of it is tied to the return of the idea of national power. With that comes the democratic reality of choice. Choices for citizens. Choices for countries. Choices for coalitions of countries. And with choice comes all the uncertainty that provokes fear in some and releases the energies and imagination of others.

What is positive nationalism? First, it is a belief in the positive tension of uncertainty and the central importance of choice. It is not wedded to narrow absolutes. It is particularly dubious about broad answers to utilitarian questions. Thus, the conviction that one market view must prevail in all considerations — whether it be Marxist or neo-liberal — is of little interest. The utilitarian is a method to be used with as much variety and complexity as reality demands. Above all, it is there to be used, not worshipped.

Citizens feel comfortable with this complexity because they are anchored into a fundamental view of themselves and *others* as part of a civic commitment. This civic or positive nationalism has been with us throughout history. It is reinvented for each age. But the links between Cicero's idea of the Roman Republic, Ambrogio Lorenzetti's forty-metre-long fourteenth-century image of *good government* in Siena's town hall, Adam Smith's application of eighteenth-century Moral Sentiments, Alexis de Tocqueville's nineteenth-century democracy, Richard Rorty's twentieth-century humanism are remarkably tight.[1] And there are equivalents in the *Analects* of Confucius and the Koran, to name just two among many non-Western approaches.

Smith is perfectly clear about the good citizen's priorities: "The wise and virtuous man is at all times willing that his own private interest should be sacrificed to the public interest of his own particular order or society. He is at all times willing, too, that the interest of this order or society should be sacrificed to the greater interest of the state or sover-eignty." Tocqueville is equally clear about how democracy and choice develop — not by utilitarianism or commercial leadership: "Poetry, eloquence, and memory, the graces of the mind, the fire of imagination, depth of thought, and all of the gifts which Heaven scatters at a venture turned to the advantage of democracy." All of which dovetails into Rorty's common sense: "[T]he country of one's dreams must be a country one can imagine being constructed, over the course of time, by human hands."

What we have seen over the last decade is a renewed and growing desire to build our societies at all levels with our own hands — that is, to find ways to be involved. That was what Bernard Kouchner meant when he said that Médecins sans frontières was born of the unwillingness of young doctors to remain passive. The same could be said of the NGO movement in general.

In a way, although the NGOs are often international, they resemble nineteenth- or early-twentieth-century social and political movements. And they are linked to another trend growing out of Globalization's failure. Many people may want to have an international side to their *lives,* but they want to live in their communities.

Or rather, they do live in their communities. They want their civilization to reflect and build upon this reality. They don't want this reality to be treated as recalcitrance or an accident.

They have just lived through a period in which their elites have been obsessed by abstract theories of how economies must work at the global level. As a result it was deduced that citizens were first subjects of these theories and must do their best to fit in. There was an incapacity among our policy-creating leadership to begin their thinking with the real lives of their real citizens. When they've been faced by popular resistance, their tendency has been to wait it out or offer bagatelles, distractions.

The contempt of the theorists for human reality has been startling. Periodically, you get a glimpse of it, most often through the use of sport as a stand-in for civic participation. Even there, as Franklin Foer describes in his analysis of soccer, money and nationalism, this sort of manipulation backfires, either because it provokes negative nationalism or because people gradually turn their backs on the global commercial aspect of the sport.[2]

The desire of people to organize their lives around the reality of where they live is central to the return of nationalism. The Jordanian Prince Hassan has repeatedly argued that the key to Islamic democracy is a highly decentralized approach. The Islamic tradition is community based. A healthy democracy will be community generated. Their elites, still highly influenced by twentieth-century Western approaches, keep on centralizing. The Western model has for some time turned around managerial ideas of power, and these require centralization. But civic pluralism has always been as central to Islam as it is fundamental to Western traditions.

Globalism has been about a streamlining of the human experience, making it harder for democracy to deal with individual realities in a constructive way. International institutions like the World Bank have reformed themselves, but they are still looking for the big solutions.

If we look at our own histories, we discover that the changes that have made the biggest differences have most often been local. Public education, obligatory school attendance, clean water, sewage treatment, laws on child labour, higher adult wages — all of this and more is fundamentally local, sometimes national. These are the foundations of middle-class well-being.

You can now see some of this humanist conception of belonging beginning to re-emerge as the great Globalist sweep recedes. I remember listening by chance in Chicago in November 2003 to a remarkable new American public figure, a year before he was elected to the Senate. Barack Obama already had a calm, clear idea of how community worked and how it was the big picture that had to adjust. As he moved onto the national scene, he continued carefully pointing out that "instead of having a set of policies that are equipping people for the globalisation of the economy, we have policies that are accelerating the most destructive trends of the global economy."[3] He was rephrasing Adam Smith: "This disposition to admire, and almost to worship, the rich and the powerful, and to despise, or, at least, to neglect persons of poor and mean condition … is, at the same time, the great and most universal cause of the corruption of our moral sentiments."

What has changed is that Obama's message is increasingly common around the world. The Chinese, Indian and Brazilian obsessions with "sustainability and equality"[4] are part of this. But so are success stories such as Sweden and Finland, both of which managed to come out of the pre-global era, survive a small crisis and reform themselves on a local basis so as to be able to deal with the international situation.

They demonstrated to what an extent the Globalist crisis has been caused by a mixture of ideology, which should be taken half seriously, and bad management, which ought not to have been taken seriously at all. But the managers were so seduced by what they thought were new abstract global theories that they lost track of the people whose lives were affected by their administrative methods.

The general atmosphere now is far calmer. It is not just China that is aimed at "balanced development" in its own terms. Warnings are coming out of the WTO and the OECD that the rush to bilateral trade agreements between large developed and smaller developing economies is starting to backfire. Trade works only if the context is right. In general, apart from the true believers, a growing number of public figures are looking more carefully at what that context might be in their particular case. Only the most obsessional still believe that a simple growth in trade brings wealth.

And above all, the priorities of citizens and their governments are shifting as the Globalist myth evaporates. When Helen Clark, the prime minister of New Zealand, began to try to turn her country around without succumbing to a Globalist panic, she said her aim was a broad policy "which reduces inequality, is environmentally sustainable, and improves the social and economic well-being" of her citizens.[5] In 1999 that sounded like a risky package. Today it sounds commonplace.

Over the same period, a small number of international business sectors have actually regulated themselves. This has been in response to sustained campaigns by NGOs and local citizens' groups. Two of the most interesting involve department stores and coffee distributors. The International Association of Department Stores has now agreed on a set of ethical rules that deal with such things as child and forced labour. The process began when the Hudson's Bay Company found itself named "sweatshop retailer of the year" along with Wal-Mart. The CEO of Hudson's Bay, George Heller, was disturbed by the distinction and began to organize his industry to improve standards.[6] The difficulty with self-regulation is that only part of the industry signed on. It is an impressive list, but Wal-Mart, for example, isn't there. It doesn't need to be, because it doesn't mind its international reputation.

The agreement on coffee seems to have tougher rules and to involve most of the major players. It may even succeed in stabilizing a notoriously unstable commodity. Here is a case where, if things go well, an international, vertically integrated cartel will have been created to serve the common good. What is the common good in this case? Overproduction will be discouraged so that developing-world farmers are not penalized. A resulting reduction in production should lead to improved environmental methods. And the consumers should pay a more realistic part of the industry costs.

But again the model is hard to multiply. In 2000 the OECD came up with an industry set of Guidelines for Multinational Enterprises. It is an impressive list of rules, but they are voluntary. We know from our experiences inside nation-states that ethical standards in a competitive context have to be binding. And yet, at least there is now concrete agreement at the OECD level that the old Globalist idea of markets determining standards did not work and was not acceptable.

What we do have so far at the international level in the way of regulations with teeth is very limited: the Ottawa Treaty against land mines; the International Criminal Court; the Kyoto Protocol on global warming. Most countries have signed on to all three. A few of the key players have refused. What these treaties demonstrate is that international relations do not have to be market driven. If binding agreements on such difficult issues are possible, then international treaties setting corporate tax levels and organizing labour conditions are possible. And it is not true to say that such treaties need be to the disadvantage of developing economies. Properly calibrated, they could help those societies, just as Spain was helped during its carefully planned entrance into the European Union.

Is it realistic to expect such progress? If you look at the evolution over the last decade, you can see that the process is surprisingly fast, considering that the blockage in most cases has come from the most powerful countries. But this is just another reminder that even the remarkable power of the United States cannot be spread thinly to determine world policy. There are now too many nations and regional groups with their own agendas. If major powers choose not to join in on new international binding agreements, they will sooner or later find themselves at a disadvantage on political or economic questions.

Is this a success story for Globalism? Or for reformed Globalism? Neither. This is quite a different process, based upon different assumptions. One of them is the power of the nation-state. It is worth reiterating this by going back to the subject of Ukraine and the president's favourite poet — the national poet — Taras Shevchenko. His most famous poem is a nationalist ode, "To the Dead, to the Living":

> Come to your senses! Be human,
> Or you will rue it bitterly;
> The time is near when on our plains
> A shackled people will burst its chains.[7]

The world is filled with nation-states that have a great deal of unfinished business. The question is not what to do about global economic integration. It is how to ensure that this new nationalist era is citizen based, focused on the national common good and on developing binding treaties in a range of areas at the international level.

The thousands of NGOs around the globe seem to be logical leaders in the process. They can claim large numbers of supporters, sophisticated leadership and skill in the dogfights of international policy. In May 2004 Monsanto, the transnational agricultural products company, backed down on its plans for genetically modified wheat. Part of the credit belonged to NGOs. There are dozens of other examples apart from this one, and the coffee agreement, and the department store agreement.

But the NGOs' position is more fragile than it appears. It is one of influence, not power. And only rarely are they integrated into national democratic systems. Laws are made by parliaments, assemblies, congresses. And there are thousands of lobbyists on every side. If the victories of the NGOs are often so narrow or partial, it is because of competing influences. Were they able to take their organizations successfully into mainstream politics, their ability to make changes would be far clearer. And in an era of resurging nation-states, their power at the international level would be greater.

There are also openings for powerful practical institutions — such as reformulated cooperatives — that could play a major role in both developed and developing economies. There are openings because the transnational technocracies have abandoned or half abandoned a whole series of areas that require too much hands-on attention to interest them. In other words, there is always a need for people seeking influence. But the real need today is for existential involvement. The fact that we are in a vacuum means that the direction for the next quarter-century will be set not by those with influence but by those who win power. This is something neo-conservatives and religious activists in the United States have understood clearly. This is why Richard Rorty is so upset with what he sees as the distant, abstract approach of the American left.

And yet, the opportunity lies waiting — if only momentarily — for someone to set the agenda for a new direction. Note, for example, that *The Financial Times* of London, a conservative business paper, takes a more progressive position on international poverty and ethical issues in general than most mainstream politicians: "[Mass poverty] is, beyond doubt, the great moral imperative of our age. But a focus on global trade liberalisation, debt reduction and the International Financial Facility will not by itself be enough."[8] They are calling for the kind of non-market action that the classic Globalists, the international technocracy and most of the transnational leadership have said is unrealistic. But that is no longer the dominant public view. There is now a growing desire among citizens for their democracies to take the lead on issues of justice and inclusion. And that desire no longer comes in the standard nineteenth-century packages of left and right.

The Spanish thinker Victor Pérez-Diaz rightly reminds us that "[j]ust by being, [the *civitas*] does not persist in being."[9] He is talking about the needs of citizenship, about the self-confidence required to take on such changes.

One last aspect of this self-confident involvement awaits our energy and commitment. We are caught up in an artificial negative tension between a theory of global economics and a reality in which people live. And we do live in real places.

There is a third factor: the reality that large numbers of people are moving between these places at astonishing rates. And most of them move to change nationalities. This fluidity is perhaps unprecedented. It is certainly one of the most complex periods of human migration, because unlike the nineteenth-century version or those of other eras, it has no set pattern.

The Europeans still struggle with the impact of a small percentage of this movement, although such changes as the German citizenship reform of 1999 show that adjustments are being made. But experts in population say the 20-odd million immigrants in Europe is nothing. Given the continent's low birth rate, it will apparently need some 160 million immigrants by 2025 to keep its societies functioning. To think of such people coming to Europe merely as migrant workers would be disastrous for the continent's vision of its own ethics and its own public good. There are those who believe immigration would undermine European culture. As the last world war demonstrated, nothing can undermine it faster than acting in a manner inconsistent with that culture's own standards.

In any case, this migration is much more than a European question. Some countries, such as Canada, are on the leading edge of how to build a society with a constantly evolving set of citizens and cultures. Others are in complete denial of what is happening to them or will soon happen. The British cabinet minister Gordon Brown has attempted to reorient national debates around *values*.[10] This is now a common trend, an almost amorphous term that is meant to indicate shared cultural standards.

The challenge today is both more complex and more interesting. It may be that we are now not only at the end of the Globalist period but also at the end of the Western rationalist period and its obsessions with clear linear structures on every subject.

Perhaps we are living the beginnings of a major rebalancing in which other cultures, with more complex ideas of what makes up a society, are coming to the fore. And those of us in the West will just have to learn to keep up and to understand what makes such a major change positive for us.

One of the ideas that has been growing for some time is that we are entering an era resembling the Middle Ages — the positive side of the Middle Ages. This is a time when the nature of borders and the definition of people are neither clear nor exclusive. In many ways this was Erasmus's dream: a loose but united idea of Europe. Today this is broader and more complex than Europe, although the most sensible direction for Europe would be precisely that — a continent of peoples, separate and interwoven.

Hedley Bull once wrote about "a system of overlapping authority and multiple loyalty."[11] That is in reality what is happening on every front.

The monolithic ideology of economic truisms is fading away. We have been repeatedly told that we must accept the inevitability of that system or fall into some sort of chaos. Instead, if we are careful, we could move toward a system of intentional complexity. The nation-state will make its comeback. But we can already see that the result is quite different from the past because the obligations and dependencies of countries are so layered. The economic aspect in this complexity is important, but by no means dominant.

The factor of populations on the move is probably the primary element. The questions this will raise about social habits and beliefs will take a great deal of our time. Developing education that will work in such a complex situation will require a great deal of imagination, and a broad, inclusive approach. We have been promised or threatened with an era dominated by English. For technical and contractual purposes, this dominance will probably remain true. But if you look beyond the technical and the contractual, we are probably entering a period of multilingualism supported by all of the cultures that go with the languages.

There is no particular culture unsuited to what is happening. There are only unsuited political movements. Islam, the religion that most concerns the West these days, is fundamentally open and has a more flexible history than Christianity. As the Koran puts it,

> We ... made you into
> Nations and tribes, that
> Ye may know each other
> (Not that ye may despise
> Each other).[12]

What our situation needs is precisely Adam Smith's public interest, the imagination that Tocqueville invoked, Rorty's humanism. A traditional reading of these words would cause some to say that I began by pointing out the return of the nation-state, only then to take it away. Not at all. The more complicated our national and international relationships are, the more all of us will need to use our most complicated sense of belonging both to feel at home and to find multiple ways to be at home with the widest variety of people and situations.

The common call today is for an examination of values. I am not clear what this means. It has a slight ring of nineteenth-century self-serving nationalism. It would be better to concentrate on something more real, such as serving the public good. Adam Smith put it that "he is certainly not a good citizen who does not wish to promote, by every means in his power, the welfare of the whole society of his fellow citizens."[13]

If people who know each other well serve the welfare of their fellow citizens, they may learn something unexpected about each other, perhaps about how different they are. If people who do not know each other well, perhaps because they come from different cultures, serve the welfare of their fellow citizens, they may well discover how similar their values are.

In both cases, this would be the process of positive nationalism.

The Return of Choice

The economic collapse of 2008 represents the failure of Globalism. It is a mistake to treat this crisis as something provoked by a financial crisis. A burst boil is a symptom, not a cause: lance it fast and move on in search of the real problems.

If we draw back we can see a much more profound crisis. Empires, reichs, imperial armies, economic theories, ideologies of all sorts, come and go. Inevitable and eternal, they parade before us, grand and self-confident for a quarter century, a half, periodically a century, rarely two. What was subscribed to so seriously suddenly seems always to have been light and flimsy and dubious. How could those in charge not have seen? They did not wish to. To be blind to reality was to be loyal to your class, whatever form that class might take. And loyalty always trumps reality among the servants of ideology.

When the moment of truth comes – that sort of truth which is simply an expression of reality – there is a great deal of shifting about in search of culprits. In the case of Globalization, the obvious villain was not even directly human, but the one step removed, old-fashioned sin of greed. If people were going to insist on an actual living, breathing culprit, the obvious choice was the banker. But greed and bankers are the standard villains of every economic crisis from Athens on. This is the blame model which for centuries fed anti-Semitism and the fear of foreigners.

How could the financial sector be to blame? This is the one area in which every transgression has taken place in full public view and these practices have been broadly criticized since the early 1990s, without anything being done to change them. After all, bankers didn't choose governments or de-regulate control systems or turn a blind eye to the creation of opaque international speculation; that is, to legalized fraud. They engaged in it in full public view while everyone in authority watched complacently. Such are the hypnotic effects of ideology.

For that matter, how could the crisis in which we find ourselves be considered a financial crisis? Surely what has happened to money is merely a symptom; just as the oil crisis of the early 1970s was not about oil, but about the build up of a broad set of economic mistakes and problems.

In these moments of meltdown, the established wise men are abruptly revealed to be simpletons, pitiful figures, embarrassingly naïve. What was fascinating about Alan Greenspan's formal public *mea culpa* in the autumn of 2008 was not his admission of error – itself a refreshing occurrence – but the child-like nature of both his beliefs and his disappointments: "I made a mistake in presuming that the self-interests of organizations, specifically banks and others, were such that they were best capable of protecting their own shareholders and their equity in the firms."

What had that presumption been based upon (apart, perhaps, on a mediocre novel by his favourite novelist, Ayn Rand)? There is nothing in three thousand years of economic history to encourage such a belief. Neither conservative nor liberal, let alone Marxist or 1930s corporatist theories, would have led even a moderately attentive thinker to such a conclusion. Again, these are the characteristics of ideological hypnosis. If you believe that history has come to an end, you explicitly banish memory from your mind. Greenspan was "shocked." Like a small child who had ventured into a world beyond his experience or imagination, he did "not fully understand why it had happened." But he had been paid to be the world's ultimate financial father and so there was no one to teach him or to slap his wrist.

Each ideology is in large part established by an intellectual class. They assume the role of courtiers or priests and live from the crumbs flicked off the table of the primary beneficiaries of the truth of the day. At first glance they appear to be little more than servants of the ideology. But the role of these gatekeepers of orthodoxy is of primary importance. First, their well-being is dependent upon this ideology involving a great revelation of truth which they can advance and defend. Ideology justifies their lives.

Second, all absolute regimes, physical or theoretical, have their bullies, their armed knights, their trusted, discreet counselors. But the power of systems is unsustainable unless there is a generalized willing suspension of disbelief. What they all need is some version of The Sacred Congregation for the Propagation of the Faith, whose job it is to work for that suspension of our critical senses. It is the job of the priests and courtiers to make all of us believe that today's truth always was true and always will be. They are the merchants of the inevitable and the eternal. Then one day the reckoning with reality comes and that particular ideology implodes. As it fades we forget the role of the Inquisition's inquisitors, of the Jesuits, the court propagandists, the compliant intellectuals, the various courtiers. But the power of any important court lies as much with the courtiers as with the kings and barons. Why? Because they are the ones who deform the word in order to prevent doubt and healthy debate and the use of intelligence. They were and remain central guilty parties in what is happening to the world today.

Who are the sacred congregations of Globalization? First they are the vast majority of professors in the Economics departments of our universities. At a more mundane level there are the business schools and their professors. Their graduates in turn have created a third, much more engaged structure for the propagation of the faith through the consulting industry.

But the management schools and the consultancy businesses are mere utilitarian expressions of the conformity which faith requires. The real heart of the Sacred Congregation beats in the departments of Economics. There, beginning in the mid-1970s, the possibility of alternate thought has been slowly marginalized, even eliminated. Of course there have always been fascinating pockets of resistance and imagination. But today, the failed ideologues of the last three decades remain in charge of what passes for economic thought in our universities. They are now angrily on the defensive and largely unrepentant. And they are still in control of the transferral of economic thought and method to new generations. As for public policy, these economists are still feeding at best marginally altered ideas into the structures of power. Cabinet ministers ask their deputies, who ask their directors for new ideas and policies. What comes back cannot help but be, at best, a superficially disguised expression of failed policies.

Even in the United States, where there is the greatest political push for fresh ideas, you can sense the difficulty the economic mainstream is having in thinking, as opposed to shuffling their few traditional cards. With great effort they are dragging out the ideas which preceded the current ideology. But this is not at all the same as reconsidering their basic assumptions.

In Britain people joke that the chancellor who put the failed policies in place – those policies which pushed their country towards reliance on the financial fantasies of the City – is now the prime minister in charge of saving the day, according to him, saving the world. And his courageous list of the things to be done is made up without exception of facing problems which have been perfectly evident for the last decade.[1] But his opponents, within his party and in the other parties, are just as guilty of scratching about in the intellectual refuse of the last thirty years. Why? Because there are thousands of economists and managers, spread through every layer of the private and public system, who have made their way precisely upon a belief in and loyalty to the failed system. They resemble the medieval scholastics, "whose profession was to tie down debate in minutiae as a way of making themselves relevant to power." It is not surprising that they have few intellectual mechanisms in their skill set with which to rethink their belief system.

If you look at Germany or Canada and listen to the very minimal things being proposed, you realize that the intellectual problem goes well beyond the reticence of a particular government. This is part of the explanation for the French president's explosive attempts to dislodge the reigning complacency when faced by 'Globalization as a Trojan horse'.[2] And his refusal to imagine his becoming a service industry country. "Je ne ferai pas de la France une simple reserve pour tourists."[3] [I will not allow France to be reduced to a tourist theme park.]

Beyond the economists, the managers and the consultants, there is a fourth group of propagandists: the many economic and business journalists who, on a daily basis, drove us on until it was too late. Now they are urgently raising red flags to warn us off protectionism and to praise, yet one more time, free trade as the only, indeed the sacred way out of the crisis. And so they are busy reanimating their old Manichean proposition that all will stand or fall in this battle of opposites – walls up or walls down – as if there were no other more sophisticated approaches to prosperity than a continual growth in trade; as if our problems were not broader and more profound.

A few of these journalists can indeed claim to have pointed out technical mistakes made by the Globalist movement over the last few decades. Some of them admit to having missed the cumulative effect. But in general these are false apologies. They are arguing that our problems are merely a matter of micro-economics – the area of their skills – and that further attention to detail will get us through.

To be fair, why should they be criticized for making a self-serving argument. Why wouldn't they? They don't want people to stop reading their columns, buying their books, newspapers and magazines, paying them to give prophetic and reassuring speeches. We talk with despair of CEOs and their inflated incomes. But there is a much more basic battle for economic survival going on inside this failed class of economic propagandists.

It matters that we carefully identify these four categories of economic scholastics – the economists, the managers, the consultants and the propagandists – because they are central to how we deal with the collapse of Globalism. It is important to point the finger accurately, otherwise we will all resemble the citizens of a country coming out of a disastrous war – in 1919 for example – and leaving the architects of trench warfare massacre in place.

What is confusing to most citizens is that abruptly, as if out of nowhere, studies are announcing that half the world population cannot satisfy its basic needs. Or that over thirty countries are at risk of falling into genocide or that countries are in some way defaulting on their debts, as if it were normal. Abruptly it seems that democracy, having been on the rise around the world for decades, is now in sharp decline. Suddenly the effects of deforming our measurements of inflation and employment and income over the last few decades are rising to the surface. As a result it is now revealed that middle class wages have been in decline for sometime; that in the United States wages in the bottom tier have declined 30% in thirty years.[4] These phenomena are not the sudden outcome of Globalization's collapse.[5] Rather, as it has collapsed, so people have begun to interpret parallel realities in a different way. It is as if the disappearance of the economic inevitability of Globalization has revealed the self-evident: that the world has truly contradictory tendencies. No longer is every question we face, from healthcare to education to culture, first dragged through an economic prism to ensure it is elevated in a Globalist context. Suddenly the obvious becomes clear: Globalization was just an economic theory, not a replacement for all concepts of internationalism.

But if the obvious is merely observed, if not fully understood, if we don't get a handle on the ideological process we have just been through, we may simply fall back into some marginally reformed version of the failed school. We might even find ourselves trapped in a whole new closed belief system.

I have a clear memory of what it felt like standing up in public for the first time to suggest that Globalization was on the way out. It was in 1999 in Sydney, during a speech that was being broadcast on Australian national television.

What was it that pushed me the last step into believing this could happen? Earlier in the day I had had a conversation with I.J. Macfarlane, the conservative Governor of the Australian reserve bank. He explained that he no longer believed in the stability of the international financial system. He had been trying for a good year to communicate this fundamental concern to a larger audience.

As a reserve banker he had to speak carefully and so in a world of hypnotized elites, those he could properly speak to were those least likely to listen. However, he did make it clear, if you paid attention, that many of his colleagues around the world agreed with him. Not all of them. And, as the U.S. reserve bankers have demonstrated, this consensus did not necessarily include the richest countries.

As I listened to him his words came on top of a series of observations I had been making, in apparently unrelated areas, since the middle of the 1990s. If you put them together it became clear that the Globalization ideology had never been more than a rather ramshackle, oversized bus. Parts of it were brand new and exciting. But the chassis was cobbled together from old-fashioned and often contradictory nineteenth-century concepts. And since its high point in 1995, wheels had been falling off as the contraption heaved and shook its way forward; gears stripping, bolts shearing, windows cracking. In other words, the faulty financial system was only the expression of a myriad of other more basic problems.

Yet the public discourse coming from those meant to know remained smooth and certain. They remained calm in the face of a constant public argument. But that disagreement was mainly about whether you were for or against Globalization, which missed the most basic point – that perhaps the whole movement was self-destructive. And that if we waited for that moment to come, the effect on all of us, whether we had been for or against, would be equally destructive.

As I began to describe this to the thousand people in the hall and sensed the words going out around the country, I felt the almost unbearable inner tension that comes when you put your reputation on the line in a way that can leave you looking like a fool.

In the year or two that followed, even those who wanted to be supportive couldn't really bring themselves to believe that the era – or rather, the ideology – was coming to an end. Of course, there were others here and there making similar arguments in various ways. If they were in the economics guild, even their most severe critiques of public policies were couched in a language shared with their colleagues, and so their arguments were artificially limited by a discourse designed to produce professional agreement. Meanwhile, on the front lines of propaganda, the courtiers were insisting that all was well, that the world was flat, the movement unstoppable. The growth in trade, they continued to insist, demonstrated that good was being done. Later, as the crisis of 2008 became painfully obvious, many of them made what appeared to be astonishing reversals – *The Economist*, for example, calling for bank nationalizations.[6] But this was only a reversal in the context of the old Manichean arguments. If the banks could be propped up, the old arguments of how the economy functioned could be maintained. What was missing was any sense of a new approach to the use of capital.

At the centre of my argument in the original 2005 edition of this book was a simple idea. Economic ideologies run out of steam several years before the elites they produce can bring themselves to admit there is a problem. Globalization was effectively over by somewhere around the year 2000. We then slipped into a vacuum – a period of disorder in which the bus had stopped moving, but the elites were pretending to themselves that this wasn't the case. These vacuums tend to last up to ten years. They are actually periods of opportunity. The old idea is dead. There is no dominant new idea. The crisis has not yet struck. The ideologues are still nominally in charge, but their ideologies are virtually powerless. These are the moments when it is relatively easy for leaders to set new directions without having to devote themselves to fighting off disaster. If they wait too long, the disaster strikes and they are then reduced to largely reactive behaviour.

Why do elites ignore danger signs and wait too long? Because they are the third or fourth generation to hold power in the era of their particular ideology. They have no real memory of other possible choices. They believe themselves to be the product of inevitability. And so, while the official discourse of leadership in the latter years of Globalization was all about risk and individualism, the reality was one of passive, soft leadership, with no experience of a world unchained in its anger.

In classic social analysis this is often described as degeneracy.

Economic theories always include elements of exaggeration or delusion and an insistence on the importance of trust. Economics of the left or the right, the past or the future are all highly speculative. They are not fact based. Globalists have often stated that their ideology is not an ideology at all, but an expression of the inevitable and unstoppable forces of technology and international market forces. Any attempt to claim inevitability for an economic theory is just a pseudo-scientific approach to the old *God is on my side* argument. What this reveals is first that the claimant is afraid their ideology will fail and second, that they lack imagination.

Systems that work are all about balancing imagination with reality. The last three decades have seen the abandonment of that search for balance and the replacement of imagination with a sort of delusional certainty.

That the international crisis should have begun in the area of finance is not surprising. Throughout history this has been the economic sector most susceptible to delusion. What we have seen from the radical collapse in paper value in 2008 and 2009 is that the effects – bad though they are – have been far less than they would have been had the values borne any relationship to reality. In other words, before and after the initial crisis, money has had the actual value of Weimar currency in the 1930s.[7] It's just that we haven't been acting as if we lived in Weimar. Billions upon billions of private, followed by public money have now simply evaporated, and so reduced the extreme imbalance between value and paper. One of the curious outcomes is that the old principle of money as a necessary but imaginary servant of real activity and real wealth – and nothing more – has been more or less reestablished.

An economy is like a cake. You whip in egg whites – money – to make it rise. You need a bit of meringue on top for extras. Globalization simply whipped up ever more egg whites to create a gigantic soufflé on top, dwarfing the cake. In the 1970s, six times more currency was traded than real goods. By 1995 it was fifty times. Who knows what it was by 2005. By any other name this was little more than old-fashioned inflation. What justified it? The Globalists claimed they had a new recipe. They insisted that thanks to their sophistication and to the new economy, money had changed character. It was no longer David Hume's "oil that renders the motion of the wheels more smooth and easy."[8] It was now an actual wheel. Many wheels. It was now a real asset; intangible perhaps, but nevertheless real. And then, as Hume would have expected, as any sane economist would have expected, the soufflé fell. The delusionary response of the economist establishment was to stuff in more egg whites. But soufflés don't re-rise or even stabilize. And so the public's money began to disappear with a great woosh. Only their debt obligations remained.

And so each of the ideology's strengths has somehow turned out to have an opposing meaning. The lowering of national residency barriers for corporations has turned into a tool for massive tax evasion.[9] The idea of a global economic system somehow made local poverty seem unreal, even normal. The decline of the middle class – the very basis of democracy – seemed to be just one of those things. That the working class and lower middle class, even parts of the middle class, could only survive with more

than one job per person seemed to be the normal punishment for not keep-
ing up. The contrast between unprecedented bonuses for mere managers at
the top and the four job families below them seemed inevitable in a glob-
alized world. For two decades an elite consensus insisted that unsustainable
third-world debts could not be put aside in a sort of bad debt reserve without betraying the essential principles and moral obligations of international
contracts. It took the same people about two weeks to propose bad debt
banks for their own far larger debts in 2009.

Even a brief reading of history tells us that such contradictory situations
cannot last. But beneath the injustice and the contradictions something
more profound lurks. Take two other phenomenon of this era that illus-
trate what I mean.

First, there was the idea that *making things* was beneath the dignity of
people in the Western democracies and that we should promote ourselves
to the level of service industries. This promised rise to sophistication turned
out to be in good part a flight from the complexities of trade competition
and from reality. All of this was accompanied by a denigrating discourse
about Western workers who were defined as either insufficiently educated
and doing low-end jobs destined to disappear or were educated but paid
too much. Meanwhile, a large percentage of these people were being shifted
over to service jobs which required almost no education, were badly paid
and insecure. There was never any attempt to work out how a large percentage of the workforce could both do sophisticated jobs appropriate to their
education and be properly paid.

Second, the Globalist movement was meant to deliver unprecedented
levels of individual autonomy and personal freedom. Yet the result in the
end has been unprecedented levels of security control and surveillance, all
of which was well underway before September 11. The service industries, for
example, are built upon the constant electronic surveillance of workers. And
Britons, historically perhaps the people most allergic to surveillance, are
now in everyday life the most watched Westerners by cameras and other
means.[10] Other democracies are rushing to catch up. It is almost as if the
message were: You don't need to fear markets, but you should fear people;
as if the markets were not people; as if this were the natural outcome of a
theory which gave precedence to global markets over the reality of people

living in real democracies. Underpinning all of this was a pseudo Darwinian idea that if the rich-poor divide was growing, well, it would provoke the poor into doing better. Thirty years later the divide was still growing. We had chosen to ignore the lessons of Western democracy which told us that egalitarian societies do better. Richard Wilkinson's 2005 study demonstrating this was one of the signs that Globalization was running out of steam.[11]

These two odd outcomes of Globalization tell us that the language of the ideology was, from its beginnings, disconnected from the reality of its policies.

Take this disconnect one step further. If you examine the attitudes of the Globalist leaders to China and India over the last decade they make no sense at all. On the surface it was all about integrating these two countries into the global trading system while the West rose to the higher levels of the service industry. In reality there was never any attempt to understand the realities of either China or India. They were treated as romantic outstations of Globalization.

Anyone who looked closely knew that they would not become serious markets for Western products. They knew that both countries' home markets were their own internal fall back for development once Western orientated Globalization had gone wrong. The Chinese in particular were convinced from the beginning that it would all go wrong. I have noticed in conversations with Chinese leaders and officials the clarity with which they see today's Globalist policies in the context of the last 150 years. Their experience is that the West is for open trade, so long as it is to the West's advantage. Not a moment longer. And indeed the relationships quickly began to sour as the trade imbalance became impossible for Western governments to justify at home.

But above all, no one in the West was listening to the Chinese and Indian leaders. In both countries they said clearly and repeatedly that given the unbearable levels of domestic poverty they could not open up their own territories to unregulated international activity without provoking explosions at home. That was why the Chinese government introduced its plan of the Five Equilibriums in 2005 to protect their citizens against the instability of open markets. That is why they set twenty-five benchmarks for their civil service to protect against a worsening of social and environmental disasters. That is why in 2007 Premier Wen said: "The speed of a fleet is not determined by the ship which travels the fastest, but the one that travels the slowest." In other words, he would not allow the market to shape the rich-poor divide. That is why the Indian government has been focused first upon the dangers of that divide and second upon the short-term opportunities within Globalization. That is why India today is the world's "biggest imitator of anti-dumping action", as a way of stabilizing internal markets.[12]

Underneath all of these oddities and misunderstandings has lain something which strikes at the language of Globalization and explains a good part of today's crisis. We have been told since the beginning of the Globalization movement that its purpose was the creation of new real wealth through constantly expanding trade. Yet the most spectacular growth of the last few decades has come in paper transactions, mergers, restructurings and speculation. And the most obvious beneficiaries have been managers, not workers or real capitalists. In areas such as agriculture, the outcome has been a decline in farmer income, a growing reliance on subsidies and massive profits to middlemen who, in a mercantilist manner, both control and deform the market.

Suddenly, with the economic collapse, trade has shrunk radically in almost every sector. Often the shrinkage has been dramatic. Yet no one is suffering from a lack of goods. They may suffer from a lack of jobs or of income to buy goods. There may be a failure to distribute goods fairly. But there is no lack of goods.

Why? Because for decades we have had a large surplus of goods in the West. And in those few large markets where there is a need for more goods – China and India in particular – the internal market is not and will not become fully international.

Given current economic theory, our principle problem is not the threat of protectionism, but the quandary of a permanent surplus in goods. This is perhaps our single biggest problem. Why? Because our economic systems are designed to work on the basis of competition and a constant improvement in technology. But these two factors can only do their job in an open market if there is some level of scarcity. In other words, the fatal flaw in Globalization has always been that it advanced an eighteenth to nineteenth-century market concept based on a growing real demand – ie. overall scarcity – which no longer applied. In the name of progress the believers were advancing a reused version of the old concept of constant growth. The constant growth in trade was supposed to create a constant stream of new wealth.

In other words, the West's economic leaders threw us into an old-fashioned Globalist trading ideology just at the point when a combination of technology, capitalism and regulation had produced a permanent glut in trade goods. I repeat, competition and wealth creation don't work in the market unless there is real demand.

What happens when you push unneeded trade? First, you may convert consumers into speculators. They can *take it or leave it* in the profound sense that they don't have a real need. Second, you drive prices down beyond the production costs of a middle-class, educated civilization. You then develop a false moral argument which argues that the consumer's principal right is to buy cheaper goods. And you argue that they are cheap because of competition from cheap labour – which is in reality only a secondary factor. They are cheap principally because of the surplus. By ignoring this reality we are left with the argument that it is all right for wages in the bottom third or half of society to go down because goods are cheap. This means we have been following a global economic theory flying the flag of wealth creation, but ends up pushing cheaper goods as an excuse for lower wages, which means wealth reduction.

And so behind the old-fashioned language of trade and competition, and the new ideological language of inevitability, we have fled in the opposite direction – off into paper speculation and tenuous services. Was there also a growth in real trade? Absolutely. There was an explosion in both production and trade. But the growth in solid, dependable demand was limited. And the low costs of production encouraged a mass approach towards sales which has meant that a growing percentage of goods sit around until they are simply crushed, pulped, buried or abandoned. So the statistics on production and trade growth have been a bit of a fiction when compared to actual consumption.

The direct result was an ever-growing drive to manage the surplus by cutting back on competition. The old-fashioned way to do this was to build large global conglomerates which were horizontally integrated around the world. This was dressed up in the new rhetoric of takeovers, consolidations, efficiencies, mergers and acquisitions. The intent of this rhetoric was to make us feel that we were participating in a great tsunami of modernization driven by unleashed competition, when precisely the opposite was happening. Strip away the rhetoric and what you have is seventeenth-century Mercantilism. The opposite of Capitalism. Mercantilism – the British East India Company and so on – was all about managing the market from production to consumption in order to avoid the dangers of competition. In other words, Globalization by the mid-1990s was becoming a contra-diction between rhetoric and reality.

And now it has collapsed. But it has collapsed without there being any attempt to understand the pattern which led us into crisis. What we are concentrating on are the superficial outcomes of something far more profound. If we examine the roots of what has gone wrong, we will also find that the problem is the outcome of a great success story.

The last seventy years have seen remarkable breakthroughs in production quantities, speed and cost. These were continued inducements to more production and trade. And we are still stuck in those outdated nineteenth-century theories which require the maximizing of trade. Looked at in a more contemporary way, the surplus in production means we should be imagining wealth creation and growth in a different way.

And so today's collapse represents the failure of Globalization. Seen in another light it represents the ultimate success of the old capitalist model of competition and risk built on technology in the context of a scarcity of goods. Of course, this success was made possible by the dominance of democracy and the resulting programs and regulations aimed at shaping the common good and helping the market to act in a responsible manner. The result has been enough long-term stability and enough inclusion and fairness to make our societies work.

The Globalists have turned this success into failure by their inability to understand two things. First, how this success was achieved. And second, if we have solved the problem of scarcity, then the old capitalist model will no longer work. We have turned a page in economic theory. We have been freed to make new choices, to develop new approaches.

In the first edition of this book I described my conversation early in the century with a local rising U.S. politician called Barack Obama, not yet known in Washington. In essence he was already talking about new choices. In his inaugural address as president he warned: "What the cynics fail to understand is that the ground has shifted beneath them." It is not just the cynics who need to pay attention to the deep shift. Above all it is those who have risen to authority in university, business and government by gliding along on old economic ideas dressed up as new.

A production system which has solved the problems of scarcity can turn to other challenges. The first challenge would involve dealing with the real costs of production. That would mean developing an inclusive approach towards economics; one which includes the full social and environmental costs of production. Redesigning how we do things in this light would mean the opening of an enormous opportunity to create new wealth, solid wealth, but in a fresh and more balanced way.

Much of the West's rise to wealth after the last world war was the result of having to rebuild a European continent flattened by war. We had a free hand to create anew. What looks like a crisis today is actually an equivalent opportunity. We must not waste it by using up our financial flexibility in the propping up of hollow paper institutions. If we do that we will remain prisoners of romantic economic rhetoric from the nineteenth century.

Around the late eighteenth to early nineteenth centuries there was a major shift in the world's social and economic habits. Some of this was for the better, some for the worse. But it was a remarkable breakthrough. Around the late nineteenth to early twentieth centuries there was another major shift in social policy and organization which changed the way the world worked. Ever since, in a truly scholastic manner, we have been scribbling in the margins of those ideas. Had it not been for the apparent early successes of Globalization we would have escaped its outdated approaches several decades ago. By doing what?

By rethinking how we organize both education and work in a civilization which has almost doubled life expectancy in a mere century. After all, our education, work and retirement patterns were all set in place in the late nineteenth century when average life expectancy in the West was fifty. Much of what seemed to be the essential speed of individual action simply no longer applies as life expectancy approaches ninety. Instead, a whole series of new social and economic choices are now available to us. We are stumbling unconsciously towards them, in part because the Globalist movement has dragged us back into debates more than a century out of date. But such new choices offer us radically different opportunities, as radical as the new choices of the late nineteenth century. These are invitations to use our imagination.

By rethinking the shape of work for the longest-lived and best-educated population ever to exist. Debates over the length of a work week are now arcane on both sides of the argument. The question is not how long we work. Some may wish to work more, others less. The real question is how to develop less linear approaches to work. You can sense how much fear the possibility of more fundamental choices is raising by the call throughout the Globalist era for an old-fashioned narrow approach to education, one focused on training, when precisely the opposite is needed.

By using the surplus in production as a base upon which to progress from mass production to quality production. The idea of progress in this case could mean integrating all the implications and costs into how we view production, which would include integrating the full environmental cost. Perhaps our production surplus has been artificially created by our narrow utilitarian approach to defining those implications and costs. Properly defined we would rediscover scarcity, but in a new and more sophisticated form. We would have the basis for a more stable and inclusive form of wealth creation.

Everyone can now see that the Globalist approaches of the last three decades were old fashioned. And most of us can see how the ground has shifted. The key to dealing with this crisis is not to rebuild the old structures based on the old assumptions. We have an opportunity to build a more sophisticated sort of wealth based upon a balancing of social, environmental and market needs. This could easily be the project of a century.

NOTES

I: CONTEXT

1. A SERPENT IN PARADISE

1. John Morley, "Democracy and Reaction," *Nineteenth Century*, April 1905.

2. John Maynard Keynes, *The Economic Consequences of the Peace* (London: Macmillan and Co., 1919), 1.

3. Ibid., 9–10. My emphasis.

3. WHAT THEY SAID IT WOULD DO

1. Michael Oakeshott, *Rationalism in Politics and Other Essays* (Indianapolis: Liberty Fund, 1991), 403.

Karl Polanyi, *The Great Transformation: The Political and Economic Origins of Our Time* (Boston: Beacon Press, 1944), 3.

2. Alfred E. Eckes, "Is Globalization Sustainable?" speech given at CMRE meeting, Charlotte, N.C., 27 October 1999.

3. Anthony Giddens, see Martin Wolf, *Why Globalization Works* (London: Yale University Press, 2004), 14.

Jagdish Bhagwati, *In Defense of Globalization* (New York: Oxford University Press, 2004), 3.

Anne Krueger, *Financial Times*, 16 April 2004, 15.

James Rosenau and Ernst-Otto Czempiel, eds., *Governance without Government: Order and Change in World Politics* (Cambridge: Cambridge University Press, 1992), 23, see also 3.

Thomas Friedman, cited in Franklin Foer, *How Soccer Explains the World: An Unlikely Theory of Globalization* (New York: HarperCollins, 2004), 2.

Daniel Yergin, Richard Vietor and Peter Evans, "Fettered Flight: Globalization and the Airline Industry" (Cambridge, MA: Cambridge Energy Research Associates, 2000), 1–2.

George Soros, *On Globalization* (New York: Public Affairs, 2002), 1.

Kenichi Ohmae, see Eckes, "Is Globalization Sustainable?"

William Watson, "Globalization: Resting, But Not Dead," *Literary Review of Canada* (June 2004): 9.

4. Wolf, *Why Globalization Works,* 14.

5. Alfred E. Eckes, "Is Globalization Sustainable?", quoting the British activist Norman Angel writing in 1911.

6. These numbers are drawn from a variety of sources, including Alfred Eckes and Thomas W. Zeiler, *Globalization and the American Century* (New York: Cambridge University Press, 2003); Wolf, *Why Globalization Works;* John Gray, *False Dawn: The Delusions of Global Capitalism* (London: Granta Books, 1999); statistical research by the German Bundestag, the OECD, UNCTAD and others.

7. See Wolf, *Why Globalization Works,* Table 8.1. The world figure for the Globalization period is 1.33 versus 2.93 for the Keynesian period. Western Europe is 1.78 versus 4.08. The rest of the West is 1.94 versus 2.44.

8. *U.S. News and World Report,* 11 February 2002, 41.

Eckes, "Is Globalization Sustainable?"

9. Prince El Hassan bin Talal, *To Be a Muslim: Islam, Peace and Democracy* (Brighton: Sussex Academic Press, 2004), 44.

See the remarkable book by Joshua Cooper Ramo, *The Beijing Consensus* (London: Foreign Policy Centre, 2004), 12. The book involves a radical recentring of the Chinese point of view of international affairs, particularly economic.

10. K. Natwar Singh, *Heart to Heart* (New Delhi: Pupa Co., 2004), 164.

11. Aga Khan, speech given at Governor General's Leadership Conference, Ottawa, 19 May 2004.

12. Vaclav Havel, interviewed in the *International Herald Tribune,* 22 October 2004, 1.

13. Samy Cohen, *Le Monde,* 7 February 2004, 8.

4. WHAT SOMEBODY FORGOT TO MENTION

1. Iris Origo, *The Merchant of Prato: Francesco Di Marco Datini* (London: Penguin Books, 1957), 64.

2. George Steiner, *The Idea of Europe* (Tilburg: Nexus Institute, 2004), 37.

3. "Congress of Vienna, June 9, 1815," in *Major Treaties of Modern History 1648–1967,* ed. Fred L. Israel (New York: Chelsea House Publishers, 1967), vol. 1, 519.

4. Gray, *False Dawn,* 23.

5. See, for example, Hedley Bull and Adam Watson, *The Expansion of International Society* (Oxford: Clarendon Press, 1984); Ole Waever, "Imperial Metaphors," in *Geopolitics in Post-Wall Europe: Security, Territory and Identity,* ed. Ola Tunander, Pavel K. Baev, Victoria Ingrid Einagel (Thousand Oaks, Calif.: Sage Publications, 1997), 59–87.

6. "Article VI," Congress of Vienna, 9 June 1815, in *Major Treaties of Modern History 1648–1967,* vol. 1: 522.

7. Sven Lindqvist, *Exterminate All the Brutes: One Man's Odyssey into the Heart of Darkness and the Origins of European Genocide,* trans. Joan Tate (New York: The New Press, 1996), 110–15, 122–23.

8. Primo Levi, *The Periodic Table,* trans. Raymond Rosenthal (New York: Schocken Books, 1984), 42.

9. Quoted by John Cassidy in *The New Yorker,* 2 August 2004, 26.

10. This section is based on an explanation by the great Socratic scholar Gregory Vlastos. See "Slavery in Plato's Thoughts," in *Slavery in Classical Antiquity,* ed. M.I. Finley (Cambridge: W. Heffer and Sons Ltd., 1960), 289, 303, 291.

11. Joseph E. Stiglitz, *Globalization and Its Discontents* (New York: W.W. Norton, 2003), 222.

Amartya Sen, *Development as Freedom* (New York: Anchor Books, 2000), 240.

12. Singh, *Heart to Heart,* 113.

13. Milton Friedman, "Nobel Speech," Stockholm, 10 December 1976.

14. See Lewis Lapham, "Tentacles of Rage," *Harper's* 309, no. 1852 (September 2004): 31–41.

15. For example, John Ruggie, "International Regimes, Transactions, and Change: Embedded Liberalism in the Postwar Economic Order," in *International Regimes*, ed. Stephen D. Krasner (Ithaca, N.Y.: Cornell University Press, 1983). Or the clear interpretation in Timothy Lewis, *In the Long Run We're All Dead: The Canadian Turn to Fiscal Restraint* (Vancouver: UBC Press, 2003), 36–38.

16. See John Williamson:

"What Washington Means by Policy Reform," paper presented at the Institute for International Economics Conference, Washington, D.C., November 1989,

"What Should the World Bank Think about the Washington Consensus?" *The World Bank Research Observer* 15, no. 2 (August 2000): 251–64, and

"Did the Washington Consensus Fail?" speech given at the Center for Strategic and International Studies, Washington, D.C., 6 November 2002.

17. Fareed Zakaria, *Newsweek,* 2 February 2004, 41.

18. Alexis de Tocqueville, *Democracy in America,* vol. 1 (New York: Vintage Books, 1945), 6. Originally published 1835.

5. A SHORT HISTORY OF ECONOMICS BECOMING RELIGION

1. Margaret Thatcher, speech given to the National Press Club, Washington, D.C., 5 November 1993.

Margaret Thatcher, cited in Fredrik Östman, "Potatis," 12 December 2001, http://members.mcnon.com/potatis/Q.Thatcher.html (accessed 21 February 2005).

2. R.H. Tawney, *Religion and the Rise of Capitalism* (London: Penguin Books, 1990), 44, 45. Originally the Holland Memorial Lectures, 1922.

3. Andrew Morrison, ed., *Free Trade and Its Reception 1815–1960: Freedom and Trade* (London: Routledge, 1998), 3. See also, among many books, P.J. Thomas, *Mercantilism and the East India Trade* (London: Frank Cass and Co., 1963), originally published 1926; H. Martyn, *The Advantages of the East-Indian Trade* (London: J. Roberts, near the Oxford Arms in Warwick-Lane, 1720).

Margaret Thatcher, speech to Bombay Chamber of Commerce, Bombay, 18 April 1981.

4. Richard Cobden, *Speeches on Questions of Public Policy by Richard Cobden, M.P.,* ed. John Bright and J.E. Thorold Rogers (London: T. Fisher Unwin, 1908), 187. Originally published 1870.

5. For a good account, see Bernard Semmel, *The Rise of Free Trade Imperialism: Classical Political Economy and the Empire of Free Trade and Imperialism, 1750–1850* (Cambridge: Cambridge University Press, 1970), chapter 7; Francis W. Hirst, ed., *Free Trade and Other Fundamental Doctrines of the Manchester School* (New York: Augustus M. Kelley, 1968), chapters 5 and 6; G.R. Searle, *Entrepreneurial Politics in Mid-Victorian Britain* (Oxford: Oxford University Press, 1993), chapter 5; Morrison, *Free Trade and Its Reception.*

Specifically:

Cobden, 15 May 1843.

Bright, 10 June 1845.

Cobden, quoted in Leone Levi, *History of British Commerce* (London: John Murray, 1872), 294–95.

Cobden, Manchester Town Hall, 4 July 1845.

Cobden, 28 September 1843.

6. Gustave Flaubert: "Quand le peuple ne croira plus à l'Immaculée Conception, il croira aux tables tournantes." Letter to Mademoiselle Leroyer de Chantepie, 16 January 1866.

7. "17th Ecumenical Council of 1447," www.catholicism.org/pages/ecumenic (accessed 20 January 2005).

8. Peter Marsh, *Bargaining on Europe: Britain and the First Common Market, 1860–1892* (New Haven, Conn.: Yale University Press, 1999), 208.

9. Gregory Bresiger, "Laissez Faire and Little Englandism," *Journal of Libertarian Studies* 13, no. 1 (Summer 1997): 45–79.

Charles de Secondat, Baron de Montesquieu, *De l'esprit des lois,* vol. 1, 316: "Où il a du commerce, il y a des moeurs douces."

10. Anna Augustus Whittall Ramsay, *Sir Robert Peel* (Freeport: Books for Libraries Press, 1928), 220–21.

11. For a fascinating, depressing analysis, see Lindqvist, *Exterminate All the Brutes.*

12. Regarding the term *informal empire,* see Dr. C.R. Fay in *Cambridge History of the British Empire* (Cambridge: Cambridge University Press, 1940), II: 399; John Gallagher and Ronald Robinson, "The Imperialism of Free Trade," *The Economic History Review* (London: Cambridge University Press, 1953), Second Series, 6, no. 1; Bernard Semmel, *The Rise of Free Trade Imperialism.*

13. Semmel, *Free Trade Imperialism,* 4.

14. Jack Beeching, *The Chinese Opium Wars* (London: Hutchinson, 1975), 39, 162.

15. Alfred E. Eckes, *Opening America's Market: US Foreign Trade Policy since 1776* (Chapel Hill, N.C.: University of North Carolina Press, 1995), xvii.

16. Edmund Morris, *Theodore Rex* (New York: Random House, 2001), 431.

17. This argument owes a great deal to Eckes's analysis as laid out in *Opening America's Market.* See all of his chapter 4.

18. Eckes, *Opening America's Market,* 137, 139.

Susan Strange, cited in Eckes, *Opening America's Market,* 137.

19. Friedrich August von Hayek, "Lecture to the Memory of Alfred Nobel," Nobel Prize lecture, Stockholm, 11 December 1974.

20. Francis Fukuyama, *The End of History and the Last Man* (New York: Free Press, 1992), 48; my emphasis.

21. George Steiner, *Errata: An Examined Life* (London: Phoenix, 1997), 121.

22. "Economic Growth Is Reducing Global Poverty." Press release from the National Bureau of Economic Research, October 2002, www.nber.org/digest/oct02 (accessed 5 November 2004).

23. Xavier Sala-i-Martín, "The World Distribution of Income," May 2002.

24. Paul Krugman, *The Return of Depression Economics* (New York: W.W. Norton, 1999), 25.

Margaret Thatcher, "The Walter Heller International Finance Lecture," lecture given at Roosevelt University, Chicago, 22 September 1975.

II: THE RISE

6. 1971

1. John Kirton's G8 Research Group at the University of Toronto has developed an invaluable long-term body of research and interpretation on the creation and

performance of the G 6-7-8. It is one of the few groups to look at modern crisis management in a historical but also political and economic manner.

The other standard interpretation of the crises leading into the G7 is Robert Putnam and Nicholas Bayne, *Hanging Together: Cooperation and Conflict in the Seven-Power Summits* (Cambridge, Mass.: Harvard University Press, 1987).

7. THE VACUUM

1. Henry Kissinger, "The Industrial Democracies and the Future," address to Pittsburgh World Affairs Council. Pittsburgh, Pa., 11 November 1975, published in *The Department of State Bulletin* 73, no. 1901, 1 December 1975: 758.

2. John Gimbel, *The Origins of the Marshall Plan* (Stanford, Calif.: Stanford University Press, 1976), 5.

3. Albert Camus, *Actuelles: Écrits politiques* (Paris: Gallimard, 1950), 92. "[L]a France et l'Europe ont aujourd'hui à créer une nouvelle civilisation ou à périr."

Victor Pérez-Diaz, "The Underdeveloped Duty Dimension of the European Citizenship," *ASP Research Paper,* vol. 53, no. 6 (2004): 1.

Kissinger, "The Industrial Democracies and the Future," 760.

4. Henry A. Kissinger, *A World Restored: Metternich, Castlereagh and the Problems of Peace, 1812–22* (Gloucester, Mass.: Peter Smith, 1973), 11, 322, 325. Kissinger drew his description from Napoleon, Prince von Hardenberg and Friedrich von Gentz.

5. Stiglitz, *Globalization and Its Discontents,* 216.

6. Friedrich August von Hayek, speech at the Nobel banquet, 10 December 1974.

7. Richard Cobden, Parliamentary Debate, 3rd Ser., 134, 784: 27 June 1854.

8. See my own description of this in *On Equilibrium* (Toronto: Penguin, 2001) and Sen, *Development as Freedom,* 63–67.

9. Hugh Corbet, "Commercial Diplomacy in an Era of Confrontation," in *In Search of a New World Economic Order,* ed. Hugh Corbet and Robert Jackson (London: Croom Helm, 1974), 23.

Gerard Curzon, "Crisis in the International Trading System," in Corbet and Jackson, *In Search of a New World Economic Order,* 33–45.

Robert Jackson, "Divergent Philosophical Approaches to Foreign Policy," in Corbet and Jackson, *In Search of a New World Economic Order,* 48–50.

8. THE KING'S FOOL

1. Business International S.A. in conjunction with the Centre d'études industrielles, Geneva, *Managing the Multinationals: Preparing for Tomorrow* (London: George Allen and Unwin Ltd., 1972), 28.

2. Courts are given more to gossip and short memories than to in-depth studies, so there are fewer examinations of the Davos phenomenon than you might think. Two worth reading are

Jean-Christophe Graz, "How Powerful Are Transnational Elite Clubs? The Social Myth of the World Economic Forum," *New Political Economy* 8, no. 3 (November 2003); Geoffrey Allen Pigman, *Shar-pei or Wolf in Sheep's Clothing? The World Economic Forum from Le Défi American to the Bill-Bill Summit,* Centre for International and European Studies, 21 February 2001.

9. SELECTED ROMANTIC ENTHUSIASMS

1. Michael King, *The Penguin History of New Zealand* (Auckland: Penguin, 2003), 488–89.

2. Peter Conway, "The New Zealand Experiment," Paper presented at the GPN Asia/Pacific Regional Meeting, Bangkok, 2–4 September 2002, 17.

3. Brian Easton, *Listener* (New Zealand), 17 July 2004, 38.

Douglas Myers, Business Roundtable chairman, *The Dominion,* 26 March 1997, 23.

The Economist, 19 October 1996, 19.

4. Margaret Thatcher, speech to the Australian Institute of Directors, Sydney, 2 October 1981.

5. Frank Freidel, *Franklin D. Roosevelt: A Rendezvous with Destiny* (Boston: Little, Brown, and Company, 1990), 147.

Oakeshott, *Rationalism in Politics and Other Essays,* 405.

6. Quoted in Jane Clifton, "Days of Thunder," *Listener* (New Zealand), 24 July 2004, 21.

7. Polanyi, *The Great Transformation,* 10.

Eric Helleiner, "Democratic Governance in an Era of Global Finance," in *Democracy and Foreign Policy: Canada among Nations,* ed. M.A. Cameron and M.A. Mohot (Ottawa: Carleton University Press, 1995), 283.

8. John Ruggie, "Embedded Liberalism Revisited: Institutions and Progress in International Economic Relations," in *Progress in Postwar International Relations,* ed. Emanuel Adler and Beverly Crawford (New York: Columbia University Press, 1991), 215.

9. See Helleiner, "Democratic Governance in an Era of Global Finance," 284–85.

10. Ruggie, "Embedded Liberalism Revisited," 215.

11. *Independent* (London), 3 June 1993, 29.

Bank for International Settlements, *62nd Annual Report* (Basel, Switzerland: BIS, 1992), 230.

12. George Williams, *The Airline Industry and the Impact of Deregulation* (Brookfield, Vt.: Ashgate, 1993), 10, 11. Most analyses are in some way tied to airline industry interests. There is virtually no difference of opinion: deregulation has been a success. A selection of these industry support documents published as books or papers include

Robert Andriulaitis, David L. Frank, Tae H. Oum, Michael W. Tretheway, *Deregulation and Airline Employment* (Vancouver: Centre for Transportation Studies, UBC, 1986).

Steven Morrison and Clifford Winston, *The Economic Effects of Airline Deregulation* (Washington: The Brookings Institute, 1986).

Nawal K. Taneja, *The International Airline Industry* (Lexington, Mass.: Lexington Books, 1988).

Elizabeth E. Bailey, "Airline Deregulation Confronting the Paradoxes," *Regulation — The Cato Review of Business and Government* (Washington, D.C., 1990).

Kenneth Button, *Airline Deregulation: An International Perspective* (New York: New York University Press, 1991).

Aisling J. Reynolds-Feighan, *The Effects of Deregulation on US Air Networks* (New York: Springer-Verlag, 1992).

"Statistical Information on Air Passenger Numbers and Characteristics," Parliamentary Office of Science and Technology (U.K., October 2000).

13. Oakeshott, *Rationalism in Politics and Other Essays,* 405.

14. Paul Bracken, "Engines of Change," *The Politic* 1, no. 1 (Spring 2004): 48, 50. Soros, *On Globalization,* 1.

15. Bhagwati, *In Defense of Globalization,* 182.

Hedley Bull, *The Anarchical Society* (New York: Columbia University Press, 1977), 254–55.

Lewis Lapham, "Dungeons and Dragons," *Harper's* 288, no. 1725 (February 1994): 9–11.

There is a good description of Roman Clientship in Anthony Everitt, *Cicero* (New York: Random House, 2001), 30–31.

16. Benito Mussolini, *Fascism: Doctrine and Institution* (Rome: Ardita Publishers, 1935), 50.

17. United Nations Development Programme, *Making Global Trade Work for People* (Sterling, Va.: Earthscan Publications, Ltd., 2003), 109–12.

10. THE GATHERING FORCE

1. See Global Economic Prospects 2005, www.worldbank.org.

2. See John Kirton's many descriptions of this process and his assessments of G7 successes and failures.

3. Quoted in Charles Webster, *The Congress of Vienna 1814–1815* (London: Thames and Hudson, 1963), 163.

Harold Nicolson, *The Congress of Vienna, A Study in Allied Unity: 1812–1822* (London: Constable, 1948), 244.

Kissinger, "The Industrial Democracies and the Future," 763.

4. Octavio Paz, *The Labyrinth of Solitude* (New York: Grove Press, 1985), 228.

5. Eckes, "Is Globalization Sustainable?"

6. M.G. Smith, *Corporations and Society* (London: Duckworth, 1974), 28.

Albert Camus, *L'Homme révolté* (Paris: Gallimard, 1951), 18. "Rien n'étant vrai ni faux, bon ou mauvais, la règle sera de se montrer le plus efficace, c'est-à-dire le plus fort. Le monde alors ne sera plus partagé en justes et en injustes, mais en maîtres et en esclaves."

7. *Financial Times* (London), 16 April 2004, 15.

Lindqvist, *Exterminate All the Brutes,* 65.

8. Lawrence Lessig quoted in *Business Week* online, "Lawrence Lessig: The 'Dinosaurs' Are Taking Over," 13 May 2002. See also Lessig, *The Future of Ideas: The Fate of the Commons in a Connected World* (New York: Random House, 2001).

Lessig, *Code and Other Laws of Cyberspace* (New York: Basic Books, 1999), 25.

9. United Nations Development Programme, *Making Global Trade Work for People,* 95.

11. CRUCIFIXION ECONOMICS

1. David Malin Roodman, "Ending the Debt Crisis," *State of the World 2001* (New York: W.W. Norton, 2001), 143–65.

2. Ray Brooks et al., "External Debt Histories of Ten Low-Income Developing Countries: Lessons from Their Experience," *A Working Paper of the International Monetary Fund,* May 1998, www.imf.org/external/pubs/ft/wp/wp9872.pdf (accessed 25 October 2004).

3. Freidel, *Franklin Roosevelt*, 164.

4. Roodman, "Ending the Debt Crisis," 150.

5. Margaret Thatcher, opening speech, London G7 Summit, 8 June 1984.

6. Joseph E. Stiglitz, "More Instruments and Broader Goals: Moving toward the Post-Washington Consensus," *WIDER Annual Lectures 2* (UNU/WIDER: Helsinki, 1998), 6, http://www.wider.unu.edu/publications/annual-lectures/annual-lecture-1998.pdf (accessed 27 November 2004).

7. There is an interesting explanation of this in Barry Riley, *Financial Times* (London), 29 January 1994. See also John Ralston Saul, *Voltaire's Bastards* (New York: The Free Press, 1990), chapters 2 and 27.

International Herald Tribune, 2 February 1995, 9.

8. *Le Monde* (Paris), 6 January 2000, 4.

"[U]ne éthique de la solidarité" and "Si tel était le cas, la France pourrait proposer que le prochain sommet, en juillet à Okinawa, décide de porter à 100% le taux d'annulation de la dette de ces pays."

9. Gerard Baker, *Financial Times* (London), 25 March 2004, 13.

III: THE PLATEAU

12. SUCCESS

1. Nicolson, *The Congress of Vienna*, 262.

2 Piotr Dutkiewicz, "Asymmetric Power, Heresy, and Post-Communism — A Few Thoughts," *New Europe* 4 (October/December 2004): 42–56. See also Shimshon Bichler and Johnathan Nitzan, "New Imperialism or New Capitalism?" (December 2004), http://bnarchives.yorku.ca/ (accessed 26 December 2004).

3. Eckes, "Is Globalization Sustainable?"

Alex Trotman, quoted in the International Chamber of Commerce 1997 brochure (Paris: International Chamber of Commerce, 1997), 1, 3.

4. Margaret Thatcher, speech to the Malaysian Institute of Public Administration, Kuala Lumpur, Malaysia, 6 April 1985.

13. 1991

1. Conversation with Vasa Cubrilovic, Belgrade, 1988. "Les pays qui font la guerre encore ne sont pas développés."

2. Bernard Kouchner, address on Leadership, Diversity and Nationalism at the Governor General's Leadership Conference, Winnipeg, Manitoba, 9 May 2004. "Il est plus facile de s'appuyer sur le nationalisme pour supprimer la diversité que de s'appuyer sur la diversité pour fair reculer le nationalisme."

Louise Arbour, "The Truth to Be Told," address to the Canadian Journalists for Free Expression, Toronto, 15 November 1999.

14. THE IDEOLOGY OF PROGRESS

1. *New Patterns of Industrial Globalization: Cross-Border Mergers and Acquisitions and Strategic Alliances*, OECD, 2001.

2. Graz, "How Powerful Are Transnational Elite Clubs?"

3. *Sydney Morning Herald*, 3 March 1997, 7.

Henry Carey, quoted in Semmel, *The Rise of Free Trade Imperialism*, 179.

4. John Ruggie, "Trade, Protectionism and the Future of Welfare Capitalism," *Journal of International Affairs* 48, no. 1 (Summer 1994): 9.

5. Tobias Jones, *The Dark Heart of Italy: Travels through Time and Space across Italy* (London: Faber and Faber, 2003), 133.

6. Confucius, *The Analects of Confucius,* trans. Arthur Waley (New York: Vintage Books, 1938), 116.

    The Economist, 5 November 1994, 13.

7. *Financial Times* (London), 21 July 2004, 11.

8. See, for instance, Chad Hills's "Lotteries in the United States: An Overview." *Family.Org: A Web Site of Focus on the Family* (22 January 2004), http://www.family.org. (accessed 23 August 2004). See also "The Stakes Get Higher," *Forbes.com,* 29 April 2002, http://www.forbes.com (accessed 23 August 2004), and *Financial Times* (London), 25 November 1999, 23.

9. Cobden in the House of Commons, 15 May 1843. Hirst, *Free Trade and Other Fundamental Doctrines of the Manchester School,* 159.

15. 1995

1. *The Economist,* 14 March 1998, 81.

2. For a good description, see Krugman, *The Return of Depression Economics,* 38–59.

3. "Income and Wealth," Joseph Rowntree Foundation. See *The Globe and Mail,* 25 March 1995, D4.

4. *Times* (London), 17 February 1995, 12.

IV: THE FALL

16. A NEGATIVE EQUILIBRIUM

1. See, for example, Shimshon Bichler and Jonathan Nitzan, "Dominant Capital and the New Wars," *Journal of World Systems* 10, no. 2 (Summer 2004): 255–327; and "New Imperialism or New Capitalism?" 38, 44. While my interpretation differs in many ways from theirs, Bichler and Nitzan are almost alone among economic thinkers — or in the old sense, political economy thinkers — to be attempting to understand what is happening and why it is not having the expected effect.

2. Alexandre Lamfalussy, general manager, Bank for International Settlements, "The Restructuring of the Financial Industry: A Central Banking Perspective," SUERF Lecture, City University, London, 5 March 1992.

    Paul Krugman, "For Richer," *The New York Times Magazine,* 20 October 2002, 62.

    George Anglade, *Éloge de la Pauvreté* (Montreal: Les éditions ERCE, 1983), 17. "[R]ejeter la croissance du superflu, pour le développement du nécessaire."

3. Jacques Chirac at the G7 in Halifax, 1995. *Le Monde* (Paris), 12 May 1996, 26. "[L]a spéculation, ce sida de nos économies."

    Sophocles, "Antigone," *The Theban Plays,* trans. Don Taylor (London: Methuen Drama, 1986), 144.

    Keynes, *Economic Consequences,* 17.

4. See Robert Menschel, *Markets, Mobs & Mayhem: A Modern Look at the Madness of Crowds* (New Jersey: John Wiley & Sons, Inc., 2002).

5. John Galt, "Bandana on Emigration," *Blackwood's Magazine* 20, no. 114 (September 1826): 471.

Kofi Annan, Address to the World Economic Forum, Davos, Switzerland, 31 January 1999.

6. OECD statistics from a variety of sources. See *Guardian Weekly* (London), 30 July 1995, 10; *Le Monde* (Paris), 21 July 1994, 19; see also current OECD "Economic Outlook" reports, as well as Andreas Botsch's revised "Employment and Labour Markets," originally presented at the Friedrich Ebert Stiftung International Conference, Bali, Indonesia, 25–26 November 1996, http://www.itcilo.it/actrav/actrav-english/telearn/global/ilo/standard/tuacempl.html (accessed 7 August 2004).

7. President Clinton quoted in Eckes, *Opening America's Market,* 283–84.
See *The Economist,* 5 November 1994, 19.

8. Dr. John Martin, quoted in *Financial Times* (London), 2 May 1995, 4. See also *The World Health Report 1995,* WHO, Geneva.

9. *Financial Times* (London), 8 June 1994, 1.
See also Andrew Glyn and Bob Rowthorn, "West European Unemployment: Corporatism and Structural Change," *AEA Papers and Proceedings* 78, no. 2 (May 1988): 194.

10. See Preamble to the ILO Constitution.

11. Milton Leitenberg, "Deaths in Wars and Conflicts between 1945 and 2000," Centre for International and Security Studies, University of Maryland, revised 7 December 2004. I have been monitoring these sorts of statistics for decades. They are obviously always soft numbers. But there is a certain consistency even in their range. This particularly detailed report appears to be more exact than others.

12. Bhagwati, *In Defense of Globalization,* 64.

17. NGOs AND GOD

1. Morris, *Theodore Rex,* 500.

2. Singh, *Heart to Heart,* 121.

3. Kouchner, address on Leadership, Diversity and Nationalism.

18. A CHRONOLOGY OF DECLINE

1. *Globe and Mail* (Toronto), 19 September 1994, B10.

2. *New York Times,* 6 August 1997, A18.
Observer (London), 28 January 1996.

3. Stiglitz, *Globalization and Its Discontents,* 99, 91.

4. Krugman, *Depression Economics,* viii, 85.

5. *The Economist,* 27 September 1997, 91.
The Economist, 14 March 1998, 81.

6. Richard Gwyn, *Sunday Star* (Toronto), 23 November 1997, F3.

19. A CHRONOLOGY OF DECLINE: THE MALAYSIAN BREAKOUT

1. *International Herald Tribune,* 5 February 1998, 17.

2. Stiglitz, WIDER Lecture.

3. "On ne négociera plus après l'AMI comme avant l'AMI.... Les peuples n'admettant plus d'être gouvernés comme par le passé."

4. Mahathir bin Mohamad, speech at Davos, 1999.
Al Gore, Remarks at the APEC Business Summit, Kuala Lumpur, Malaysia, 16 November 1998.

5. I.J. Macfarlane speeches: The East Asia Economic Summit, Singapore, 14 October 1998; the International Conference of Banking Supervisors, Sydney, 21 October 1998; the CEDA Annual General Meeting Dinner, Melbourne, 25 November 1998.

Financial Times (London), 31 October/1 November 1998, 2.

6. *International Herald Tribune,* 1 February 1999, 11, 13.

7. Krugman, *Depression Economics,* 158.

8. *Financial Times,* 4 February 2000, 5.

9. Joseph Stiglitz, address to the American Economic Association, Boston, 9 January 2000.

Kofi Annan, Bangkok, 12 February 2000. "Les manifestations de rue ont reflété les angoisses ressenties par beaucoup de gens face à la mondialisation. Il faut répondre à ces angoisses."

10. *Financial Times* (London), 4 February 2000, 5.

20. THE END OF BELIEF

1. Samuel Taylor Coleridge, from Chapter 14 of the *Biographia Literaria.* 1817. *Selected Poetry and Prose of Coleridge,* ed. Donald A. Stauffer (New York: Random House, 1951), 264.

2. Sophocles, "Oedipus at Colonus," *The Theban Plays,* 89.

3. Jean-Cyril Spinetta, president of Air France–KLM. *Le Monde* (Paris), 31 October–1 November 2004, 12.

4. Alfred E. Kahn, "Airline Deregulation," *The Concise Encyclopedia of Economics,* 2001, www.econlib.org/library (accessed 19 July 2004).

Kahn, "Change, Challenge, and Competition: A Review of the Airline Commission Report," *Regulation: The Cato Review of Business & Government* 3 (1993), http://www.cato.org/pubs/regulation/reg16n3d.html (accessed 4 June 2004).

Rigas Doganis, *The Airline Business in the 21st Century* (London: Routledge, 2001), 17, 79.

George Williams, *The Airline Industry and the Impact of Deregulation,* xii, 49, 143, 145.

5. Elizabeth I, Golden Speech to Parliament, London, 30 November 1601.

6. Bhagwati, *In Defense of Globalization,* 183.

7. Marcia Angell, *The Truth about the Drug Companies* (New York: Random House, 2004), 3, xv–xviii. This remarkable book lays out in great detail the growing problem with the pharmaceutical industry.

8. David Kessler, quoted in *Guardian Weekly* (London), 10–16 April 2003, 23.

9. *Le Monde* (Paris), 17 April 2003, 18. "Le fait est que l'Europe, le Canada et le Japon ne payent pas la part qui leur revient des coûts de recherche."

10. Angell, *The Truth about the Drug Companies,* xv–xvii.

11. Joan-Ramon Laporte, "The Supposed Advantages of Celecoxi and Rofecoxib: A Scientific Fraud." *Butlleti Groc,* the Catalan Institute of Pharmacology.

See *The Canadian Medical Association Journal,* 17 February 2004, and *The Lancet* 363, no. 9818 (24 April 2004).

International Herald Tribune, 22 October 2004, 13.

David Graham, associate director for Science and Medicine in the FDA's Office of Drug Safety, 18 November 2004, testifying before the Senate Finance Committee. *USA Today,* 19 November 2004, 1.

The Economist, 27 November 2004, 63.

12. Ibid., 64.

13. For example, the World Economic Forum 2003 survey of 36,000 people in forty-seven countries.

Financial Times (London), 5 February 2003, 13.

14. Morris, *Theodore Rex,* 507.

15. *Dresden Post,* 8 January 2005.

16. Aristotle, *The Ethics of Aristotle: The Nicomachean Ethics,* trans. J.A.K. Thompson (London: Penguin Books, 1976), 317.

17. Riva Krut, "Globalization and Civil Society: NGO Influence in International Decision-Making," UN Research Institute for Social Development, April 1997.

18. Walter van de Vijver, exploration director, to Sir Philip Watts, chairman. See *Guardian Weekly* (London), 22–28 April 2004, 11.

19. *New York Times,* 2 September 2004, A22.

20. G7 1998 communiqué.

21. *International Herald Tribune,* 5 June 1998, 17.

22. *Financial Times* (London), 22 November 2001, 6.

23. Conor Cruise O'Brien, *The Great Melody,* 365.

24. *New York Times,* 13 April 2004, A26.

Financial Times (London), 20 September 2004, 1.

Wall Street Journal, 27 January 2003.

Financial Times (London), 9 August 2004, 15.

Financial Times (London), 5 May 2003, 1.

Joseph Conrad, *The Arrow of Gold* (New York: Doubleday, Page and Co., 1927), 38. Originally published 1919.

25. "The Profit Motive Goes to War," *Financial Times* (London), 17 November 2004, 19.

26. Global Policy Forum, "Comparison of Revenues among States and TNCs," 10 May 2000, www.globalpolicy.org/socecon/tncs/tncst (accessed 13 December 2004).

27. Robert Cooper, *The Breaking of Nations: Order and Chaos in the Twenty-First Century* (New York: Atlantic Monthly Press, 2003), 7.

28. *New York Times,* 8 April 2004, A16.

29. *The Economist,* 1 January 2005, 35.

30. Ibid.

31. *Guardian* (London), 22 November 2000.

32. See, for example, the lengthy report "Exposed: The Utility Chief Millionaires," in the *Observer* (London), 14 May 1995.

Daily Express (London), 13 June 2002, 12.

Financial Times (London), 22 January 2005, 4.

33. Peter Conway, "The New Zealand Experiment," 4.

Listener (New Zealand), 24 July 2004, 21.

Stiglitz, WIDER Lecture.

34. Report by Ransom Myers and Boris Worm, Dalhousie University, Halifax, 2003. See *Toronto Star,* 17 July 2004, H5.

35. "Malaysian Recovery Proves Critics Wrong," *Wall Street Journal* (New York), 9 January 1999.

Mahathir bin Mohamad, address at the East Asia Economic Summit, Putrajaya, Malaysia, 6 October 2002.

Financial Times (London), 26 March 2004, 6.

36. I.J. Macfarlane, speech at the International Conference of Banking Supervisors.

Ibid., address at the CEDA Annual General Meeting Dinner.

37. Harold James, *The End of Globalization: Lessons from the Great Depression* (Cambridge, Mass.: Harvard University Press, 2001), 222.

Lamfalussy, "The Restructuring of the Financial Industry."

Helleiner, "Democratic Governance in an Era of Global Finance," 288.

38. Fareed Zakaria, *The Future of Freedom* (New York: W.W. Norton, 2004), 240.

39. *Financial Times* (London), 24 September 1992, 1.

40. Phil Angleides quoted in *Financial Times* (London), 26 July 2002, D3.

41. Zakaria, *The Future of Freedom,* 240.

42. *New York Times,* 25 March 2002, C1.

43. From a speech given 10 November 2004 in Sydney on the launch of Michael Keating's book *Who Rules: How Government Retains Control of a Privatised Economy,* quoted in *The Sydney Institute Quarterly* 8, nos. 3 & 4, (December 2004): 24.

44. Martin Wolf, "Location, Location, Location Equals the Wealth of Nations," *Financial Times* (London), 25 September 2002, 23.

21. INDIA AND CHINA

1. Stiglitz, *Globalization and Its Discontents,* 125.

2. Ramo, *The Beijing Consensus,* 4.

3. *Le Monde* (Paris), 26 June 2004, 4. "La croissance [économique] n'est pas une fin en soi. C'est un moyen de créer des emplois, de bannir la pauvreté, la faim et l'absence de toit, d'améliorer les conditions de vie de la masse de notre peuple." "Cap sur l'équité et la justice sociale."

4. Singh, *Heart to Heart,* 164.

Ramo, *The Beijing Consensus,* 37.

5. Ibid., 40.

6. Business International, S.A., *Managing the Multinationals,* 26.

22. NEW ZEALAND FLIPS AGAIN

1. Helen Clark, speech from the Throne, Opening of Parliament, Wellington, NZ, 21 December 1999.

2. Jane Kelsey, *The New Zealand Experiment: A World Model for Structural Adjustment* (Auckland: Auckland University Press, 1995), 5.

3. Gray, *False Dawn,* 42.

Graham Kelly, *Economic Apartheid: Growing Poverty in the Nineties* (Wellington: Parliament, 1998), 3.

King, *History of New Zealand,* 490.

4. Ruth Richardson, quoted in *The Economist,* 19 October 1996, 19.

5. *The Economist,* 19 October 1996, 19.

6. Don Brash, governor of the Reserve Bank of New Zealand, speaking notes on the release of the 13 March 1997 *Economic Projections.*

7. King, *History of New Zealand,* 513, 507.

8. Jane Clifton, *Listener* (New Zealand), 24 July 2004, 21.

9. Clark, Speech from the Throne, 21 December 1999.

10. Seneca, *On the Shortness of Life*, trans. C.D.N. Costa (Toronto: Penguin Books, 2004), 1.

11. Helen Clark, post-budget speech to Parliament, Wellington, NZ, 16 June 2000.

Helen Clark, speech on the social dimension of Globalization to the ILO, Geneva, Switzerland, 8 June 2004.

V: AND WHERE ARE WE GOING NOW?

23. THE NEW VACUUM: AN INTERREGNUM OF MORBID SYMPTOMS

1. Richard Rorty, *Objectivity, Relativism, and Truth* (Cambridge: Cambridge University Press, 1991), 1.

2. International Labour Organization, Summary of the Final Report of the World Commission on the Social Dimension of Globalization. Published as *A Fair Globalization: Creating Opportunities for All* (Geneva: ILO, 2004), x.

Immanuel Wallerstein, *The Decline of American Power* (London: The New Press, 2004), 17.

Keith Suter, *Global Order and Global Disorder: Globalization and the Nation-State* (Westport, Conn.: Praeger, 2003), 2.

3. *Le Monde* (Paris), 4 January 2000, 6. "Le monde n'est pas qu'un marché, nos sociétés ont besoin de règles, l'économie doit être au service de l'homme, et non l'inverse. La liberté des échanges ne doit pas s'imposer lorsque la santé publique est en jeu."

4. Kissinger, "Industrial Democracies and the Future," 760.

Camus, *Actuelles*, 117. "De plus, si la peur en elle-même ne peut être considérée comme une science, il n'y a pas de doute qu'elle soit cependant une technique."

5. Georgi Arbatov quoted by Anthony Sampson, *Independent* (London), 7 August 2004, 37.

6. Samuel P. Huntington, *The Clash of Civilizations and the Remaking of World Order* (New York: Simon and Schuster, 1996), 21, 28.

7. Transcript of the Aga Khan's interview with the *Globe and Mail* (Toronto), 30 January 2002.

http://www.ismaili.net/timeline/2002/20020130trgm.html (accessed 14 May 2004).

8. Jan Peter Balkenende, speech by the Dutch prime minister to the European Parliament, Strasbourg, 21 July 2004.

9. See Graz, "How Powerful Are Transnational Elite Clubs?" 332–37.

10. Colin Powell, remarks at the World Economic Forum, Davos, Switzerland, 26 January 2003.

11. See *Financial Times* (London), 22 January 2005, 7.

12. *New York Times*, 29 January 2005, C4.

13. *International Herald Tribune*, 25 November 2000, 9.

14. Joseph Conrad, *Nostromo* (London: Penguin Books, 1982), 122–23. Originally published 1904.

Aristotle, *The Ethics of Aristotle*, 209.

Gouverneur Morris, *A Diary of the French Revolution*, vol. 1 (London: Harrap and Co., 1939), 148.

15. *Deutsche Welle* (Bonn), 6 April 2004, http://www.dw-world.de/dw/article/0,1564,1163753,00.html (accessed 2 November 2004).

16. Martin Wolf, *Financial Times* (London), 10 May 2004, 11.

17. Ramo, *The Beijing Consensus*, 14, 21.

18. See the survey in *The Economist*, 27 November 2004.

19. Sen, *Development as Freedom*, 6.

20. Stiglitz, WIDER Lecture.

Tim Hazeldine, quoted in Kelsey, *The New Zealand Experiment*, 361.

21. Nelson Mandela, public address in Trafalgar Square during the G7 finance ministers' meeting, London, England, 3 February 2005.

24. THE NEW VACUUM: IS THE NATION-STATE BACK?

1. *Le Monde*, 24 November 1959, 4.

2. See Heinrich August Winkler, "The Long Shadow of the Reich: Weighing Up German History," 2001 Annual Lecture of the German Historical Institute (London: The German Historical Institute London, 2002).

3. Heinrich August Winkler, "Europeans of All Countries, Remember," *Deutschland* E6, no. 3 (June–July 2004): 19, 16.

4. Karl E. Meyer, *The Dust of Empire: The Race for Mastery in the Asian Heartland* (New York: Century Foundation Book, 2003), 4–5.

5. Quoted by François Fetjö in his remarkable *Histoire de la destruction de l'Autriche-Hongrie — Requiem pour un empire défunt* (Paris: ÉDIMA/Lieu Commun, 1988), 377. "[L]a vraie Europe, sa quintessence."

6. *International Herald Tribune*, 22 October 2004, 1.

7. Gordon Brown, British Council annual lecture, London, 7 July 2004.

8. Jan Zielonka, "Enlargement and the Finality of European Integration," Jean Monnet Working Paper No. 7/00, Symposium: Responses to Joschka Fischer, 2000, http://www.jeanmonnetprogram.org/papers/00/00f0801.html (accessed 9 September 2004).

Robert Cooper, *The Breaking of Nations*, 60.

Jan Peter Balkenende, address to the European Parliament.

9. Jan Zielonka, "How New Enlarged Borders Will Reshape the European Union," *Journal of Common Market Studies* 39, no. 3 (September 2001): 507–36, 508.

10. Aleksander Smolar, The NEXUS conference, Washington, D.C., 18–20 November 2004.

11. Joshua Micah Marshall, *The New Yorker*, 2 February 2004, 84.

12. *The Economist*, 4 December 2004, 9.

13. *Financial Times*, 25 January 2005, 6.

Michael Lind, "How America Became the World's Dispensable Nation," *Financial Times* (London), 25 January 2005, 17.

14. *Financial Times* (London), 18 February 2005, 13.

15. Winkler, "Long Shadow," 21.

Oskar Lafontaine, cited in Winkler, "Long Shadow," 21.

16. Kouchner, address on Leadership, Diversity and Nationalism.

17. *Sunday Times* (London), 16 January 2005, 7.

18. Richard Rorty, *Achieving Our Country: Leftist Thought in Twentieth-Century America* (Cambridge, Mass.: Harvard University Press, 1998), 7–8.

19. Liah Greenfeld, *Nationalism: Five Roads to Modernity* (Cambridge, Mass.: Harvard University Press, 1992), 10, 11.

25. NEGATIVE NATIONALISM

1. *The New Science of Giambattista Vico,* unabridged translation of the 3rd ed. (1744) Book 1: 120, 121; 2, 122, trans. Thomas Bergin and Harold Fisch (Ithaca, N.Y.: Cornell University Press, 1968), 60.

2. Erich Fromm, *The Sane Society* (London: Routledge and Kegan Paul, 1963), 57. James McConica, *Erasmus* (Oxford: Oxford University Press, 1991), 33. Greenfeld, *Nationalism,* 12.

3. Rorty, *Achieving Our Country,* 37–38.

4. *International Herald Tribune,* 2–3 April 1994, 1.

5. *Le Monde* (Paris), 10 December 2003, 1.

6. *Le Monde* (Paris), 28 January 2005, 14. "C'est à nous tous ensemble de mener la confrontation politique avec les néonazis et les vieux nazis."

7. Israel Singer in *Financial Times* (London), 26 January 2005, 19.

Kjell Magne Bondevik, address at "The Politics of European Values" NEXUS Conference, The Hague, 7 September 2004.

8. *Financial Times* (London), 25 January 2005, 7.

9. Ian Buruma, "The Rest Is History," *FT Magazine,* 22 January 2005, 23.

10. Statement by UN Secretary General Kofi Annan, *Globe and Mail* (Toronto), 22 April 2004.

Simon Schama, *Guardian Weekly,* 19–25 September 2002, 6.

11. Richard Rorty, in Jürgen Habermas, Richard Rorty and Leszek Kołakowski, *Debating the State of Philosophy,* ed. Józef Niżnik and John T. Sanders (Westport, Conn.: Praeger, 1996), 29.

12. Francis Fukuyama, *State-Building: Governance and World Order in the 21st Century* (Ithaca, N.Y.: Cornell University Press, 2004), ix, 99, 120.

Milton Friedman, quoted in Martin Wolf, *Financial Times* (London), 3 November 2004, 17.

13. Mussolini, *Fascism: Doctrine and Institutions,* 50.

14. Jane Kramer, "All He Surveys," *The New Yorker,* 10 November 2003, 95.

15. Arbour, "The Truth to Be Told."

16. Cooper, *The Breaking of Nations,* 103.

17. Huntington, *The Clash of Civilizations,* 20.

18. Aga Khan, speech given at the Governor General's Leadership Conference.

19. Tim Lahaye and Jerry B. Jenkins, *Left Behind: A Novel of the Earth's Last Days* (Wheaton, Ill.: Tyndale House Publishers, 1995).

20. *International Herald Tribune,* 22 October 2004, 8.

21. See Nicolson, *Vienna,* 253–54.

Édit de Nantes: "[Ô]ter la cause du mal et troubles qui peut advenir sur le fait de la religion qui est toujours le plus glissant et pénétrant de tous les autres."

26. THE NORMALIZATION OF IRREGULAR WARFARE

1. Jack Straw, "Order out of Chaos: The Challenge of Failed States," *Reordering the World,* ed. Mark Leonard (London: The Foreign Policy Centre, 2002), 99.

2. General Michael Rose, quoted in the *International Herald Tribune,* 4 August 2004, 7.

3. Mahathir bin Mohamad, address during a plenary session, "Trust and Governance for a New Era," Davos, Switzerland, 23 January 2003.

4. Pascal Lamy, quoted in the *International Herald Tribune,* 22 July 2003, 7.
   See Karl E. Meyer, *The Dust of Empire,* 205.

5. Xenophon, *Memorabilia Oeconomicus,* trans. E.C. Marchant (Cambridge, Mass.: Harvard University Press, 1992), 17.

6. See Jessica Warner, *Craze: Gin and Debauchery in an Age of Reason* (New York: Four Walls Eight Windows, 2002), 212.

27. POSITIVE NATIONALISM

1. Greenfeld's differentiation between nationalism is different, but perhaps more due to her fascinating exercise in definition than any real difference. See also
   Adam Smith, *The Theory of Moral Sentiments* (Indianapolis: Liberty Fund, 1984), 235, based on 6th ed., 1790, originally published 1759.
   Tocqueville, *Democracy in America,* 5.
   Rorty, *Achieving Our Country,* 102.

2. Foer, *How Soccer Explains the World.*

3. Barack Obama quoted in the *Financial Times* (London), 31 July 2004, 7.
   Smith, *Moral Sentiments,* 61.

4. Ramo, *The Beijing Consensus,* 12, 21.

5. Clark, Speech from the Throne, Opening of Parliament.

6. *Globe and Mail* (Toronto), 19 May 2004, B1.
   International Association of Department Stores Declaration of Common Principles, IADS 43rd General Assembly, Singapore, October 2002.

7. Taras Shevchenko, *Poems* (Kiev: Edition "Prime," 2001), 119.

8. Lead editorial, *Financial Times* (London), 5–6 February 2005, 6.

9. Pérez-Diaz, "The Underdeveloped Duty," 3.

10. Gordon Brown, British Council annual lecture.

11. Quoted in Ronald J. Deibert, *Parchment, Printing and Hypermedia: Communication in World Order Transformation* (New York: Columbia University Press, 1997), 214.

12. "Al Hujurāt" 49: 13. 'Abdullah Yūsuf 'Alī, *The Meaning of the Holy Qur'ān,* 4th ed. (Brentwood, Md.: Amana Corporation, 1991), 1342–43.

13. Smith, *Moral Sentiments,* 231.

AFTERWORD. THE RETURN OF CHOICE

1. Statement by Gordon Brown, 18 October 2008.

2. *The Times* (London), 28 April 2007.

3. *Le Monde,* 22 November 2008, p.15.

4. *The Times* (London), 18 February 2007, p.48.

5. *Le Monde,* 21 January 2009. A more complex interpretation of poverty not based on the $1 a day approach.
   Ottawa Citizen, 9 December 2008, A11. An analysis of Genocide Risks based on five separate analyses.

6. *The Economist*, 28 February 2009, p.73.

7. For a particularly fine analysis of how bad things became, see Michael Lewis, "The End," on *Portfolio.com*, December 2008.

8. "Of Money," in *Essays: Moral, Political and Literary* (Indianapolis: Liberty Classics, 1985), p. 281

9. *Guardian Weekly*, 2 February 2009, p.13.

10. See the House of Lords Report on Surveillance, February 2009.

11. Richard G. Wilkinson, *The Impact of Inequality: How to Make Sick Societies Healthier* (London: Routledge, 2005).

12. *The Economist*, 28 March 2009, p.80. A long analysis of the return of protectionism.

ACKNOWLEDGMENTS

Globalization has to be written about and judged in its own global context. David Davidar of Penguin Canada and Michael Levine were central to this book being conceived in a borderless way, and I am very grateful for their advice, imagination and support. With them I want to thank Toby Mundy and Bonnie Chiang of Atlantic Books, Peter Mayer of the Overlook Press, Christophe Guias of Payot, Bob Sessions at Penguin Australia, Geoff Walker at Penguin New Zealand, and, in particular, Lewis Lapham and Luke Mitchell of *Harper's*, who were at the heart of the publishing and editorial approach.

And none of this, as they say, would have been possible without the intellectual advice, research skills and research imagination, speed, precision and calm of Thomas Hodd. I also want to thank Carrie Hodd for lending him at all hours on all days.

Many thanks for their comments and help to Timothy Lewis, Maurie Barrett, Thomas de Konninck, David Young, Jordan Bishop, Yves Chevrier, Lachlin McKinnon, Bob Jickling on the Snake River, Marci MacDonald, Piotr Dutkiewicz, Jonathan Nitzan, David Longworth at the Bank of Canada, John Kirton and Madeline Koch at the G8 Research Group. And to David Staines.

As well, I am grateful to Joe Ingram at the World Bank, High Commissioner Graham Kelly, Shaohua Chen at the World Bank Development Research Group, Mark Leonard who is at the Centre for European Reform, the historian Heinrich Winkler in Berlin. Also in Berlin, the Globalization advocate Hans Olaf Henkel, Ingrid Spiller of the Heinrich-Boell Foundation, Jürgen Stetten of the Friedrich-Ebert Foundation, Jean Fredette and Heike Echterhölter of the Canadian Embassy.

Eternal gratitude to those who lent me places where I could write hidden from all forms of communication: Greg and Donna Horton of Double H Ranch, Beverley McLachlin and Frank McArdle of Lake Brogan, Bill and Cathy Graham in the Hockley Valley, and Laura and Sandro Forconi in Siena.

And thank you to everyone who has had to put up with me through this process, particularly Adrienne, with my love.

INDEX